CHRISTIAN WORSHIP

Its Theology and Practice

God is spirit,
And those who worship him
Must worship in spirit and truth.
—JOHN 4:24

CHRISTIAN WORSHIP

Its Theology and Practice

Franklin M. Segler

BROADMAN PRESS

Nashville, Tennessee

© Copyright 1967 • BROADMAN PRESS
Nashville, Tennessee
All rights reserved

4223-09

ISBN: 0-8054-2309-5

All Scripture quotations in this volume are
from the *Revised Standard Version of the Bible* unless otherwise indicated.
© Copyright 1946, 1952

Dewey Decimal Classification Number: 264
Library of Congress Catalog Card Number: 67-22034
Printed in the United States of America

To the people of God, called to be saints
with whom I worshiped in the churches
where I served as pastor

Preface

This book has grown out of a lifetime of searching for a more mature grasp of man's relationship to God, particularly as experienced in public worship. I was found by God's grace in a small church in southern Oklahoma which met for worship in a country schoolhouse. The services were spontaneous (unplanned) and were led by an untrained minister. I have always been grateful for what I received there. Only in later years did I realize how much more I might have received if more understanding and planning had been invested in the church's ministry of teaching and worship.

As leader of worship for eighteen years in the local church, I often yearned for more knowledge of how to plan and lead worship services. How could one make the prayers more meaningful and less repetitious? What could be done to encourage the congregation to become more involved in a meeting with God? How could the service bring inspiration and strength to the worshipers?

I am grateful for what experiences of worship in many churches have taught me. I have visited and observed worship services in many different traditions—Baptist, Roman Catholic, Greek Orthodox Catholic, Disciples, Lutheran, Methodist, Congregational, Episcopal, Presbyterian, Jewish, Christian Science, Unitarian, Holiness, and Quaker. In most of them I was able to participate in a genuine spirit of worship. The extent to which I could worship was determined by my doctrinal beliefs, my cultural and aesthetic insights, my traditional practices, and my desire to enter without prejudice into the existential experience.

Here at Southwestern Baptist Theological Seminary I have taught a course in worship for fifteen years and have shared some of the same materials in pastor's conferences and denominational assemblies. Now I venture to present in print the results of my experience gained in leading in worship, in research, and in teaching.

Writing primarily from the viewpoint of Free Church worship, the author is indebted to many resources in the liturgical tradition as well as in the Puritan tradition. All churches are mutually indebted to many historic treasures to which no one denomination or tradition can lay exclusive claim.

A debt of gratitude is due many persons who encouraged and aided me in the writing of this book. In a course in Parish Church Leadership in Harvard University, 1958, Dr. George A. Buttrick gave a strong emphasis to the necessity of adequate planning of all elements in the worship service, particularly the prayers. Over a period of fifteen years two pastors, H. Guy Moore and J. P. Allen in Broadway Baptist Church, Fort Worth, have enriched our lives by their genuine artistry and depth of spirit in creative planning and effective leadership in worship.

Several colleagues on Southwestern Seminary's faculty have read parts of the manuscript and served as interested critics. Allen Graves, for many years an effective pastor and now serving as a dean and professor in Southern Baptist Theological Seminary, Louisville, Kentucky, read the entire manuscript and offered valuable suggestions. James McClendon, professor of theology in the University of San Francisco and Edgar N. Jackson, minister, author and lecturer, gave wise counsel. Numerous pastors and churches have made significant contributions toward a more mature understanding of the needs of the churches in worship leadership. William J. Fallis and Joseph F. Green, Jr., of Broadman Press and Clifton J. Allen, editorial secretary of the Baptist Sunday School Board, have given generous counsel and encouragement.

FRANKLIN M. SEGLER

Contents

Introduction

E. C. Dargan, a leading Baptist theologian of the nineteenth century, declared that a study of worship is indispensable for an understanding of the church and its ministry.[1] One of the duties and privileges of the Christian church is that of providing for and maintaining the worship of God. The first order in the church's mission is worship. All other aspects of ministry are motivated by worship, and without worship the church will die.

The purpose of this book is both theological and practical. It is written with the hope that it will help to interpret the meaning of worship and provide guidelines for planning and leading worship. It is meant to be a source book for pastors and other leaders in the churches, and especially for college and seminary students, pointing to many treasures both old and new in the literature of the church.

Part One, *The Meaning of Worship,* seeks to interpret worship from the standpoint of its biblical and historical foundations, its theological basis, and its psychological principles. The attitudes involved in the act of worship are also discussed.

Part Two, *The Means of Expressing Worship,* discusses the nature of the various elements used in expressing worship and shows how they are related to the entire worship service. These include music, prayers, preaching, the reading of the Scriptures, and others.

Part Three, *Planning and Conducting Worship,* proposes to provide principles for relating form and freedom in worship. Form should never be so rigid as to restrict the spirit of freedom or spontaneity. Neither should a spirit of spontaneity ignore the need for some concrete form for the expression of our common praise.

There is no set form suggested which man must follow in worship. However, it is natural, indeed inevitable, that he will use some form in his efforts to commune with God. It is better to use sound

[1]*Ecclesiology* (Louisville: Charles T. Dearing, 1897), p. 517.

1

principles than to be careless and indifferent. God is a God of order, and man lives in a universe of law and order. His worship will of necessity follow some form and order.

There are various types of worship—formal and informal, public and private, planned and spontaneous. The spirit and motive are always the same: the desire to commune with God, to have a new and fresh encounter with the Lord of life. The attitude and spirit are primary. The form, as a secondary essential, is meant to aid in disciplining and expressing the attitude.

The concluding chapter, "Worship and Church Renewal," shows worship to be the motivating dynamic for the life and mission of the church. Worship is the life stream of the church. Vital worship provides the motivation and inspiration for righteous living, fervent evangelism, and the total stewardship of life. The hope for church renewal depends upon a renewal of genuine worship.

Part One

The Meaning of Worship

Here we stand, as an innumerable company before us have stood, at the last outpost of human endeavor, seeking God. We have done our utmost in the world, failing or succeeding, and now we stand within the sanctuary, before the Eternal, and what we have done or not done is swallowed up in mystery. We have worked, laying our wills against the world; now we worship, that God may lay his will against us. We have entered into the making of the world, but that is not enough; we desire God to enter into the making of our life.

SAMUEL H. MILLER
The Life of the Church

1

What Is Worship?

Worship is an end in itself; it is not a means to something else. Karl Barth has appropriately declared that the "church's worship is the *Opus Dei,* the work of God, which is carried out for its own sake." When we try to worship for the sake of certain benefits that may be received, the act ceases to be worship; for then it attempts to use God as a means to something else. We worship God purely for the sake of worshiping God.

To worship is:

> To quicken the conscience by the holiness of God,
> To feed the mind with the truth of God,
> To purge the imagination by the beauty of God,
> To open the heart to the love of God,
> To devote the will to the purpose of God.[1]

Why does man worship? Because he cannot help worshiping. Worship is not a human invention; rather, it is a divine offer. God offers himself in a personal relationship, and man responds. God's offer of love elicits man's response in worship. A vision of God demands a worship response because God is worthy of worship. God often surprises man by breaking in on his experience, in which case man often spontaneously responds in adoration and praise. In his meditations Pascal discovered that in his seeking after God, God had already found him.

As the worshiper has sought for ways of speaking about worship, he has developed a vocabulary which has been adopted widely. The terms in the following paragraphs may assist in the interpretation of worship for modern Christians.

---

[1]William Temple, *The Hope of a New World* (New York: The Macmillan Co., 1942), p. 30.

Preliminary Terminology

The English word "worship" is derived from the Anglo-Saxon "weorthscipe"—"worth" and "ship"—meaning one worthy of reverence and honor. When we worship, we are declaring God's worth. The angels sang, "Worthy is the Lamb who was slain," and every creature answered, " 'To him who sits upon the throne and to the Lamb be blessing and honor and glory and might for ever and ever!' And the four living creatures said, 'Amen!' and the elders fell down and worshiped" (Rev. 5:12,13-14).

The biblical term "glory" is often attributed to God as man proceeds to worship him. The Hebrew term *kabōd,* translated "glory," means the "honor" or "weight" of God. When Isaiah saw the Lord high and lifted up, he declared, "The whole earth is full of his glory" (Isa. 6:3). The New Testament term *doxa,* translated "glory," expresses the estimate that God is worthy of praise and honor. At the birth of Jesus the angels sang, "Glory to God in the highest, and on earth peace among men with whom he is pleased!" (Luke 2:14).

The principal Old Testament term translated "worship" is *shachah,* which means to "bow down" or to "prostrate" oneself. The Old Testament idea conveyed in this term and other similar terms is the reverential attitude of mind or body or both, combined with the notions of "religious adoration, obedience, service." When the people of Israel heard that God had spoken to Moses, they believed and "bowed their heads and worshiped" (Ex. 4:31).

The Greek term most often indicating worship in the New Testament is *proskuneō,* meaning literally to "kiss the hand towards one" or to "prostrate oneself" before another in token of reverence. Jesus used this word when he said to the woman of Sychar, "God is spirit, and those who worship him must worship in spirit and truth" (John 4:24).

The term liturgy is derived from the Greek *leitourgia,* translated "ministry" or "service." In the New Testament it does not occur in connection with ceremonial affairs. It denoted the work of the priestly office under the old covenant (cf. Luke 1:23, Heb. 9:21) and also the ministry of Christ (Heb. 8:6) and the worship of the church (Acts 13:2). Literally it means an "action of the people," and more particularly the service which the Christian renders to God in faith and obedience.

For Paul the true *leitourgia* of God is a life of faith that shows forth fruits of the Spirit (Gal. 5:22). Worship is meant essentially in his exhortation, "I appeal to you therefore, brethren, by the mercies of God, to present your bodies as a living sacrifice, holy and acceptable to God, which is your spiritual worship [*leitourgia*]" (Rom. 12:1). In later centuries the term "liturgy" has come to be used to designate the order of worship in the churches.

It has been affirmed that religion appears in three main aspects: as cult or worship, as doctrine or beliefs, and as behavior or morals.[2] This does not mean that the three are unrelated or separate parts. Rather, they are forms of expression or manifestations of religion. The entire living content of a religion is present in all three. The term "cult" or "cultus" has long been used to define the content and practices of a people's worship. Mowinckel defines "cult" as the "socially established and regulated holy acts and words in which the encounter and communion of the Deity with the congregation is established, developed, and brought to its ultimate goal." The cult appears in all religions, even in the most "anti-cultic" sects, although it may appear in traditional, unwritten practices rather than in adopted and fixed liturgies.

Descriptive Propositions

Christian worship defies definition; it can only be experienced. However, like every other kind of experience, it calls for analysis and understanding. For the Christian, theology is always an attempt to describe the experience of God's grace applied in a redemptive relationship. A living experience may be analyzed, but it can never be completely contained in formulas and creeds and liturgies.

The sensitive soul may feel with Paul, "I had such an experience that it cannot be told; in fact, it does not seem appropriate to speak about it" (see 2 Cor. 12:3-4). Certain experiences in worship are so intimate that the worshiper cannot share them. On the other hand, when men worship together they need not only a unity of spirit but

---

[2]Sigmund Olaf Plytt Mowinckel, *The Psalms in Israel's Worship,* trans. D. R. Ap-Thomas (New York: Abingdon Press, 1962), p. 15.

also a unity of understanding. Although the majesty and holiness of God cannot be comprehended, and the feeling of awe cannot be strictly defined, man cannot help reflecting on the meaning of worship. The clearer man's total understanding of worship, the more meaningful will be his experience of worship. Even though the *esse* (the reality) of worship cannot be defined or contained in formulas, the *bene esse* (well-being), or those things which aid worship, can be set forth.

Although the innate desire to worship is universal in man, there is often confusion as to the meaning and nature of worship. While all efforts at defining worship seem inadequate, certain aspects of worship need to be described. The essence of worship as inner experience and the outward acts of worship which aid man in the experience are interrelated. The following descriptive propositions may aid in clarifying this relationship.

Mystery.—Worship is both revelation and mystery. Man experiences the presence of God in revelation and stands in awe of God in the face of mystery. God both reveals and withholds himself at the same time. Man can be conscious of God in his life, but he can never comprehend the ultimate meaning of God. In worship we experience both mystery (God's transcendence) and meaning (God's immanence).

Man's communion with God is always a miracle, just as the revelation of Jesus Christ himself was a miracle, and the continuing work of the Holy Spirit in the church is a miracle. As Samuel Miller has put it, the miracle of worship is "sight of God seen through earthly circumstance; it is the glory of God shining through darkness; it is the power of God felt when all other strength fails; it is the eternal manifested in time." Worship in the Free Churches will become more serious when ministers lead their churches to approach worship with a sense of mystery and awe and wonder in the face of what they are doing.

Writing on the testimony of the soul eighteen hundred years ago, Tertullian said, "Whenever the soul comes to itself, as out of a surfeit, or a sleep or a sickness, and attains something of its natural soundness, it speaks of God." A. N. Whitehead declared that strong religious worship evokes an "apprehension of the commanding vision." He continued, "To worship God is not a rule of safety—it is an adventure of the spirit, a flight after the unattainable, . . . the high hope of adventure."[3] Man can know God in worship, but he can never fully comprehend the nature of God nor fathom the mystery of his ways with man.

Celebration.—Worship is essentially the celebration of the acts of God in history—his creation, his providences, his covenant of redemption, his redemptive revelation through Jesus Christ in the incarnation, the cross, and the resurrection, and the manifestation of his power through the coming of the Holy Spirit. Von Ogden Vogt sees worship as the interruption of work to praise and to celebrate his goodness. Worship is indeed a celebration of the gospel.

Man worships in appreciation for what God has done for him. As Henry Sloane Coffin affirmed, we worship for sheer delight. When the question is raised, "Why go to church?" one may as well ask, "Why enjoy music, why read poetry, why find happiness in being with one's dearest? A service is rightly termed a celebration."[4] As Martin Luther declared long ago, "To have a God is to worship him."

Life.—Worship is not limited to acts of devotion and rites and ceremonies. For the Christian it is synonymous with the whole of life. In its broadest aspect, worship is related to all that man does. He stands always before God to present his whole life to him. Man sees himself as a part of God's creation and offers himself and all that he has in dedication to his Creator. Every area of life belongs to the kingdom of God. In a sense, worship is practicing the presence of God in every experience of life.

There is a sense in which we may think of the "whole life of the universe, seen and unseen," as an act of worship, glorifying God as its Creator, Sustainer, and End.[5] Paul claimed the whole universe for Christ—the world of things, the world of persons in time, and the world of the eternal (1 Cor. 3:21-23). Because God is the Lord of all life, he is to be worshiped in every sphere of life. Even the

---

[3]*Science and the Modern World* (New York: The Macmillan Co., 1926), p. 276.

[4]*The Public Worship of God* (Philadelphia: The Westminster Press, 1946), pp. 15,16.

[5]Evelyn Underhill, *Worship* (New York: Harper & Bros., 1937), p. 3.

formal acts of devotion are concerned with every aspect of life. Moreover, particular acts of devotion are more meaningful if the whole of life is devoted to God.

Dialogue.—In worship man experiences God in a conscious dialogue. Worship is both revelation and response. God takes the initiative in revelation, and man responds in worship. The eternal Word comes to man through words such as the Bible, man's witness, and other symbols and actions. The eternal Person comes to man through other persons in the fellowship of believers. God comes through the witness of their words, their music, their symbols, and their actions. The eternal Person comes as Spirit directly to the spirit of man. Man responds to God through words and music and acts of celebration and dedication.

In this dialogue of revelation and response something happens in the experience of man. Worship is more than conversation; it is also encounter. In this encounter, God confronts man and makes demands upon him. The story of Jacob tells of such an encounter. In his dream, Jacob was conscious of God's coming to him in the presence of his angel messengers, who were ascending and descending on the ladder. When Jacob awoke from his sleep he said, " 'Surely the Lord is in this place; and I did not know it.' And he was afraid, and said, 'How awesome is this place! This is none other than the house of God, and this is the gate of heaven' " (Gen. 28:16-17). For the apostle Paul, it was important to know God, but it was more important "to be known by God" (Gal. 4:9). Meaningful worship leads to decisive experiences. The final moral judgment of God comes to bring man salvation. In this encounter it is only by humble faith that man realizes the crowning value of life in Christ.

Giving.—The purpose of worship is not primarily to receive blessings from God but to make offerings to God. Ancient peoples presented offerings in the form of sacrifices. In the Bible story the Hebrews made offerings in a variety of ways. The psalmist exhorted, "Ascribe to the Lord the glory due his name; bring an offering, and come into his courts!" (96:8).

The New Testament also emphasizes giving as central in worship. Man is to offer his gifts in sincere faith and total obedience, as in the days of Abel and Cain (Heb. 11:4). The "holy priesthood," the congregation of believers, is to "offer spiritual sacrifices acceptable to God through Jesus Christ" (1 Peter 2:5).

As Winward points out, the almost exclusive stress of the Free Churches on the "downward movement" of worship, the revelation of God in his Word, has led to the virtual exclusion of the "upward movement," the offering in the response of the worshipers.[6] In the practice of public worship the concrete, objective offering is essential for the conscious enforcement of the meaning of spiritual worship. Jesus Christ as God's sacrificial offering is the basis for man's response in making an offering to God (Eph. 5:2). Worship is not just something said; it is something done. It is acting on the word of God in faith. As God has acted toward believers, so believers are to act toward God.

Worship is primarily the offering of our total selves to God—our intellects, our feelings, our attitudes, and our possessions. Our outward gifts are the result of our inward dedication. The gifts of money sent by the Philippian church to Paul were seen as "a fragrant offering, a sacrifice acceptable and pleasing to God" (Phil. 4:18). The highest expression of giving is the offering of the person himself, the presentation of "your bodies as a living sacrifice, holy and acceptable to God" (Rom. 12:1). What God wants is ourselves. Coffin declares, "We present him our thoughts, our penitence, our thanksgiving, our aspirations for our own lives, for those dear to us, for our land and our world. Our selves is the gift he seeks."[7]

Eschatological fulfilment.—Worship is the eschatological function of the church. According to Delling, "It is, in its very essence, the continuing decisive working out of salvation in history, which ends in the eternal adoration of God."[8] The church is charged to continue its worship. Paul said, "As often as you eat this bread and drink the cup, you proclaim the Lord's death until he comes" (1 Cor. 11:26). The church sees in its celebration of worship eschatological fulfilment of God's redemption, awareness of itself as the eschatological church, and hope of eschatological consummation.

---

[6]Stephen F. Winward, *The Reformation of Our Worship* (Richmond: John Knox Press, 1965), p. 33.

[7]*Op. cit.,* p. 21.

[8]Gerhard Delling, *Worship in the New Testament,* trans. Percy Scott (Philadelphia: The Westminster Press, 1962), p. 182.

Reality in Worship

There is no possibility of the church's being Christian without worship. Worship is in its essence the self-portrayal of the congregation, whom God has called to be his people in the world. In fact, worship is the power from God that enables the church to be the church.

People too often attend church with the mistaken idea that when they worship they leave the "real world" behind and enter some ghostly realm of "auras, ectoplasms, disembodied spirits, and unattainable ideals."[9] Willard L. Sperry says, "A service of worship is a deliberate and disciplined adventure in reality. In Church, if anywhere, we are under moral bonds to be real."[10]

The term "reality," to be intelligible, must have certain points of reference. Religious experience is a real experience. It has a firm basis. There are at least three points of reference essential here: (1) To Christian philosophy the ultimate reality is personal, and to Christian theology and experience the ultimate expression of the personal is God's manifestation of himself. Worship is in the realm of the personal. (2) Another point of reference is historical manifestation. Christian worship is related to the acts of God in history. These acts are observable in time and place, and man's experience of God in history verifies the reality of divine revelation, especially in the person of Jesus Christ. (3) Worship may also be judged by the reality of its dynamic effects. Man's serious dialogue with God produces transforming results. A clear vision of God brings a realistic picture of man's need and a desire for God's cleansing and forgiveness. Life is most real when man finds his true self in Christ.

Finally, to reiterate, definitions and propositions cannot adequately delineate the experience of worship, for worship is an act of faith. It is not adherence to propositions, declares Carl Michalson, for "faith's propositions are always invocations. Not, 'I consent to agree intellectually, but a *sursum corda,* a lifting up of the heart in willing response.' "[11]

---

[9]Willard L. Sperry, *Reality in Worship* (New York: The Macmillan Co., 1925), p. 206.

[10]*Ibid.,* p. 221.

[11]"Authority," *A Handbook of Christian Theology,* ed. Marvin Halverson (Cleveland, Ohio: The World Pub. Co. [Meridian Books, Inc.], 1958), p. 28.

Worship is not a mere preparation for action. It is the *Opus Dei,* the adoration of God as man's highest privilege. Without this sense of the priority of worship, God will be served as a means to an end, not for himself alone.

Such a utilitarian approach is not valid even if the end in view be as admirable as service to the community, or building the morale of a nation, or the making of individuals with greater integrity, health, or sensitivity. God must be worshiped for his own glory, or it is idolatry, however relatively worthy its motivations.

As I have previously written, then, "Christian worship is man's loving response in personal faith to God's personal revelation of himself in Jesus Christ."[12] In essence, worship is man's communion with God in Christ, this conscious relationship being effected by the Holy Spirit in the spirit of the worshiper. This is the reason why true worship "never palls on the reverent soul," for "he who is weary at worship is not worshiping, just as he who tires of loving is not loving."[13]

After more than forty years in the ministry, one pastor acknowledged that he could not define worship, but he gave the following description: "If you leave church with your faith stronger, your hope brighter, your love deeper, your sympathies broadened, your heart purer, and with your will more resolute to do the will of God, then you have truly worshiped!"[14]

----

[12]*A Theology of Church and Ministry* (Nashville: Broadman Press, 1960), p. 195.

[13]Edgar S. Brightman, *The Spiritual Life* (New York: Abingdon Press, 1942), p. 157.

[14]Perry F. Webb, formerly pastor of the First Baptist Church, San Antonio, Texas. Used by permission.

2

Biblical Foundations

Christians generally claim to look primarily to the Bible for the norms of worship. Even churches of strong ecclesiastical traditions believe that the Bible provides the basic principles for worship. The Free Churches particularly stress biblical authority for their principles of worship. Perhaps all churches tend to develop their patterns of worship partly from biblical principles and partly from tradition. Patterns and practices in public worship should be tested constantly by the spirit and practice of men who have faith in the Bible story, especially in New Testament Christianity. This chapter proposes to examine certain abiding principles of worship as found in the Bible. Perhaps a brief look at primitive practices of worship will aid in understanding biblical foundations.

Ancient Backgrounds

Man is by nature religious and must have some object of worship. Worship in some form is, therefore, universal, ranging from superstitious fear or fetishism in paganism to the highest spiritual exercise in Christianity. Primitive history indicates that all people have worshiped some object. In the oldest monuments of civilized man, as shown in the pyramids of Egypt and the early Vedic scriptures of India, for example, there are evidences of religious convictions, inspirations, and worship.[1]

Primitive practices often took the form of nature worship. This was usually polytheistic, making a god of every object, or else pantheistic, considering everything in nature of divine essence. For example, the Egyptians worshiped Ra, the sun-god, and Osiris, the god of the Nile and of fertility.[2]

---

[1]David Hume, *The World's Living Religions* (New York: Charles Scribner's Sons, 1924), p. 1.

[2]*The International Standard Bible Encyclopedia, op. cit.,* V, 3110. See also *Encyclopedia Britannica,* 1942 ed., VIII, 58.

The forms of primitive worship usually consisted of sacrifices and superstitious rites intended to ward off evil spirits or to placate angry gods. Primitive worship was prompted by the innate needs of man. Objects of worship were gods created by man in an effort to fulfil his needs. For example, Baal was imagined to be the god of the crops who provided for man's material needs. The worship of this god of materialism was often encountered by Old Testament peoples (see Judg. 2:11-14; 1 Sam. 7:3-4; 1 Kings 18:17-19).

Archaeologists and anthropologists have discovered artifacts and other indications of the types of worship followed by ancient peoples. Many primitive peoples did not distinguish between spiritual deities and natural phenomena. There were gods of the fields, of rivers, of the sun and moon, of fertility and barrenness, and of birth and death. Certain of the peoples even believed in the hope of reincarnation. Man has always had a sense of the supernatural in his life struggle with the problem of good and evil.[3]

In some ancient cultures, human beings were offered as sacrifices, slain upon altars, burned, or buried alive. For example, certain of the Canaanite people worshiped the god Moloch by offering their own children as sacrifices to him on an altar of fire. Although the facts are too meager to give definite conclusions concerning many of these intimations, it is clear that man has been a worshiper from ancient times. He has always sought to understand himself and the complex world in which he lived. However paganistic or polytheistic his attitudes have been, he has always reached out for the "unknown god."

Primitive worship had social implications. Sometimes it took the form of ancestor worship. Religious rites were set forth in the public worship of the tribe or clan. Coleman suggests that either fear or veneration is a predominant sentiment in the attempt to enter into communion with superhuman beings.[4]

---

[3]See James F. Frazier, *The Golden Bough* (1 vol.; New York: The Macmillan Co., 1930); Sigmund Freud, *Totem and Taboo,* trans. A. A. Brill (New York: Moffat, Yard and Co., 1918); and Edward B. Tyler, *Primitive Culture* (2 vols.; New York: Holt, Rinehart, & Winston, Inc., 1874).

[4]A. I. duP. Coleman, "Worship," *The New Schaff-Herzog Encyclopedia of Religious Knowledge, op. cit.,* XIII, 435.

Worship in the Old Testament

The difference between pagan worship in the ancient world and the worship of the people of God in the Old Testament is the fact of God's revelation of himself to a particular people and his choice of them for his service. According to Roland de Vaux, the worship of Israel was distinguished from Oriental cults as follows: (1) Israel's God was the only God; (2) he was a personal God who intervened in history; (3) Israel had no image in its worship.[5]

G. Ernest Wright also contrasts the worship of Israel with that of the polytheistic religions: "In the faith of Israel the basis of worship lay in historical memory and in spiritual communion."[6] Although there are no strict lines of demarcation, it is evident in the Old Testament story that worship in the life of Israel was a developmental process. That is, a definite cultus developed, and the practices of worship varied throughout the history of Israel.

The ancient story always assumes that God desires man to commune with him. In the Garden of Eden God asked, "Adam, where art thou?" (Gen. 3:9, KJV). The sons of Adam, Cain and Abel, worshiped God. Cain was a tiller of the soil, and Abel was a keeper of sheep. Cain brought the fruits of the soil as an offering to the Lord, and Abel brought the firstlings of the flock as an offering. The Lord accepted Abel's offering but rejected Cain's, evidently because of the motivations in their hearts (4:2-5).

Enoch lived in constant fellowship with God. "Enoch walked with God; and he was not, for God took him" (5:24). The Hebrew word "walked" suggests an intimate fellowship between Enoch and God. The literal translation says they "walked back and forth together." Enoch not only worshiped God at stated times, but he lived in continuous relationship with his Creator.

Several generations later we find Noah worshiping God. God again took the initiative and called Noah to serve him and to represent him before the people. Noah obeyed God and built an ark of safety into which he took his family. After the flood, at God's command, Noah

---

[5] *Ancient Israel: Its Life and Institutions* (London: McGraw-Hill Book Co., Inc., 1961), pp. 271 ff.

[6] "The Faith of Israel," *The Interpreter's Bible*, ed. George Buttrick (Nashville: Abingdon-Cokesbury Press, 1952), I, 375.

left the ark and "built an altar unto the Lord . . . and offered burnt offerings on the altar" (8:20) in celebration of his deliverance. This episode of communion between God and man was sealed with the rainbow of promise (9:11-12).

The Patriarchal Period—Private and Family Altars

The Pentateuch took shape as a "priestly edition of Israel's sacred history."[7] The atmosphere of worship pervades the whole work. Its design and religious symbolism, hallowed by centuries of worship, produce a solemn sense of the holiness and majesty of God. The Old Testament story begins with the idea of a personal God who created man for the purpose of communion with himself. From the beginning God claimed man and took the initiative in seeking him. Man's worship response included the building of altars and the dedication of places and objects. These altars or "sanctuaries" were always established with reference to some manifestation of Yahweh at particular places.

God appeared to Abraham and called him to leave his own country and go to a land of promise. God promised to bless Abraham, to make of him a great nation, and to make his name great (Gen. 12:1-30). Abraham responded with faith and obedience and built an altar unto the Lord and worshiped him (12:7). Later Abraham worshiped God when he indicated his willingness to sacrifice his own son, Isaac, to the Lord (22:9-10).

Isaac learned to worship God from his father, Abraham. He built an altar and called on the name of the Lord (26:24-25). Jacob's experiences in worship were as numerous as they were glorious. He dreamed that God appeared to him through angels descending and ascending upon a ladder that reached up into heaven. In the morning he declared, "Surely the Lord is in this place; and I did not know it. . . .How awesome is this place! This is none other than the house of God" (28:16-17). He set up a stone for an altar which he dedicated to the Lord and called it Bethel, "house of God."

Thus, before the ritual law of Leviticus was given, the Old Testament stresses the necessity of worship.

---

[7]Bernard W. Anderson, *Understanding the Old Testament* (2d ed.; Englewood Cliffs, N. J.: Prentice-Hall, Inc., 1966), p. 382.

The Mosaic Period—The Covenant of
Revelation and Response

Israel's worship consisted in the celebration and proclamation of the covenant that God ordained. God revealed himself to Israel as Jehovah, the covenant God. The covenant was delivered to Moses in Sinai as God's claim upon Israel (Ex. 20:1-18). He demanded sincere worship: "You shall not bow down to them [idols] nor worship them, for I the Eternal, your God, am a jealous God" (v. 5, Moffatt). Jehovah, who delivered the tablets to Moses, is the God who acts in history. From that time forth the tablets of stone became for Israel the revealed Word of God. Perhaps the matrix of the meaning and purpose of worship in the Old Testament is best summed up in Deuteronomy 6:4, "The Lord our God is one Lord."

Some forms of public worship were surely observed in the wilderness under the direction of Moses. The primitive sanctuary or "tent of meeting" probably resembled an ordinary shepherd's tent, having both outer and inner compartments. The tent of meeting seems to have been pitched outside the camp (Ex. 3:7; Num. 11:26).

Ultimately God directed Moses to build a sanctuary for worship and an ark in which the Ten Commandments should be kept (Ex. 25:26). With the building of the tabernacle, congregational worship was established as an institution. God then commanded Moses to consecrate Aaron and his sons to the office of priesthood (28:2-3). The duties of the priests were set forth in detail. The people were to bring offerings unto God continually as an act of worship (29:30).

Concerning the history of the tabernacle, James Strong has the following to say:

It appears (Exodus 33:7) that the name "Tabernacle of the Congregation" was originally applied to an ordinary tent, probably the one officially occupied by Moses himself; and that this was first set apart by the token of the divine presence at its doorway as the regular place of public communication between Jehovah and the people. This was prior to the construction of what was afterwards technically known as the Tabernacle, which of course superseded such a temporary arrangement.[8]

---

[8]*The Tabernacle of Israel* (Grand Rapids: Baker Book House, 1952), p. 9.

The Period of the Judges

As Israel proceeded with the conquest of Canaan, they encountered the worship of the nature deities known as the "Baalim." In this environment, God's people were influenced by the tribes who worshiped false gods. Consequently, the worship of Jehovah was not always kept in its purest form. Some of the people forsook the God of their fathers. Many of them transferred to the worship of Jehovah the rituals and ceremonies of the popular shrines, where false gods were worshiped. Doubtless Hannah's prayers were genuine (1 Sam. 1), but the corrupt acts of the priests (2:12-27, 22-25) and the fetish value placed upon the ark (4:3) indicate false acts of worship.[9] It should be pointed out, however, that biblical traditions present us with a religion which was much more than, and quite different from, Canaanite worship.

Jehovah was not forgotten by all his people, and worship of him continued at numerous shrines during the period of the judges. Gilgal was likely the first place established for the worship of Jehovah in the new land of Canaan. Saul was crowned in the Gilgal sanctuary, and annual celebrations of Israel's crossing into Canaan may have taken place there. Altars at Gilgal (Judg. 2:1), Ophrah (6:24), Shiloh and Dan (18:29-31), Hebron (2 Sam. 5:3), and Gibeon (1 Kings 3:4) indicate that Israel's conquest of the land for Jehovah was going forward constantly.

Temple and Cultus

In the historical books the king appears several times as the leader in worship, for he was a sacred person, sanctified by his anointing and adopted by Yahweh. David set up the first altar for Yahweh in Jerusalem (2 Sam. 24:25) and also conceived the plans for building him a temple (7:2-3).

In Solomon's Temple at Jerusalem Old Testament worship reached its climax. The Temple was the most magnificent and elaborate of Isarel's holy places dedicated to the worship of God. It was erected in Jerusalem, where God had previously appeared (24:16-

---

[9]Horton Davies, "Worship in the Old Testament," *The Interpreter's Dictionary of the Bible,* ed. George Buttrick (Nashville: Abingdon Press, 1962), IV, 882.

25). Thus it became the central sanctuary of Israel. King David had it in his heart to build a house of rest for the ark of the covenant of the Lord and for the footstool of God (1 Chron. 28:2). He had made elaborate preparations for the building of the Temple, but God would not allow him to build the house, because he had been so warlike. God informed David that his son Solomon, who would succeed him as king, had been chosen to build the house of God. Having delivered into Solomon's hands elaborate plans for the building of the Temple, David said to Solomon, "Be strong and of good courage and do it. Fear not, be not dismayed; for the Lord God, even my God, is with you. He will not fail you or forsake you, until all the work for the service of the house of the Lord is finished" (v. 20).

The Temple was elaborately furnished with dedicated vessels: "the golden altar, the table for the bread of the Presence, the lampstands and their lamps of pure gold; . . . the flowers, the lamps, and the tongs of purest gold; the snuffers, basins, dishes for incense, and firepans, of pure gold; and the sockets of the temple for the inner doors to the most holy place and for the doors of the nave of the temple were of gold" (2 Chron. 4:19-22). Then Solomon commanded the elders and the Levites to bring up the ark to the Temple.

Second Chronicles gives an account of the dedication of the Temple. The priests and the Levitical singers, arrayed in fine linen, with cymbals, harps, lyres, and trumpets, together with many singers, made themselves heard in unison, praise, and thanksgiving to the Lord. They sang, "For he is good, for his steadfast love endures for ever" (5:13). The house of the Lord was filled with a cloud, and the priests could not stand to minister, because the glory of the Lord filled the house of God (vv. 13-14). Then Solomon knelt before the assembly and prayed a prayer of dedication. Again God manifested himself, and his glory filled the Temple. When the people saw the glory of the Lord upon the Temple, they bowed their faces to the earth and worshiped and gave thanks to the Lord. Solomon and the people offered sacrifices before the Lord. Then the priests offered praises and the Levites sounded their trumpets and all Israel stood (7:3-6).

With the magnificent Temple came a further development of the

cultus. It developed largely around the feasts celebrated throughout
the land. For example, the Feast of Unleavened Bread, with the
eating of unleavened cakes, the offering of firstfruits, and the waving
of the sheaf of firstfruits preceded by the Passover with its slain
lamb and the blood-sprinkled doorposts, was celebrated annually.
The Feast of Weeks included the waving of two leavened loaves
before the Lord. It came between the barley and wheat harvests.
The Feast of Booths was the greatest of all. It was a harvest of
thanksgiving which included the use of lights and dancing (Isa.
30:29). Israel lived seven days in booths and celebrated the new
year, offering prayers for the coming of the rains.

The Temple at Jerusalem was the central place of worship for
the entire land. The people came up to Jerusalem to rejoice before
God. They brought their tithes and sacrificial offerings to the sanctuary. Their acts of worship included music, solos, anthems, shouting,
dancing, processions, the playing of instruments, preaching in elemen-
tary form, sacred recitations of the stories of Israel—her fathers,
heroes, saints, and soldiers—interspersed with petitions, prayers,
vows, promises, sayings of creeds and confessions, sacred meals, and
washings.

There was silence also in Israel's worship. Habakkuk exclaimed,
"The Lord is in his holy temple; let all the earth keep silence before
him" (2:20). The psalmist spoke for God: "Be still, and know that
I am God" (46:10).

Elaborate rituals and ceremonies, with feast days and sacrificial
offerings, were developed to remind the people of their sinfulness and
also of God's mercy and love. The entire book of Leviticus is devoted
to this sacrificial and priestly system. Sacrifice was understood to
be a necessary condition of effective worship.[10]

Roland de Vaux gives a detailed explanation of Israel's ritual of
sacrifice, which includes the "holocaust" or burnt offering "taken
up" to the altar, whose smoke "goes up" to God (1 Sam. 7:9; Deut.
33:10); the "communion sacrifice" in which the victim is shared be-

---

[10]See John B. Ascham, *The Religion of Israel* (New York: Abingdon Press,
1918), p. 92. Part of this priestly code probably goes back to more ancient
times. See John Bright, "Modern Study of Old Testament Literature," *The
Bible and the Ancient Near East,* ed. G. Ernest Wright (Garden City, N. Y.:
Doubleday and Co., Inc., 1961), p. 18.

tween God and the persons offering the sacrifice (Lev. 3); the "expiatory sacrifice" offered for sin (4:1 to 5:13) and as reparation for sin (5:14-26); the "vegetable offerings" presented as a memorial of a pledge made (Lev. 2); the "offering of shewbread" or "bread of the presence" symbolizing a pledge of the covenant between God and Israel (24:5-9); and the "offerings of perfumes" or incense (Ex. 30: 34-38; Lev. 16:12,13), fragrant aromas presented to God. Paul speaks of the gifts of the Christians at Philippi as a "fragrant offering, a sacrifice acceptable and pleasing to God" (Phil. 4:18).

The Prophets and the Psalms—Personal and Ethical Religion

As a corrective in Israel's worship, numerous prophets vigorously protested the empty ritualism and mixed motives of the people in their acts of worship. The herdsman Amos abhors their feast days, solemn assemblies, burnt offerings, and meat offerings, and calls Israel back to a sincere worship of Jehovah (5:21-24). Hosea prophesies for God, "I desired mercy, and not sacrifice; and the knowledge of God more than burnt offerings" (6:6, KJV). The book of Micah conveys a similar exhortation regarding sacrificial practices: "With what shall I come before the Lord, and bow myself before God on high? . . . Will the Lord be pleased with thousands of rams, with ten thousands of rivers of oil? . . . He has showed you, O man, what is good; and what does the Lord require of you but to do justice, and to love kindness, and to walk humbly with your God?" (6:6-8). This does not mean, however, that the prophets rejected the forms and content of the cultus as such. They called not for the abolition of ritual, but for sincerity in the performance of the ritual.

Several of the prophets called for a general reformation of worship. For example, Jeremiah insisted on the personal or experiential element in worship. Jehovah is personal and desires that his people worship him in sincerity. "My people . . . have forsaken me, the fountain of living waters, and hewed out cisterns for themselves, broken cisterns, that can hold no water" (2:13). Both blessings and judgments are connected with their worship. "Blessed is the man that trusteth in the Lord, and whose hope the Lord is" (17:7, KJV). " 'Woe to the shepherds who destroy and scatter the sheep of my pasture!' says the Lord" (23:1).

Ezekiel, priest and prophet, also called for reform: "Because you have defiled my sanctuary with all your detestable things . . . therefore I will cut you down" (5:11). False prophets were prophesying peace for Israel when there was no peace (13:16). Individual responsibility on the part of fathers and sons was declared: "The soul that sins shall die" (18:20). Because false shepherds were concerned only about feeding themselves, the hungry sheep looked up and were not fed (34:8). Having denounced their sins and condemned their false worship, Ezekiel challenges Israel to return to genuine worship by means of a vision which God revealed to him. This magnificent vision of the measureless temple of God included a detailed account of a meaningful cultus—a chamber for washing the offering (40:38), tables for slaughtering the sacrifice (vv. 39-41), chambers for the priests' preparation (vv. 44-46), the most holy place (41:4), carved likenesses of cherubim and palm trees (vv. 17-18), the table before the Lord (v. 22), chambers where the priests consumed the offering (42:13), the priests' holy garments (v. 14), a visitation of the spirit and a vision of the glory of the Lord filling the temple (43:4-5), the voice of God speaking his word (vv. 6ff.), the altar for the burnt offerings with details for making the sacrifice (vv. 18-27), detailed instructions to the priests as to their garments, their consecration and their ministries (44:15 ff.), and detailed instructions concerning the people's worship (46:3 ff.). The vision of the temple and the acts of worship climaxed with the blessings of God flowing out from the sanctuary like fresh waters to bless the land with ever-bearing trees producing fruit for food and leaves for healing (47:1-12).

The classic example of worship is found in the experience of Isaiah recorded in the sixth chapter of his prophecy. In a vision of the temple of worship Isaiah saw the Lord in all his majesty and glory. Confronted by the God who is holy, he confessed his sins, received cleansing, and committed himself to the will of God.

The book of Malachi is particularly concerned with worship. The prophet was burdened about the deterioration of worship among the people of Israel. Their polluted bread, diseased animal sacrifices, and unrighteous attitudes had perverted God's covenant and profaned his altars. Malachi calls for repentance and dedication to the Lord. To those who turn from their wickedness and fear his name, Jehovah promised healing and renewal of life (4:2).

The book of Psalms is rich in content of personal worship. The personal element does not necessarily mean individual or private, for many of the psalms were written to be used in common worship. The Psalter has always been the most used and best beloved book of the Old Testament. The psalms have been the foundation of Christian hymnody. The title of the book of Psalms in Hebrew is *Tehillim,* which means "cultic songs of praise." Mowinckel says that the great majority of the Psalms are really cult psalms composed for use in the actual worship services in the Temple.[11]

Above many of the Psalms appear headings or terms indicating the liturgical aim of the particular psalm. A few examples will illustrate: Psalm 100, "For thanksgiving"; Psalm 88, "For Penance" or "To humiliate" one's soul; Psalm 38, "For reminder" or "For a memorial sacrifice." "To the Chief Musician" appears above several with certain instructions as to how the music is to be rendered in the worship of God.

Many of the Psalms are "songs of ascent" sung by pilgrims on their way up to the temple of worship located on Mount Zion. "I will lift up mine eyes to the hills. From whence does my help come? My help comes from the Lord, who made heaven and earth" (121:1-2). "I was glad when they said to me, 'Let us go into the house of the Lord!' " (122:1). Another song acknowledged dependence upon the Lord: "Unless the Lord builds the house, those who build it labor in vain" (127:1). Still another gives assurance of God's blessings upon those who worship him: "Blessed is every one who fears the Lord, who walks in his ways!" (128:1).

Samuel Terrien observes that the Hebrew Psalms constitute the core of personal prayer and corporate worship for all forms of Judaism—Orthodox, Conservative, Reform—and for all churches of Christendom—Greek, Roman, Protestant.[12] They were the liturgical food of the inner life of Jesus and provided support for Paul and Silas in prison (Acts 16:25). The Christians in the catacombs,

---

[11]*Op. cit.,* I, xxiii.

[12]*The Psalms and Their Meaning for Today* (New York: Bobbs-Merrill Co., Inc., 1952), p. vii.

the preachers of the Reformation—John Hus, Martin Luther, John Calvin—the Huguenots, the Puritans of the seventeenth century, and contemporary Christians all give a central place to the Psalms in their worship.

Terrien says the secret of the vitality of the Psalms may be explained by the following facts: (1) the sense of worship which animated their poets; (2) the poets' boldness and honesty in prayer; (3) their theological certainty concerning God's ultimate victory; (4) their sense of historical and social responsibility; (5) and their elegant literary and aesthetic form.[13] The poetry of the Psalms as the vehicle of spiritual intuition and devotion is related to the entire history of our worship.

Worship in the New Testament

According to the New Testament story, Christian worship is rooted in Jewish practices. The earliest Christians were first of all Jews who had been faithful in their worship at the Temple and in their synagogues. Jesus himself followed the practices of his people in worship. The first Christians followed the Hebrew manner of worship to some extent, such as they were accustomed to in the Temple and in the synagogue.

From the beginning Christian worship was filled with the use of biblical ideas and images. The early Christians made constant use of Jewish liturgical forms with no sense of incongruity. The raw material of Christian worship was a common religious inheritance—the practice, teaching, and symbolism of the Temple and synagogue, together with the special practices and teachings of Jesus. Although there is a distinct element in Christian worship not found in Old Testament worship, there is no radical discontinuity between worship in the Old Testament and that in the New.[14]

Dargan asserted that there was "no sudden jar in passing from the Old Testament to the New" in worship.[15]

It is generally conceded that there are three merging types of

---

[13]*Ibid.*, pp. xi-xiv.

[14]See Massey H. Shepherd, Jr., *Worship in Scripture and Tradition* (New York: Oxford University Press, 1963), p. 32.

[15]*Op. cit.*, p. 528.

worship in the New Testament: worship in the Temple, worship in the synagogue, and Christian worship in the homes and other places where Christians met as a distinctive group.[16]

The Temple—Traditional Place of Worship

There are numerous associations of New Testament activity in the Temple. There Zechariah had a vision that assured him he would not die childless (Luke 1:11 ff.). On his presentation in the Temple by Mary, the infant Jesus was greeted by Simeon and Anna (2:27 ff.). In his twelfth year Jesus was found talking with the Temple rabbis (vv. 46ff.). Jesus cleansed the Temple of the dealers that profaned his Father's house of prayer (Mark 11:15-17; John 2:13 ff.). Jesus was observed at various feasts in the Temple (John 5; 7; 8; 10:22 ff.). The first days of the closing week in the life of Jesus he spent largely in the Temple (Matt. 21:12-16; Mark 12:41 ff.; Luke 21:5). At the Temple he announced that not one stone would be left upon another. This prediction was fulfilled in the destruction of the Temple by the Romans in A.D. 70.

Luke observes that the Christians were continually in the Temple blessing God (Luke 24:53). After Pentecost they were found in the Temple day by day continuing steadfastly in prayer (Acts 2:46). The apostles continued to teach daily in the Temple (4:1 ff.). Although Paul attended the Temple for ceremonial purposes (21:26), he proclaimed that "the Most High does not dwell in houses made with hands" (7:48; 17:24). Jesus himself had predicted, "The hour is coming when neither on this mountain nor in Jerusalem will you worship the Father" (John 4:21). The Christians no longer needed the Temple in Jerusalem, for Christ himself had become their Temple, their place for meeting God in worship. Paul saw the church as a "holy temple" in the Lord (Eph. 2:14,21).

The Synagogue—Worship in Transition

The fall of Jerusalem and the destruction of Solomon's Temple, the long period in exile away from the central place of worship, the decline of the prophetic ministry, and the accelerated emphasis

---

[16]See Ilion T. Jones, *A Historical Approach to Evangelical Worship* (Nashville: Abingdon Press, 1954), p. 61.

on the Scriptures gave rise to new modes of worship. New centers of worship known as synagogues began to arise. Although no mention of the synagogue appears in the Old Testament, it was probably established by the third century B.C.[17]

Since the Temple with its majestic architecture and elaborate symbolism was destroyed in A.D. 70, its influence did not strongly prevail in the development of Christian worship. The synagogue, with its plain building and simple services, had greater influence on Christian practices. The Greek word for "synagogue" meant a "gathering-place" (Luke 7:5).

The synagogues were first established as institutions for teaching. However, later they probably were used as places of worship for the Jews. Even in Jerusalem there were many synagogues, and in all parts of the Dispersion there were particular synagogues for community worship (Acts 6:9). In Palestine synagogues were scattered all over the country, the larger towns—including Nazareth (Matt. 13:54) and Capernaum (12:9)—having one or more.

According to the Gospels, Jesus, a good Jew, made use of the synagogues for teaching and worship (see Luke 4:16-21). Paul and others of the disciples were also accustomed to going to the synagogue for worship (Acts 14:1).

Worship in the synagogues differed a great deal from worship in the Temple. The following differences have been pointed out: (1) synagogue worship was less formal; (2) the didactic or teaching element was foremost in the synagogue; (3) priestly functions were not as prominent; (4) the teacher was the central figure in the synagogue; and (5) lay participation was more prominent.

The chief elements of synagogue worship have been outlined as follows: (1) reading of the Scriptures and their interpretation; (2) recitation of the Jewish creed, the Shema (Deut. 6:4); (3) the use of the Psalms, the Ten Commandments, the Benediction, and the Amen; (4) the prayers; (5) and the Jewish Kedushah, or prayer of sanctification, which became in the Christian tradition the *Ter Sanctus* ("Holy, Holy, Holy").[18]

---

[17]*Interpreter's Dictionary of the Bible, op. cit.,* IV, 882.
[18]W. O. E. Oesterley, *The Jewish Background of the Christian Liturgy* (Oxford: Clarendon Press, 1925), chap. 2.

The practices of worship in the Old Testament have been variously summarized as follows: (1) Everything was prescribed, such as the prayers, the offerings, and the ceremonies. (2) Worship was built largely around a sacrificial system in which blood was a symbol representing life for the people. (3) The Hebrew year was given much prominence. (4) The priest played an important part in the system, for he dramatized the offering of sacrifices. (5) The place of worship was prominent in that it symbolized the presence of God. (6) There was a great deal of emphasis on the feasts, especially the Passover, Pentecost, Trumpets, Day of Atonement, and Tabernacles.

Obviously, the sacrificial system in Old Testament worship included many rituals which are not appropriate for Christian worship. There are, however, many abiding principles, as well as certain rituals and symbols, which are valid for Christian worship.

New Testament Distinctives

Although early Christian worship grew out of the Jewish practices of the Temple and the synagogue, it must not be construed that there was nothing distinctive about Christian worship. Phifer has pointed out numerous distinctions in the materials used in worship.[19]

1. The Christians used writings of their own leaders, such as the Epistles of Paul and the Gospel accounts of the life of Jesus, and perhaps verbal recollections concerning them. These writings soon took precedence over the Law and the Prophets.

2. Although the Psalms were used to express praise in Christian worship, new hymns were added by Christian writers, such as those found in the Epistles of Paul. The classic passage on the humiliation of Christ seems to be an early hymn or a confession of faith (Phil. 2:5-11). Paul encourages the Christians to speak to one another "in psalms and hymns and spiritual songs, singing and making melody in your heart to the Lord" (Eph. 5:18-19).

---

[19]Kenneth G. Phifer, *A Protestant Case for Liturgical Renewal* (Philadelphia: The Westminster Press, 1965), p. 23. See also Gerhard Delling, *op. cit.,* chap. 1.

3. Baptism and the Lord's Supper are distinctive additions to Christian worship. Beasley-Murray shows the distinction between Christian baptism and the earlier practices of baptism.[20] Oscar Cullmann believes the Lord's Supper was the "basis and goal of every gathering."[21] There are numerous references to Christians breaking bread together. The so-called love feasts seem to bear some relationship to the Lord's Supper. How large a place the Lord's Supper played in the early worship services cannot be known for certain, but we can be sure that it was a vital experience in Christian worship.[22]

4. There was a spirit of zeal in Christian worship produced by the consciousness that the Holy Spirit had come to make Christ regnant in their midst. Worship became primarily a celebration of the acts of God manifested in Jesus Christ. The resurrection struck a triumphant note in the hope which had been planted in their hearts by the Lord himself. An unbounded enthusiasm is seen in the spontaneous spirit of early Christian worship. The emphasis was upon the presence of the risen Christ. Paul expressed this in the words, "Now the Lord is that Spirit: and where the Spirit of the Lord is, there is liberty" (2 Cor. 3:17, KJV). From the first there was a devotion to the living Christ that gave a deep sense of mystery and awe and triumphant joy.

5. Christian worship also differed from Jewish worship as to times and places. The Jewish sabbath as the day of worship was fulfilled and abrogated by Christ himself. The Lord's Day, the first day of the week, became the Christian day of worship in commemoration of the Resurrection. The Christian Sunday is not a continuation of the Jewish sabbath, yet it does symbolize the fulfilment of the promises which the sabbath foreshadowed.

Although the early Christians at first worshiped in the Temple and in the synagogues, the place for meeting God was no longer limited to the central sanctuary. The living Christ was present wherever two or three gathered in his name (Matt. 18:20). The

---

[20]George R. Beasley-Murray, *Baptism in the New Testament* (London: Macmillan & Co., Ltd., 1962), pp. 27 ff.

[21]*Early Christian Worship* (London: SCM Press, Ltd., 1953), p. 29 f.

[22]See Joachim Jeremias, *The Eucharistic Words of Jesus,* trans. Norman Perrin (New York: Charles Scribner's Sons, 1966).

early Christians met in homes or "house-churches" and in other places designated for Christian worship. It was not so much that they repudiated the importance of church buildings; they simply had no central meeting places at first. From about the third century onward, Christians began to build their own buildings for the services of worship.

Elements of New Testament Worship

Although there is no prescribed order for worship in the New Testament, there is evidence of some kind of order and planning. As Paul warns against the excesses expressed in ecstatic utterances and speaking in tongues, he concludes with the exhortation concerning worship, "Let all things be done decently and in order" (1 Cor. 14:40, KJV). Henry C. Vedder says that the traces of ritual are found in the New Testament, not only in the Lord's Prayer and the doxologies, but also in rhythmical passages in the apostolic writings.[23]

No exact order can be found in the worship of New Testament times, but the following elements of worship are found throughout the New Testament.

1. Music had a central place in the Christians' expression of praise. They sang psalms and hymns and spiritual songs, making melody in their hearts unto the Lord (Eph. 5:18-21; Col. 3:16; 1 Cor. 14:15). Among the earliest Christian hymns were the Magnificat of Mary in Luke 1:46 ff, the Nunc Dimittis of Simeon in Luke 2:29-32, and the Benedictus of Zechariah in Luke 1:68 ff. These were probably used in early Christian worship services. Other great hymns of the New Testament are found in Revelation 5:9,12-13; 12:10-12; 19:1-2,6.

2. The reading of the Scriptures was definitely an element in early Christian worship. We are told that Jesus stood up in the synagogue to read the Scriptures (Luke 4:16). Paul makes numerous references to the reading of the Scriptures (Col. 4:16, 1 Thess. 5:27; 1 Tim. 4:13). Paul's letters were written to be read in the churches. Doubtless they came to be a part of regular instruction in worship. Selections from the Old Testament Scriptures con-

---

[23] *A Short History of the Baptists* (Philadelphia: American Baptist Publication Society, 1907), p. 32.

tinued as a part of Christian worship, especially passages from the Prophets and the Psalms.

3. There is abundant evidence of prayers in early Christian worship. Luke's narrative of the early church tells us they devoted themselves to teaching, to fellowship, to the breaking of bread, and to prayers (Acts 2:42). There were prayers of thanksgiving, petition, intercession, and benediction. Examples of these may be seen in Philippians 4:6; Colossians 2:7; 2 Timothy 2:1-2; 2 Corinthians 13:14. One of the oldest liturgical prayers is the Aramaic *Maranatha,* "Come, Lord Jesus" (Rev. 22:20.). The classic example of prayer is the Model Prayer given by Jesus to his disciples (Matt. 6:9-13). It is the standard of devotion for Christians of all time. According to this Model Prayer, genuine worship begins in the act of adoration and ends in filial devotion.

4. The people's "amens" are seen in numerous places in the New Testament. "Amen" is a term used by the congregation to express approval of what the leader says (see 1 Cor. 14:16).

5. The sermon or exposition of the Scriptures seems to have been an important part of early Christian worship. On the day of Pentecost Simon Peter stood up and preached the gospel to the people (Acts 2:40). Paul exhorted Timothy to be faithful in preaching the Word (2 Tim. 4:1-4). The kerygma, or the acts of God in history revealed in Jesus Christ, was preached wherever Christians went.[24]

6. Exhortation was held to be essential in worship. The writer of Hebrews felt that it was important for Christians to "provoke one another unto love and to good works" (Heb. 3:13; 10:24, KJV). Paul urged his fellow Christians to exhort one another and to reprove one another with authority in the Lord (1 Thess. 3:2; 2 Thess. 3:12; Titus 2:15).

7. It was customary for Christians to give offerings in public worship. Paul exhorted the Christians at Corinth to share their material goods with their less fortunate brethren in Philippi (1 Cor. 16:2; 2 Cor. 9:6-7, 10-13). He implied that giving is motivated by worship of the Lord Jesus Christ who, though he was rich,

---

[24]See C. H. Dodd, *The Apostolic Preaching* (New York: Harper & Bros., 1936).

became poor so that by his poverty believers might become rich (2 Cor. 8:1-8). Jesus commended the poor widow for presenting her offering in sincere worship, for out of her deep poverty she gave all she had (Mark 12:42).

8. New Testament worship is filled with doxologies. In the midst of his writings Paul continually breaks forth with doxologies unto God. For example, he exults, "Blessed be the God and Father of our Lord Jesus Christ, who has blessed us in Christ with every spiritual blessing in the heavenly places" (Eph. 1:3).

9. Open confessions seem to have been a practice of Christians in the early church. There was the public confession of one's sin in the presence of witnesses (1 Tim. 6:12). Paul says that confession of faith in Jesus Christ with one's lips is a part of the process of salvation (Rom. 10:9). James urged his fellow Christians to confess their sins one to another and to pray for one another (James 5:16).

10. Christian worship included the ordinances of baptism and the Lord's Supper. Jesus commanded his followers to practice the observance of baptism and the Lord's Supper. Baptism followed immediately upon one's belief in Jesus Christ as Saviour and Lord; it was an act of confession that Christ is Lord (Matt. 28:18-20; Acts 2:38-41; Gal. 3:27). The Lord's Supper had an important place in early Christian worship. At the institution of the Supper Jesus commanded his disciples to practice the observance of the Supper in remembrance of him (Matt. 26:26-28). In his treatment of worship, Paul deals at length with the observance of the Lord's Supper (1 Cor. 11:20-34).[25]

Neither Jesus nor Paul laid down a particular order for worship. However, both of them implied that there is a logical order for public worship. Perhaps the Model Prayer includes a logical sequence of attitudes in worship. As we have seen, Paul insists upon orderliness and thoughtful discipline in the worship service (1 Cor. 14:40). Moffatt says, "This practical wisdom, or cool, quiet handling of supernatural powers and functions in the spiritual sphere, with its stress upon the permanent influence of the

---

[25]For further study see A. J. B. Higgins, *The Lord's Supper in the New Testament* (London: SCM Press, Ltd., 1960), pp. 70 ff.

Spirit as opposed to any exaggeration of intermittent ebullitions, is one of Paul's great services to the Christianity of his day."[26]

> Resign the rhapsody, the dream,
>   To men of larger reach;
> Be ours the quest of a plain theme,
>   The piety of speech.[27]

---

[26]James Moffatt, *Moffatt's Commentary: First Epistle to the Corinthians* (London: Hodder & Stoughton, 1943), p. 225.

[27]*Ibid.*, p. 220.

3

Historical Backgrounds

The primary objective of this historical study of worship is to discover those resources which have been most helpful in making worship vital throughout the history of Christianity. A secondary objective is to evaluate the errors and weaknesses evident in certain traditional practices of the churches in their worship. Contemporary practices may then retain the strengths and avoid the weaknesses in seeking to maintain vitality in the life of the churches at worship. No effort will be made here to give a detailed history of the development of liturgy, but simply to portray Christian practices with a few illustrations of various forms of liturgy.[1]

Worship in the Early Churches

There are very few literary sources of information concerning the development of Christian worship in the early centuries. There are no strictly liturgical manuals or texts. In Clement's personal letter to the church of Corinth, written about A.D. 96, there are a number of exhortations concerning various elements found in worship services, but there is no specific instruction concerning the worship service as such. For example, Clement encourages the people to read and revere the Word of God, to repent and confess their sins, to show humility before God's majesty, to acknowledge the Holy Spirit in their presence, to acknowledge their salvation in Jesus the High Priest, to proclaim faithfully the Word of God, and to present offerings for the support of those who serve among them. The letter concludes with a prayer which would be fitting for a worship service.[2]

---

[1]For a more detailed study of the history of worship see Dom Gregory Dix, *The Shape of the Liturgy* (London: A & C Black, 1945), and W. D. Maxwell, *An Outline of Christian Worship* (New York: Oxford University Press, 1936).

[2]See *Library of Christian Classics, Early Christian Fathers*, ed. Cyril C. Richardson (Philadelphia: The Westminster Press, 1953), I, 43 ff.

Pliny, Roman governor of the Province of Pontus and Bithynia, wrote to the Emperor Trajan (about A.D. 112) requesting a clear policy on how to deal with the problems which the Christians were creating within his province. He describes the worship of the Christians on Sunday, mentioning two rites. First, they meet "before daybreak" when a hymn is sung to Christ as God, and the Christians bind themselves by a "sacramentum" to abstain from evil. They meet later to eat food described as "common and harmless"; this is the second rite.[3]

Part of a paragraph from Pliny's letter reads as follows:

They were in the habit of meeting before dawn on a stated day and singing alternately a hymn to Christ as to a god, and they bound themselves by an oath, not to the commission of any wicked deed, but that they would abstain from theft and robbery and adultery, that they would not break their word, and that they would not withhold a deposit when reclaimed. This done, it was their practice, so they said, to separate and then to meet again together for a meal.

The *Didaché,* probably written between A.D. 120 and 150 and purported to be "The Teaching of the Twelve Apostles," was discovered in 1873 at Constantinople.[4] This manual, the first of the fictitious church orders which claim apostolic authorship, was divided into two parts: (1) a code of Christian morals, and (2) a manual of church order. It gave instruction concerning baptism as follows: "Baptize in running water in the name of the Father, and of the Son, and of the Holy Spirit. If you do not have running water, baptize in some other. If you cannot in cold, then in warm. If you have neither, then pour water on the head three times in the name of the Father, and of the Son, and of the Holy Spirit." Moreover, it instructed the one who baptizes and the one being baptized to fast one or two days beforehand. It instructed believers to pray three times a day the Model Prayer which Jesus gave to his disciples.

The *Didaché* gave instructions concerning the observance of the Lord's Supper as follows:

---

[3]Maxwell, *op. cit.,* p. 8.
[4]See *Library of Christian Classics, Early Christian Fathers,* I, 161.

Now about the Eucharist: This is how to give thanks:

(1) First in connection with the cup:

"We thank you, our Father, for the holy vine of David, your child, which you have revealed through Jesus, your child. To you be glory forever."

(2) Then in connection with the piece (broken off the loaf): "We thank you, our Father, for the life and knowledge which you have revealed through Jesus, your child. To you be glory forever.

"As this piece (of bread) was scattered over the hills and then was brought together and made one, so let your Church be brought together from the ends of the earth into your Kingdom. For yours is the glory and the power through Jesus Christ forever."

(3) You must not let anyone eat or drink of your Eucharist except those baptized in the Lord's name. For in reference to this the Lord said, "Do not give what is sacred to dogs."

(4) After you have finished your meal, say grace in this way: "We thank you, holy Father, for your sacred name which you have lodged in our hearts, and for the knowledge and faith and immortality which you have revealed through Jesus, your child. To you be glory forever.

"Almighty Master, 'you have created everything' for the sake of your name, and have given men food and drink to enjoy that they may thank you. But to us you have given spiritual food and drink and eternal life through Jesus, your child.

"Above all, we thank you that you are mighty. To you be glory forever.

"Remember, Lord, your Church, to save it from all evil and to make it perfect by your love. Make it holy, 'and gather' it 'together from the four winds' into your Kingdom which you have made ready for it. For yours is the power and the glory forever."

"Let Grace come and let this world pass away."

"Hosanna to the God of David!"

"If anyone is holy, let him come. If not, let him repent."

"Our Lord, come!"

"Amen."

In the case of prophets, however, you should let them give thanks in their own way.[5]

---

[5]*Ibid.* pp. 175-76.

The first broad outline of worship is given in Justin Martyr's *Apology* written about A.D. 140. In his *Manual of Church History,* A. H. Newman calls Justin's outline of worship "one of the most detailed and life-like views of the ordinances and worship of the early Christians that we have." The following is Justin's description of Christian worship:

(1) The Reading of the Scripture—On the day which is called Sunday we have a common assembly of all who live in the cities or in the out-lying districts, and the memoirs of the Apostles or the writings of the Prophets are read, as long as there is time.

(2) The Address of the President—Then, when the reader has finished, the president of the assembly verbally admonishes and invites all to imitate such examples of virtue.

(3) The Prayer—Then we all stand up together and offer up our prayers, and, as we said before, after we finish our prayers, bread and wine and water are presented.

(4) Thanksgiving and Amen of the people—He who presides likewise offers up prayers and thanksgivings, to the best of his ability, and the people express their approval by saying "Amen."

(5) Distribution of the bread and the wine—The Eucharistic elements are distributed and consumed by those present, and to those who are absent they are sent through the deacons.

(6) Collection for the Poor—The wealthy, if they wish, contribute whatever they desire, and the collection is placed in the custody of the president. (With it) he helps the orphans and widows, those who are needy because of sickness or any other reason, and the captives and strangers in our midst; in short, he takes care of all those in need.[6]

Justin states, "Sunday, indeed, is the day on which we all hold our common assembly because it is the first day on which God, transforming the darkness and matter, created the world."

In the early centuries there must have been considerable latitude, since the choice of psalms and hymns would vary and the earliest prayers were probably extemporary.

Worship During the Medieval Period

The development toward ritualism with an established liturgy

---

[6]Justin Martyr, *The First Apology,* trans. Thomas B. Falls (New York: Christian Heritage, Inc., 1948), p. 107.

was soon begun in the early Christian churches. According to Adolph Harnack's *History of Dogma,* in the third and fourth centuries the free usages of primitive Christianity passed over into the beginning of a formal system, which was to be thoroughly developed later by the Roman Catholic Church. In evaluating this change, Harnack speaks of the "sanctifying power of blind custom."[7]

The emphasis upon outward form and ceremony was due to the theological system of sacramentalism and sacerdotalism. Medieval worship reverted to the priestly system of the Old Testament, with certain customs of the mystery and pagan religions added. Much superstition was enforced by use of sensory appeals.

From the fifth century until the Reformation emphasis was placed upon buildings designed to fit set forms of worship performed at certain times. Hence, the development of the Mass, a certain way of celebrating the Lord's Supper with elaborate artistic forms. The service included numerous Scripture readings, an endless number of prayers with versicles and responses, a growing number of hymns, and the commemoration of the saints. A great number of books were necessary in the conduct of the service: the psalter, the antiphonal, the hymnal, the Bible, the collect book, the processional; and for direction, the Consuetudinary, the Ordinal, and the Directorium. The liturgy was devised to serve an authoritarian church in its claim to a bestowal of grace through a sacramental system.

By the sixth century different Christian centers had developed their own liturgies. The main divisions were the Eastern and the Western. In the East were three major types of rites known as the Alexandrian, the Syrian, and the Byzantine. The Byzantine liturgy became the adopted liturgy of the Orthodox Church in the East. In the West the primary classifications were the Gallican and the Roman liturgies.

During the early part of this period the Roman Catholic method of worship began to dominate throughout the West. Baker delineates this development as follows: (1) Worship was centered in the observance of the Mass (the Lord's Supper), which was looked upon as the "unbloody sacrifice" of Christ again. The symbolism was now completely literal. The wine was not yet withheld from

---

[7](London: Williams and Norgate, 1899).

the people. The Supper was now considered to be a sacrament. (2) An extensive system of mediating saints had developed. (3) The worship of the virgin Mary had also become more widespread. (4) Relics became an important part of the religious life. (5) The number of sacraments was increasing, although it was not yet fixed. Some contended for simply two, some for five, and others for as many as a dozen. (6) Auricular confession was already fairly well established. (7) The idea of merit from the sacraments and from external works was widespread.[8]

The Roman liturgy will serve as an example of the fixed order of worship which had developed by the Middle Ages. Sometime between the period of New Testament worship and A.D. 500 the order of worship had been divided into two parts, *The Liturgy of the Word* and *The Liturgy of the Upper Room*. All members of the congregation were invited to the Liturgy of the Word, but only the initiate or baptized Christians were invited to remain for the Liturgy of the Upper Room. All unbaptized persons were dismissed before this second part, which has been called "the liturgy of the faithful." According to Maxwell, the Roman Mass was the simplest of all rites. It was comparatively brief, austere, and rigid in the economy of words, structure, and ceremony.[9] A brief outline of it follows.

Liturgy of the Word

Introit by two choirs as clergy enter
Kyries
Celebrant's salutation
Collect (s)
Prophecy or Old Testament lection
Antiphonal chant
Epistle
Gradual (Psalm sung originally by one voice)
Alleluia
Gospel, with lights, incense, responses
Dismissal of those not communicating (Greg. Dialog. I.ii.23)

---

[8]Robert A. Baker, *A Summary of Christian History* (Nashville: Broadman Press, 1959), pp. 92-93.
[9]*Op. cit.,* p. 56 ff.

Liturgy of the Upper Room

Offertory: Collection of elements, spreading of corporal on altar, preparation of elements for communion, offering of gifts, admixture, psalm sung meanwhile

Salutation and *Sursum corda*

Prayer of Consecration:
  Preface
  Proper Preface
  Sanctus
  Canon

Kiss of Peace

Fraction

Lord's Prayer with protocol and embolism

Communion, celebrant first, then people (Psalm sung meanwhile)

Post-communion collect (Thanksgiving)

Dismissal by deacon

Maxwell gives a detailed description of the ceremonial and indicates there were many superstitious ideas connected with the Mass by the time of the Reformation. There were several ways of celebrating the Mass. (1) The Pontifical High Mass was a sung Mass in which the celebrant has a bishop assisted by one or more priests. (2) The High Mass was a sung Mass celebrated by a priest assisted by deacons. The High Mass required a well-trained choir to sing choral parts. (3) The Low Mass was the popular Mass celebrated by a priest with neither choir nor assistant ministers. By the sixteenth century Low Mass had become the popular service. (4) The Missa Sicca or Dry Mass was a low Mass said without consecration of the elements and without communion. Numerous Masses were said during the Middle Ages— for the dead in Purgatory, for safety on a journey, for recovery from sickness, for the capture of thieves, for the release of captives, for rain, and for fair weather. Maxwell says these "private masses became a cancer feeding upon the soul of the Church."[10]

By the sixteenth century the Roman Mass had attained uniformity. The doctrine of transubstantiation was complete. The observance of the Lord's Supper was mixed with superstition. The people were urged to participate only once a year, at Easter. The

[10]*Ibid.*, p. 68.

worship service was conducted in the Latin language, an unknown tongue to the people. Passages from the lives and legends of the saints were substituted for Scripture passages. The Scriptures were not available in the vernacular. The practice of paid masses and indulgences became a source of exploitation. Reformation became an urgent necessity in the Church.

Certain defects are obvious in the Roman rite: (1) emphasis on the propitiatory character of the Mass led to all kinds of abuses; (2) members of the congregation became mere spectators rather than participants in the service; (3) the Mass became a patchwork of prayers taken from different sources which did not fit into one another and which were not intelligible; (4) there was an absence of prayer for the Holy Spirit to dedicate the worshipers and the elements; (5) the Mass became static because it was offered in a dead language. This tended to encourage superstition among uneducated people. Davies concludes that "because Roman worship is offered in a strange tongue, it lacks one of the essential marks of true worship: edification—the building up of the faith of the worshippers."[11]

The development of the liturgy during the Middle Ages has been described as the struggle of religion with art. The spiritual became subordinate to the artistic. There was an emphasis upon the visible church as the seat of authority, upon buildings, set times for worship, set forms, a certain way of celebrating the Mass, and a growing tendency to exalt the externals. Artistic forms appealing to the five senses included vestments, bells, symbolic actions, frequent changes of posture, processions, prayers for the dead, and incense.

Reformation Worship

During the medieval period the practice of worship became too objective, centering in symbols (verbal or otherwise) which became ends in themselves. Such perfunctory worship ceased to meet the deep needs of the people, and there developed a restless spirit and a desire for reformation within the church.

---

[11]*Christian Worship: Its History and Meaning* (New York: Abingdon Press, 1957), pp. 39-40.

Long before the reformation movement actually broke with Martin Luther's nailing of his Ninety-five Theses to the church door at Wittenberg in 1517, there had been wide dissent throughout Europe. Strong evangelical beliefs prompted a stirring in the minds and hearts of many who were inclined toward evangelical faith. Evangelical parties in Germany, Austria, Italy, and Bohemia had been in correspondence for three centuries. This accounts for the rapidity with which the Reformation developed in the thirteenth century.[12]

There was a growing desire among the people for genuine religion. Manifest in the lives of outstanding Christian pietists and mystics, it found expression in some of the monastic orders. It is impossible to mention all of the leaders who contributed toward reform in worship during this period. Among the reformers who made outstanding contributions in the revision of worship were Luther, Zwingli, Calvin, and certain leaders in the Puritan and dissenting churches.

During the Reformation period, worship took three main forms. The most conservative effort at reform was the Lutheran, after which Anglican worship was patterned. The second was moderate or Calvinist which produced the Presbyterian or Reformed patterns. The third and most radical form came in the independent churches of the Puritan tradition, such as the Anabaptists and Quakers. These are the forebears of the patterns of worship among Baptists, Congregationalists, and other Free Church groups.

The Lutheran liturgy was scaled down considerably from the Roman Catholic period. Luther did not intend to break with the Roman Catholic Church but meant only to reform it. Therefore, he retained much of the structure of the liturgy. It will not be necessary to give an outline of Luther's liturgy, but only to set forth certain principles characterizing it. According to Maxwell, the following things characterize Lutheran worship.[13]

(1) There was the fellowship of Christians in and with the living Word. (2) The Lord's Supper was the central service. Luther believed it ought to be celebrated daily throughout Christendom.

---

[12]Baker, *op. cit.*, p. 185.
[13]*Op. cit.*, pp. 72 ff.

(3) Luther believed in the real presence of Christ in the elements. This doctrine has been called the theory of consubstantiation. (4) The Mass is not a repetition of the death of Christ as the Catholics claim, but Christians enter into his sacrifice, offering themselves up together with Christ. (5) Luther urged a Mass conducted in the vernacular. The first was celebrated without the vestment at Wittenberg in 1521. (6) Lutherans soon reverted to the old practice of the Roman Church, retaining the Latin, most of the ceremonial lights, incense, and vestments.

Luther did not go far enough in his reform. It should be said in Luther's behalf, however, that he gave the people a more intelligible part in worship. There was a greater emphasis upon the use of hymns. Liturgical uniformity was never a Lutheran ideal, for there were many variations and much creativeness. The Swedish, the Norwegian, and the American rites are examples of this. Luther held that all practices in the church should be patterned after the Scriptures. He proposed the principle that whatever is not forbidden by the Scriptures is allowed if, in the judgment of the church, it is helpful.

Huldreich Zwingli exerted strong influence in the reformation of worship. His approach to religion was more rational, and he sought for more simplicity and more moral reality in his worship. Zwingli's revision of the Mass was more radical. Unlike Luther, he did not consider the Mass the norm of worship. Zwingli believed that four times a year was suffcient for the celebration of the Lord's Supper. Moreover, he believed that the Lord's Supper was primarily symbolical. In the church at Zurich the Lord's Supper was stripped to its barest essentials. Zwingli rejected both the Roman Catholic doctrine of transubstantiation and Luther's doctrine of consubstantiation in favor of the memorial aspect of the Supper. He also rejected practically all symbols in worship, except those verbal symbols represented in the reading of the Word and in preaching, and abolished all music from public worship. Antiphonal recitation of the psalms and canticles was substituted.

According to Thomas M. Lindsay, Zwingli stood in freer relation to the doctrines and practices of the medieval church, and his scheme of theology was wider and fuller than Luther's. He was quicker to discern the true doctrinal tendencies of their common religious verities. But his position on indulgences and his manner of protesting against them was more radical than Luther's. He failed to see that underneath the purchase of indulgences, the pilgrimages, the adoration of relics, there was a cry for pardon of sins. He was not as sympathetic, therefore, with the Roman Catholic Church as was Luther.[14]

John Calvin made the greatest contribution to the theology of the Reformation, and therefore wielded the greatest influence in the formulation of the liturgies for generations to follow. Calvin was bolder than Luther in changing the liturgy, but he was less radical than Zwingli. Calvin did not think he was expounding a new theology or creating a new church. He considered the doctrinal beliefs of the early Christians, founded on the Word of God and held by pious people throughout the generations from the earliest centuries, to be the theology of the Reformation.[15]

In Geneva in 1537, Calvin prepared a first draft of the reforms he wished to introduce. They dealt with four things, the first two of which have to do with worship: the holy Supper of our Lord, singing in public worship, the religious instruction of children, and marriage. Calvin believed the Lord's Supper ought to be celebrated frequently and be well attended. It ought to be dispensed every Lord's Day, as was the practice in the apostolic church. But the weakness of the people made it undesirable to introduce a sweeping change at first. Therefore, he suggested that the Supper be celebrated once each month.

Calvin took a mediating position between Luther and Zwingli concerning the theology of the Lord's Supper. He was unwilling to go as far as Zwingli in considering the Supper a mere memorial or symbol. He did not agree with Luther that the real presence of Christ was in the bread and wine. He did believe in the real presence of Christ, but related it with the receptivity of the believer.

Calvin felt that congregational singing of psalms ought to be a part of the public worship of the church. Actually, psalms sung in

---

[14]*A History of the Reformation* (New York: Charles Scribner's Sons, 1916), p. 16.
[15]*Ibid.,* p. 100.

this way are really public prayers. Since the people were not trained for congregational singing, Calvin suggested that children be selected and taught to sing in a clear and distinct fashion in the congregation. If the people would listen with attention, they might little by little come to learn to sing together as a congregation.

In the development of the liturgy at Geneva, Calvin was influenced by other leaders in the Reformation. According to Ilion T. Jones, some of the most significant work pertaining to the Reformation of the liturgy took place at Strasbourg. Actually, Calvin's liturgy was a modified form of the Strasbourg Rite.[16]

Calvin was greatly indebted to Martin Bucer of Strasbourg. Bucer substituted the title "Lord's Supper" in the place of "Mass." He introduced the terms "minister" for "priest," and "table" for "altar." Special days for saints were abolished, and the vestments used in worship were discarded in favor of a black gown with cassock. Bucer insisted upon liberty in the formulation of the liturgy. He believed in the inspiration of the Holy Spirit among those who worship and felt that everyone may worship and praise without restraint.

Calvin's Genevan Service Book has served as a model for most of the Reformed churches down through the centuries. For this reason, it seems appropriate to include the outline of worship used by Calvin in Geneva.

The Liturgy of the Word

Scripture Sentence: Psalm cxxiv, 8
Confession of sins
Prayer for pardon
Metrical Psalm
Collect for Illumination
Lection
Sermon

The Liturgy of the Upper Room

Collection of alms
Intercessions
Lord's Prayer in long paraphrase
Preparation of elements while

---

[16]*Op. cit.,* p. 126.

Apostle's Creed sung
Words of Institution
Exhortation
Consecration prayer
Fraction
Delivery
Communion, while psalm or Scriptures read
Post-communion collect
Aaronic Blessing.[17]

Calvin's rite became the norm of worship in Calvinist France, Switzerland, South Germany, Holland, Denmark, and elsewhere. Calvin's influence was extended to Scotland, as may be seen in John Knox's *Book of Common Prayer* and in the "Directory of Public Worship" of the Presbyterian church of England. Calvin's order of worship has continued to influence the Reformed churches through the centuries, including the Presbyterian church in America.

John T. McNeill observed that these reformers insisted on simplicity in worship on the grounds that the "accumulation of rites in the church takes away Christian Liberty and substitutes ceremonies for faith."[18] The order of worship adopted in the different churches of the Reformation was in accord with their respective ideas of doctrine.

It was Calvin's objective to move further from the Roman liturgy than Luther had done. Calvin declared that whatever is not taught in the Scriptures is not allowable in worship, whereas Luther had said that whatever is not forbidden in the Scriptures is acceptable. Calvin's principle called for the rejection of much ceremonialism of the medieval orders of worship. However, Calvin retained dignity and order and insisted upon a structured pattern of worship and a unity which was lacking in the extremes of Zwingli's pattern of worship. Calvin was not guilty of "barrenness and ugliness" in his liturgy.[19] Simplicity was Calvin's aim, for he abhorred the unnecessary bric-a-brac of ornamentation. This did not mean that Calvin lacked an appreciation for order and beauty. Later generations who claimed to be Calvinists were guilty of extremes.

---

[17]*Maxwell*, op. cit., pp. 114-15.
[18]*The History and Character of Calvinism* (New York: Oxford University Press, 1957), p. 89.
[19]Phifer, *op. cit.*, p. 74.

During the Reformation period a third group, known as the Radical Reformers, went to greater extremes in the reformation of worship. Some historians believe that twentieth-century Christianity reflects the theology and forms of worship of the radical groups more than any of the other reformers. Because of their efforts to restore the primitive New Testament order, these radical movements, uninhibited by the political and social commitments that limited Luther and Zwingli and Calvin, tossed aside many of the practices in favor of an unstructured approach to Christianity.[20]

Post-Reformation Worship

Since these radical reformers have influenced worship in the Free Churches for generations, it is appropriate that a brief study be made of their principles of worship. The noncomformist churches were loosed from all moorings of usage and ritual.

A religious awakening has always been accompanied by a revision of the liturgy. The Free Churches sought the true genius of worship as they insisted on being free from traditional rites and ceremonies. They were weary of the old, the habitual, the established—hungry for what was radically new and untried.

In support of the principles of free worship, Andrew M. Fairbairn contrasts the ancient rituals with the Christian pattern of worship. He says, "Let us freely concede to the temple a sensuous sublimity which appeals to eye and ear; but for the church we claim a spiritual sublimity which appeals to the soul and conscience."[21] There is a spirit in worship which predominates over all the fine arts—*i.e.,* the fine art of making men. "It is not faces or dress, but souls; not manner, but men; not a multitude of possibly perfect units, but a crowd of potential persons, an epitome of mankind.[22] This is the Free Church at worship. Out of this kind of conviction the radical reformers discarded the fixed liturgies of the medieval church and insisted upon a simpler approach to worship which would emphasize the spirit rather than the form.

---

[20]Baker, *op. cit.,* p. 227.

[21]*Studies in Religion and Theology* (New York: The Macmillan Co., 1910), p. 261.

[22]*Ibid.,* p. 262.

The Christian groups known as the Radical Reformers were called by various names: Anabaptists, Puritans, Independents, Nonconformists, Separatists, and Dissenters. Prominent among these early reformers were the Anabaptists. Their movement was strong in Switzerland between 1525 and 1529.[23] Anabaptism was born January 21, 1527, in Grossmunster, Switzerland. The movement was based upon believer's baptism and the rejection of infant baptism. This earliest church of the Anabaptists was known as the Swiss Brethren. Their doctrinal conviction of the absolute necessity of personal commitment to Christ influenced the practice of Free Church worship.

Like other Free Church groups, the Anabaptists revolted against the Roman Catholic liturgies. They sought to return to primitive Christianity in their worship, as well as in their living. Some of the principles which they followed in their worship are included here. (1) The preaching of the Word was central. (2) There was an emphasis upon congregational participation in the activities of worship. (3) The clergy and laity became practically indistinguishable, except for certain functions assigned by the church to the clergy. (4) There was an emphasis upon hymn singing by the congregation. The hymns which they sang were hymns of martyrdom telling the story of suffering at the hands of their persecutors. For example, while George Blaurock was in prison in Switzerland, he wrote two hymns. The first sets forth the conditions of salvation, and the second is a hymn concerning Blaurock's personal faith in God.[24] (5) The Anabaptists adopted confessions of faith rather than creeds. The earliest of these was known as the Schleitheim Confession, written and adopted by the Swiss Brethren in February, 1527. It was composed of seven articles, two of which dealt with the way the ordinances are to be observed. These two are particularly pertinent to worship in the history of the Free Churches.[25] (6) Only two ordinances are to be observed by the church, namely baptism and the Lord's Supper. The Anabaptists rejected the sacraments of the Roman

---

[23]For an excellent treatment of the Anabaptists, see William R. Estep, *The Anabaptist Story* (Nashville: Broadman Press, 1963). See also Franklin H. Littell, *The Anabaptist View of the Church* (Boston: Star King Press, 1958).

[24]Estep, *op. cit.,* p. 34.

[25]For a copy of this confession, see William L. Lumpkin, *Baptist Confessions of Faith* (Philadelphia: The Judson Press, 1959) pp. 23 ff.

Church. Baptism was interpreted as a burial in water of those who had accepted Christ as Saviour for themselves. This excluded infant baptism. All believers who had followed Christ in baptism were welcome to partake of the Lord's table. Some of the Anabaptists observed the practice of partaking of the Lord's Supper as they sat about a round table. This was an attempt to get back to the New Testament practice of the close fellowship of believers. (7) Latin was abolished, and the vernacular was introduced so that the common people understood what was being said in church.

It may be emphasized, however, that there were failures and losses in the reforms that occurred in some of the Free Churches. Winward points out three of these. First, there was the revival of clericalism as ministers continued to dominate the service of worship as had been done before the Reformation. Even to this day in many of the Free Churches, worship is dominated by the man in the pulpit, and the congregation is reduced to the role of listening. In the second place, the error of verbalism, which assumes that worship is almost entirely a matter of words, militates against congregational participation. Without the gift of eloquence, the ordinary worshiper finds it easier to do something rather than to say something. A third serious weakness is the failure of some churches to provide for vocal participation in public prayer. There should be a place also for the congregation to participate in prayers.[26]

Phifer observes a fourth weakness: Puritanism carried individualism and subjectivity to the extreme. The concept of the church at worship as a corporate unity was practically lost. The Puritan congregation was a collection of individuals at prayer. The real meaning of the service was considered to be what happened within the individual without reference to the body as a whole. Furthermore, there was a loss of symbolism in Puritan worship. Because of the abuses of the medieval church, the reformers became suspicious of all objects appealing to the senses. Phifer says, "The rich liturgy of the Middle Ages was stripped away, and the simplicity of Christian worship revealed anew. However, the simplicity was prone to degenerate into barrenness."[27]

---

[26]Winward, *op. cit.,* p. 105.
[27]*Op. cit.,* pp. 83-86.

Among the Free Churches Baptists have insisted upon certain guiding principles for worship. Perhaps no other church has insisted as have Baptists on the centrality of the New Testament connection between baptism and personal faith as a symbolic act of surrender to God—on the realistic conversion of the whole life. They have had a passion for spiritual liberty and have shown impatience with ecclesiastical control.

The history of Baptist worship is varied. Baptists owe a great debt to the reformers Luther, Zwingli, and Calvin, to the Puritans, to the Anabaptists, and to their fellow Free Churchmen who followed in their train. Davies reminds us that in the whole range of Protestant worship, from the Quakers to the Anglo-Catholics, from the spontaneous to the formal, from the radical to the traditional, the worship of the Quakers and of the Baptists will be found furthest to the left in origin and development.[28] However, in the course of history the Baptists have been moving more to the center.

In England there were two streams in Baptist history, the General Baptists and the Particular Baptists. The former held to what is known as "general atonement," the doctrine that Christ died for all men and not for a particular few. They date to about 1609 in Amsterdam, Holland, under the leadership of John Smyth. The Particular or Calvinistic Baptists believed in a limited atonement, that Christ died only for the elect. They date from 1638 when they were organized in London under the leadership of John Spillsbury.

The manner of worship in the General Baptist Church at Amsterdam was as follows:

The order of the worship and government of our church is: (1) We begin with a prayer, (2) after read some one or two chapters of the Bible; (3) give the sense thereof and confer upon the same; (4) that done, we lay aside our books and after a solemn prayer made by the first speaker (5) he propoundeth some text out of the scripture and prophesieth out of the same by the space of one hour or three quarters of an hour. (6) After him standeth up a second speaker and prophesieth out of the said text the like time and space, sometimes more, sometimes less. (7) After him, the third, the

[28]*Worship and Theology in England: from Watts and Wesley to Maurice, 1690-1850* (Princeton, N.J.: Princeton University Press, 1961), p. 114.

fourth, the fifth etc., as the time will give leave. (8) Then the first speaker concludeth with prayer as he began with prayer, (9) with an exhortation to contribution to the poor, which (10) collection being made is also concluded with prayer. This morning exercise begins at eight of the clock and continueth unto twelve of the clock. The like course of exercise is observed in the afternoon from two of the clock unto five or six of the clock. Last of all the execution of the government of the Church is handled.[29]

It is surprising to find that these early Baptists rejected the singing of hymns by the congregation since the Anabaptists had left behind them a remarkable body of hymns dating as early as 1564. General Baptists decided that psalm singing was "so strangly foreign to the evangelical worship that it was not conceived any way safe to admit such carnal formalities."[30] A single voice might sing praise, but congregational singing was forbidden. Hymns were frowned upon even more as the singing of "men's compositions."

The Particular Baptists were closer to the Reformed tradition in worship. Many of them sang psalms and Scripture paraphrases, but reluctantly came to sing compositions not directly from the Scriptures. For many years there was a controversy in Baptist churches over congregational singing.

The general pattern of Baptist worship in England has remained about the same from the seventeenth century to the present. It has consisted of Scripture reading, prayers, and sermons, interspersed with hymns by the congregation and the choir. Payne mentions certain changes that have taken place: (1) the shortening of the sermons and prayers; (2) the occasional use of collects and set forms of prayer; (3) greater use of music by instruments (especially the organ) and choirs; (4) in some, the introduction of the children's sermon; (5) a wider use of congregational singing, especially of hymns of original composition.[31]

Baptists were probably the first English Protestants to have a special

---

[29]See Earnest A. Payne, *The Fellowship of Believers: Baptist Thought and Practice Yesterday and Today* (London: The Carey Kingsgate Press, Ltd., 1952), p. 92.

[30]Davies, *Worship and Theology in England: From Watts and Wesley to Maurice, 1690-1850*, p. 127.

[31]*Op. cit.*, p. 96.

collection of hymns for use at the Lord's Supper. In 1697 there appeared Joseph Stennett's "Hymns in Commemoration of the Sufferings of Our Blessed Saviour, Jesus Christ, Composed for the Celebration of the Holy Supper." Stennett was a Baptist minister endowed with outstanding literary gifts and widely respected for his Christian character and his learning.

J. Paul Williams says that it was through Baptists that the singing of English hymns of original composition became popular in America. He states that *The Pilgrim's Progress* was a powerful weapon in the controversy over the new hymns. Many of the songs which Bunyan put on the lips of Christians came to enjoy great popularity.[32]

Worship in America

The influence of the radical reformers was carried over from England and Scotland to North America by immigrants. This fact accounts for the dislike, until recent times, of prepared forms of worship and ornate liturgy. It should be stated that certain of these Protestant communions were semi-liturgical and continued to be bound by tradition. For example, in 1879 Charles Beard observed that in certain worship services, "The Apostle's Creed is recited without any recollection of the controversies which through six centuries have left their works upon clause after clause, and given them a meaning which present usage does little to suggest. The whole service belongs to the past; its newest word is three centuries old."[33]

The Frontier Period

Phifer gives a good description of the development of worship on the American frontier. The two denominations with a commanding position in the American society were the Congregationalists and the Presbyterians, both Calvinistic in theology and Puritan in worship. In the American colonies there was progressive rejection of any fixed order of worship among Congregationalists, Presbyterians, Baptists, and Methodists. The Puritan freedom in worship exactly suited the scene in early America where people were enjoying their newly

[32]*What Americans Believe and How They Worship* (New York: Harper & Row, 1962), p. 242.
[33]"Worship in Free Churches," *Theological Review*, XVI (1879), 221.

gained independence. The American frontier was characterized by individualism and revivalism. These churches on the American frontier considered their task to be primarily one of "snatching brands from the burning." Consequently, they did not take worship very seriously, apart from the conversion of sinners.

Worship on the American frontier may be characterized by the following principles: (1) There were no set forms for worship. (2) The observance of the ordinances was infrequent because of the lack of ordained men to conduct them. (3) There was a suspiciousness on the part of frontier people concerning an educated ministry. To them this indicated an established church. (4) Preaching was the primary emphasis in worship services. (5) The prayers were spontaneous and were participated in by laymen as well as ministers. (6) There was an informal enthusiasm on the part of the worshipers, often expressed in emotional ecstasy. (7) Worship services were characterized by exuberant singing. The songs were subjective and individualistic, while at the same time buoyant and optimistic. (8) Frontier worship was characterized by a spirit of immediacy, and little attention was given to tradition and the past. (9) The place of worship was plain and harsh. Church buildings were not intended to lend themselves to ritual.[34]

The early churches in America had no books of common worship to guide their ministers or to be used as prayer books by the worshipers. There were no fixed or standardized orders of service. The worship of the overwhelming majority of Christian churches in the United States was of the Puritan, informal, spontaneous, spirit-filled, evangelistic type of worship of the New Testament.[35]

One might question whether the type of worship described above is entirely analogous with the worship of the New Testament.

Writing in 1951, James Hasting Nichols deplored the impoverishment of public worship in the two hundred years from 1650 to 1850. He declared that Roman Catholics, Lutherans, Anglicans, and

---

[34]Phifer, op. cit., p. 103.

[35]For a more detailed description of worship in early American history, see William Warren Sweet, Religion in the Development of American Culture, 1765-1840 (New York: Charles Scribner's Sons, 1952); also Jerald C. Brauer, Protestantism in America: A Narrative History (Philadelphia: The Westminster Press, 1953).

Reformed and Puritan Protestants alike felt it in their different ways. He says there were at least four factors which affected the decline of worship in the Free Churches. First, there was an exaggerated hostility toward liturgical worship. They went to extremes to avoid any semblance of the formal worship of the liturgical churches. Second, the primitive circumstances of the American colonists and their cultural disabilities dulled their appreciation of the aesthetic aspects of worship. The low estate of musical culture and the shortage of hymnbooks added to this impoverishment. Third, the overemphasis upon revivalism caused a decline in attention to the basic elements of worship, especially among the Baptists and Disciples. This spirit of revivalism reduced all prayer and praise and reading of the Scriptures to "preliminary exercises" and risked everything else for the experienced or shared ecstasy of conversion. The fourth factor responsible for the dissolution of worship in the Free Churches was the romantic transcendentalism of such leaders as Emerson and Parker. Nichols says this produced a sort of "self-conscious artiness" seen in much of Unitarian worship as well as that of other churches. This overemphasis on aesthetics he calls "play acting with holy things."[36]

The Contemporary Period

There has perhaps never been an era in the history of the Free Churches when they took more seriously the theology and practice of worship than they are taking in this contemporary era. The worship of the Christian churches offers the best clue to their interior life, as well as an index to their state of health. The current theological ferment in the world and the prevailing modes of architecture, art and music greatly influence worship. Just as the church cannot ignore theology and ethics in its worship, theology and ethics cannot afford to separate themselves from worship.

On every hand there is a call for church renewal. Although church membership has reached a new statistical level in America, church gains are not keeping pace with population gains. Even churches and denominations which have realized great advances on

---

[36] "The Rediscovery of Puritan Worship," *The Christian Century* (April 25, 1951).

the American scene are aware of the lack of spiritual depth and concern on the part of many in their membership. An example of this concern is the group known as Southern Baptists. They have slowed down in the numerical gains in evangelism; they have not risen to their potential in stewardship; they have become satiated with an overemphasis on organization, programing, and institutionalism; they have felt a mild anticlerical revolution in favor of more participation by the laity; they acknowledge their tardiness in attacking the sprawling social issues of this era; they are seeking to correct an overemphasis on subjectivism and individualism; and they are often aware of their isolationism in relation to other Christian bodies. Perhaps this description would fit many other Free Church groups in America also.

The Free Churches realize that isolationism is no longer a tenable attitude. In theological education a Protestant dialogue is taking place among teachers and students in seminaries of various denominations. This has even crossed from the Free Churches to the Roman Catholic Church. The various ecumenical councils in the last half-century have called attention to the need for understanding among the churches. Some of the differences have been based upon doctrinal convictions, while others are due to differing aesthetic and liturgical concepts. The recent Vatican Councils called for a reformation of worship in the Roman Catholic Church and a restudy of the relationship of worship practiced in the Free Churches to the ancient forms of liturgy.

Reinhold Niebuhr attributes much of the weakness of public worship in American churches to a spirit of protest. He says the Free Churches have grown up in an atmosphere of "protest against preoccupation with theology, liturgy, and polity."[37] This period of protest, he believes, has led the churches to extreme conclusions.

Charles Seidenspinner calls for a more serious study in our contemporary worship. Describing the weaknesses in the Free Churches, he speaks of our shoddy little anthems, our shameless prayers in which a pastor exposes to public view a bad neurosis of his own, and our sermons plagiarized from assorted homiletic helps. "To such

---

[37]"The Weaknesses of Common Worship in American Protestantism," *Christianity in Crisis,* (May 28, 1951), p. 68.

material we shall have to apply the scissors," he observed.[38] Oscar Hardiman also makes a plea for the reformation of worship. He believes that aesthetic considerations, psychological insight, a growing appreciation for many of these treasures, and an earnest desire to worship more worthily promise some improvement among the Free Churches.[39]

A. W. Palmer urges better preparation on the part of ministers that they may be able to lead the churches more effectively in their worship. He says the congregation may be heard saying, "He's a sincere man, but awfully dull," or "The poor fellow means well, but I can't stand his mannerisms or his voice or his slovenly way of conducting the services."[40]

Among those writing for the renewal of worship are Baptist authors. Generally speaking, Baptists have neglected the study of worship because they have taken for granted that true worship will find its expression primarily in the spontaneous experience without regard to planning or order.

As early as 1900, T. H. Pattison, a Baptist teacher in Rochester Seminary, spoke of the extreme worship practices in the Free Churches. In his standard work *Public Worship,* he called attention to the fact that not even the Reformers were entirely agreed on how far the revolt should be carried. "The dread of popery need not preclude our using the most praiseworthy secrets of its strength in our worship." In this textbook Pattison defined and described worship, then dealt with the various elements found in a public worship service. He suggested the simple form usually followed by the Free Churches. A great emphasis was placed upon the congregation's participation in public worship. He warned against exaggerating the sermon at the expense of other parts of the service. Pattison felt there was need for preserving a settled order of service.

In his classic volume on preaching entitled *The Preparation and Delivery of Sermons,* John A. Broadus included a section on worship. Writing in 1870, he warned against the tendency to neglect worship

---

[38]"Genius of Protestant Worship," *Religion in Life* (Spring, 1949), p. 245.
[39]*History of Christian Worship* (Nashville: Cokesbury Press, 1937), p. 253.
[40]*The Art of Conducting Public Worship* (New York: The Macmillan Co., 1939), p. 5.

in favor of preaching, and urged that more attention be given to the "general cultivation and preparation" for worship.

Edwin C. Dargan included a serious discussion on worship in his book *Ecclesiology,* published in 1897. He gave a brief analysis of worship in the Bible, followed by a brief historical sketch of Christian worship, indicating the importance of the historical point of view in worship. Dargan felt that preaching occupies too large a place proportionately in worship.

Harvey E. Dana made a strong appeal for a reverent approach to worship in his book *A Manual of Ecclesiology.* He declared that the doctrines of the Free Churches have often been misused and abused so that a so-called freedom "throws reverence to the winds and degenerates into a formless profanity of conduct" in the realm of worship.

Recent writings on worship among British Baptists include S. F. Winward's *The Reformation of Our Worship, Orders and Prayers for Church Worship* by Ernest A. Payne and S. F. Winward, and *Call to Worship* by Neville Clark. H. Wheeler Robinson and W. E. Aubrey also have had strong influence on the worship of British Baptists.[41]

---

[41]See Davies, *Worship and Theology in England: The Ecumenical Century, 1900-1965* (Princeton, N. J.: Princeton University Press, 1965), p. 380.

4

A Theology of Worship

As men believe, so they worship. The doctrines we hold determine the nature of our worship. If we are sacramentalists, we will seek God through channels of doing rather than receiving. If we view God as only divine principle, we will seek to conform to the principle. If we view God as idea, we will seek to know him through intellectual understanding or reasoning. If we view God as a personal Being, we will seek to know him in personal relationship. If we conceive of him as Spirit, self-revealed in history, we will worship him in "spirit and truth."

Worship without theology is sentimental and weak; theology without worship is cold and dead. Worship and theology together combine to motivate a strong Christian faith and to empower a fruitful Christian life. J. H. Kurtz, author of *Church History*, believed that worship should be regulated and determined by doctrine. An uncritical view of Christian worship is inadequate.

Christian worship is first an experience, not an art. It is based upon a historical fact, the fact that God revealed himself in history. Evangelical worship is grounded in the great historical facts of God's creation, the incarnation, the works of Jesus Christ, his atoning death, his resurrection, and his abiding presence in the life of believers. The way men think about these historic facts is called theology. Worship that is not grounded in the knowledge and love of God is not true worship. Theology that does not lead to the worship of God in Christ is both false and harmful. A sound theology serves as a corrective to worship, and true worship serves as the dynamic of theology.

The basis of Christian worship is not utilitarian but theological.[1] Worship depends upon revelation, and Christian worship depends

---

[1] Raymond Abba, *Principles of Christian Worship* (New York: Oxford University Press, 1957), p. 5.

upon the revelation of God in Christ Jesus. Worship is therefore a revelation and a response. It springs from the divine initiative in redemption. By faith man responds to grace as he finds it in a face-to-face encounter with God.

Stauffer declared, "Theology is doxology or it is nothing at all."[2] We may further declare that unless worship is theologically sound, it becomes less than doxology. Worship and theology go together. "The reasoned idea without the worship is theology; the worship without any reasoned idea is superstition; but the two in wholesome and corporate union make religion. What theology is to the speculative reason, worship is to the popular consciousness, a form under which deity is conceived and described."[3]

Actually, worship is the experience of conscious communion with God, and theology is the effort to describe the meaning of the experience. Worship is essential to religion. Creeds, however sound, can never be a substitute for worship. Men who seek refuge and safety in creeds soon lose the vitality which issues only from a living faith kept alive by worship.

God, Worthy of Worship

The great fact of life is the human soul confronting the transcendent holiness of God. No person is ever left alone without God. An individual may try to ignore God but he cannot have peace without him; he may deny or reject him but not without a consciousness of judgment. God claims every creature. Worship is the loving response of the creature to his Creator. There is no sovereign right but God's, no other totalitarian authority.

Christian worship is God-centered. God took the initiative in worship by creating man for fellowship with himself. As the ground of being, he is the source and sustainer of life. As sovereign ruler, God confronts man. He comes to man as the one worthy of worship, and because he is worthy he stands in judgment over man and makes demands upon him. As man responds in worship God allows

---

[2] Ethelbert Stauffer, *New Testament Theology*, trans. John Marsh (London: SCM Press, Ltd., 1955), p. 88.

[3] Fairbairn, *A Philosophy of the Christian Religion* (New York: The Macmillan Co., 1923), p. 480.

him to experience new manifestations of his goodness and his love.

A personal God.—God is not an ideal or a philosophy of life or a metaphysical principle; he is a personal and spiritual Being who seeks personal relationships with men. Revelation is not acknowledged by a third-person proposition which says, "There is a God"; it is acknowledged in direct confession of the heart which says, "Thou art my God."[4] God is known not as an inference from logic nor as an essential principle, but as a personal presence continually invading our lives. He comes to man not as sheer power but as the living God seeking to commune with man. God is a thinking, purposing, loving person, however awesomely he transcends all our understanding and experience.

A transcendent God.—When we worship we do not worship an equal; we worship our Creator, the eternal, infinite God. God is the beyondness of man's existence, the absolute source of being. He is the ultimate Being for which man seeks. God's transcendence means that in his absoluteness he is above man. In all his attributes God is higher than man. "My thoughts are not your thoughts, neither are your ways my ways, says the Lord" (Isa. 55:8). God's holy character is a constant challenge to man in his sinful condition. Man stands in awe of the *mysterium tremendum* of God's presence. In worship man experiences a creature-feeling, a feeling of dependence upon God. The majesty of God is a sort of overpoweringness in response to which man can only cry, "Holy, holy, holy is the Lord of hosts; the whole earth is full of his glory" (Isa. 6:3).

Jonathan Edwards saw a qualitative difference between the rational joy of man and experience of true worship: "The conceptions which the saints have of the loveliness of God and that kind of delight which they experience in it are quite peculiar and entirely different from anything which a natural man can possess or of which he can form any notion."[5] Man's efforts at worship without this awe and adoration of the God who is worthy of praise are empty and meaningless. To believe in God implies acknowledgment of his in-

---

[4] H. Richard Niebuhr, *The Meaning of Revelation* (New York: The Macmillan Co., 1946), pp. 153 ff.

[5] Quoted in William James, *The Varieties of Religious Experience* (New York: Modern Library, 1902), p. 229.

finite worth. The man who says in sincerity, "Thou art my God," will also have to say, "Worthy art thou, O Lord, to receive glory and honor and power."

An immanent God.—God is constantly present in the life of man. As giver of life, he is also the sustainer of life. In numerous ways God makes himself known to man. The most intimate and personal expression of his revelation is his love in action. God continually offers himself in abundant love and forgiveness. Man is not left to speculate on the presence and purposes of God, for he comes to man continually. To believe in God's absolute sovereignty is to believe in the sureness of his love.

God comes to man in outgoing love in every means of revelation which he has ordained. His creative power, his sustaining providence, his special revelations to certain individuals who recorded his words, and especially his acts of sheer love in the incarnation, the cross, and the resurrection all indicate the concern of a God who is eternally present with man. Paul said, "He is not far from each one of us, for 'In him we live, and move, and have our being' " (Acts 17: 27-28). The acknowledgment of our total dependence on this free action of God, both transcendent and immanent, is therefore a true part of worship.

Man's knowledge of God is immediate, for man stands in the presence of the living God. It is a "mediated immediacy" as God sees fit to reveal himself through his Word, through Jesus Christ, and through the Holy Spirit.[6]

A trustworthy God.—The God who is worthy of worship is also trustworthy in response to man's act of worship. Man is never disappointed when he lifts his voice to God in praise or petition. The sovereign God is a God of purpose. By his grace he has elected men to be saved. "Whom he did predestinate, them he also called: and whom he called, them he also justified: and whom he justified, them he also glorified. . . . If God be for us, who can be against us?" (Rom. 8:30-31, KJV). Belief in God's electing grace releases reserves of courage and energy.

The man of faith will find God faithful and trustworthy when he

---

[6]John Baillie, *Our Knowledge of God* (New York: Charles Scribner's Sons, 1959), p. 174.

approaches him in worship. Because of God's faithfulness, nothing can separate man from the love of God in Christ. Of this Paul was firmly convinced (Rom. 8:37-39). Before religion can be known as sweet communion, it must be known as an answered summons.[7] The invitation confronts man, "If any one hears my voice and opens the door, I will come in to him and eat with him, and he with me" (Rev. 3:20). The central thing in our religion is not our hold on God but his hold on us, not our choosing him but his choosing us, not that we should know him but that we should be known of him.

Jesus Christ, Object of Faith

The basis of the church's worship is christological. The very life of Jesus is in some sense liturgical. His was a "life of worship." In every act of worship the church experiences afresh the miracle of the coming of the risen Christ. The only way in which man can meet God redemptively is by an encounter with Jesus Christ. The worship of God is made possible in the person of his Son. Christian worship is more than sentiment or idealistic reverie. As J. J. von Allmen says, Christian worship is neither the outcome of an illusion nor an exercise of magic, but a grace that is offered in Christ.[8] It has objective content. Jesus Christ is the object of man's faith. The primary distinction between Christianity and the other great religions of the world is found in the person of Jesus Christ. When Christ's finality is gone, Christianity is gone.[9] All true worship is Christocentric, for only in Christ can God be found.

To use Fairbairn's expression, Christ has become the temple where God and man meet. The divine presence which Israel once found in the tabernacle and in the Temple, man now finds in Christ. Man encounters in the heart of history the glory and grace of God manifest in flesh. "And the Word became flesh and dwelt among us, full of grace and truth; we have beheld his glory, glory as of the only Son from the Father" (John 1:14). Worship may take place anywhere by a meeting with Christ.

---

[7] *Ibid.*, p. 57.

[8] *Worship: Its Theology and Practice* (New York: Oxford University Press, 1965), p. 27.

[9] P. T. Forsyth, *The Person and Place of Jesus Christ* (Boston: Pilgrim Press, n.d.).

Manifestation.—"No one has ever seen God; the only Son, who is in the bosom of the Father, he has made him known" (John 1:18). A sound Christology is essential to a sound theology. The incarnation, with all its mystery, is the only way in which the Christian conception of God becomes credible or even expressible.[10] Whatever Jesus did in his life, in his teaching, in his cross, in his resurrection, ascension, and exaltation, it is really God who did it in Jesus. In the worship experience Jesus comes to man as "God's own Word about himself."[11] Man's vision of God comes in the challenge of Jesus, "He that hath seen me hath seen the Father" (John 14:9, KJV).

Identification.—In his humilitation Jesus identified with man in every area of man's life. To be reconciled to God in Christ is to be reconciled to life in all its concreteness. He took the form of a servant, "being born in the likeness of men" (Phil. 2:7), to bring man into fellowship with God. Man can worship a holy God because he came in lowly birth to man's lowest condition. In the real humanity of Christ God came the whole way to man. In Christ and in all the acts and manifestations of Christ, history and eternity meet. God has come to redeem man in history. That redemption is realized in worship. In worship man identifies with Jesus Christ. In Christ God and man still uniquely meet.

Redemptive power.—The atonement means that God came to meet man's moral need in Christ. The New Testament does not speak of God's being reconciled to man, but of man's being reconciled to God. God is the Reconciler taking the initiative in the cross. "Therefore, if anyone is in Christ, he is a new creation" (2 Cor. 5:17). In the cross man sees God express his concern in the act of suffering love. And that vision brings him to his knees with songs of adoration and praise in gratitude for God's matchless gift. The cross is the only deed which releases a power sufficient to meet man at the depths of greatest need in worship, the need for forgiveness of sin.

Living lordship.—Jesus Christ not only gave himself for the church

---

[10]Donald M. Baillie, *God Was in Christ* (New York: Charles Scribner's Sons, 1948), p. 65.

[11]Emil Brunner, *The Mediator: A Study of the Central Doctrine of the Christian Faith,* trans. Olive Wyon: (Philadelphia: The Westminster Press, 1947).

in his death, but he also continues to give himself to his church in worship. Paul declared, "Therefore God has highly exalted him and bestowed on him the name which is above every name, that at the name of Jesus every knee should bow, in heaven and on earth and under the earth, and every tongue confess that Jesus Christ is Lord, to the glory of God the Father" (Phil. 2:9-11). The resurrection is the eternal answer to the power of sin and death. The living Christ is present for every man at worship. The earliest Christians acknowledged the presence and lordship of the risen Christ when they met for worship. Christian worship presupposes that people come together in the "name of Jesus." Worship as man's faith-event finds reality in the Christ-event—incarnation, cross, and resurrection. The early Christians could proclaim their faith with the words *Kurios Christos*—"Christ is Lord."

Holy Spirit, the Dynamic of Worship

The chief modern heresy in worship concerning the Holy Spirit is the neglect of his presence and power. Every aspiration in the human heart and every spiritual achievement is the work of the Holy Spirit. More sermons ought to be preached about the Holy Spirit, more hymns addressed to him, and more attention paid to his works.

God's personal presence.—God appears to man as Holy Spirit. The Holy Spirit is personal and not merely an atmosphere. In man's worship God is present in his Spirit; the Holy Spirit is present as the manifestation of the Father and of the Son. Paul said, "You are in the Spirit, if the Spirit of God really dwells in you. Any one who does not have the Spirit of Christ does not belong to him" (Rom. 8:9). To ignore the Spirit is to ignore God. To quench the Spirit of God is to refuse the power of God in worship. The Spirit of God or the Holy Spirit is always God-at-hand, and the Spirit of God or the Holy Spirit is always God-at-work.[12]

The transforming power.—Man's salvation is made possible by the power of the Holy Spirit. He comes to convince men of their guilt by making them aware of sin and righteousness and judgment

---

[12] Henry P. Van Dusen, *Spirit, Son and Father* (New York: Charles Scribner's Sons, 1958), p. 19.

(John 16:8). His work is to make Christ known and to make his truth clear to men (vv.14-15). The Spirit transforms man in God's work of grace. Jesus told Nicodemus, "Unless one is born of water and the Spirit, he cannot enter the kingdom of God. That which is born of the flesh is flesh, and that which is born of the Spirit is spirit" (3:5-6). Jesus again said, "It is the Spirit that gives life" (6:63). God's saving acts can come home to men only through the inward testimony of the Holy Spirit.

Furthermore, the Holy Spirit is the agency of moral transformation by which man is changed into the likeness of Christ from one degree of glory to another (2 Cor. 3:17-18). In the discovery of God through his Spirit, the whole of man's experience is gathered into the comprehensiveness of God's being and is given a new unity.[18] God's power coming into the life of man brings a new quality of life which includes the transformation of man's total being, including his rational, emotional, and volitional powers. Through the Spirit's power it is possible for man to live the life in Christ (Gal. 2:20).

Life in the church.—It is the Holy Spirit's function to inspire and guide the church in its worship and work. The Spirit created the church, and he continues to give life to the church. Without his power the church cannot exist. It cannot function in any area of its mission without the Spirit's presence.

The Holy Spirit was central in the early church. After the Resurrection, the disciples were filled with inspiration, for the wingbeat of the Spirit was felt everywhere. Jesus commanded his disciples to tarry until they were empowered by the Spirit (Acts 1:4-5). They were not prepared for their work until they received his power. The lordship of Christ could be understood and acknowledged only if the Spirit was present. The will of Christ could be accomplished only by the Spirit's living in the church and guiding it in all its worship and activity.

Christian character is fortified by the work of the Spirit. All the virtues and fruits of the Christian life develop through his living presence. Paul implied that the fruits of the Spirit—love, joy, peace, longsuffering, gentleness, goodness, faith, meekness, temperance—are

---

[18]H. Wheeler Robinson, *The Christian Experience of the Holy Spirit* (London: Nisbet and Company, Ltd., 1952), p. 5.

possible only if we live and walk in the Spirit (Gal. 5:22-25). This harvest of the Spirit results when the Christian cooperates with the Holy Spirit in the discipline of life.

In its worship the early church was aware of God's presence through the manifestations of his Spirit. They recognized that spiritual gifts were bestowed by him. By his power they sang and prayed and preached and prophesied and spoke in tongues (1 Cor. 12:8-11). And all these diverse gifts were bestowed by the same Spirit (v. 4).

The Holy Spirit gives the church motivation for its ministry. He inspires the singing, praying, teaching, preaching, and worship of the entire body (1 Cor. 14:36; Rom. 8:26-27; Acts 4:31; Eph 5:18-20). Under the power of the Spirit the early Christians often had ecstatic experiences expressed by speaking in tongues. Paul did not oppose this phenomenon but insisted that it be guided by the principle of edification (1 Cor. 4:26). Inspiration in worship was bestowed for a higher purpose and not simply for the emotional experience itself. Paul urged that worship be carried out in an orderly manner (14:40).

The church in every generation may approach its worship with a spirit of expectancy if it acknowledges the Holy Spirit in its midst. In worship God is known as Father, Son, and Holy Spirit. God the Father stresses the ultimacy and certainty of his existence as expressed in his creation. Jesus Christ defines the character of God expressed in his redemptive love. The Holy Spirit affirms the intimacy of his life expressed in his never-failing availability.

There may be a variety of forms in worship, but there can be no mistaking the fact that the church is dependent upon the Holy Spirit for the reality of its worship. The Spirit must release the desire for praise and prayer. He must create in the minds of the congregation the consciousness of God. Genuine worship takes place only when God is worshiped for his own sake. This experience is made possible only by the creative work of the Holy Spirit in the hearts of individuals and in the entire body, the church.

The Bible, the Eternal Word Through Words

The Bible is the life book of the church. It provides objective content for worship. It points man to God, the source of truth and life. There is a depth of mystery in the Bible that causes the worshiper to wait before the Scriptures like a child who knows nothing and is waiting to be taught his ABC's. There is a mysterious vitality in the Scriptures which is a sign pointing to its hidden center. The Bible is a record of God's revelation of his life-giving salvation to his people.

Since the Bible is the church's source book of knowledge about its salvation, its guidebook for living, and the promise of its destiny, it must be kept central in the church's worship. The objective, intellectual content which guides man's worship is found in the Scriptures. As Brunner has said, we turn backward to the Bible, but also forward to the living Word of God to which the Bible bears authoritative winess.[14] By the Holy Spirit we worship the living God, and the *living* Word witnesses to us by the *written* Word, the Bible.

The Bible is a necessary textbook in matters pertaining to the spiritual life—God's purpose for man, man's relationship to God, and man's relation to his fellowman. The Bible is concerned about life's ultimates—ultimate values, ultimate causes, ultimate objectives. It is both trustworthy and authoritative for the worship of God.

Men should acknowledge the Bible for what it claims to be, the message of God concerning the redemption of man. It claims to be a trustworthy guide in redemptive truth and in redemptive relationships. If men claim less for the Bible than it claims for itself, they deny God's power and purpose in their lives. If they claim more for the Bible than it claims for itself, they deny their faith in God and seek to build for themselves a theological wooden house on the sands of bibliolatry, rather than a strong house on the rock of a dynamic faith in the Lord of the Bible.

A record of divine history.—In Israel, according to the Old Testament, all history is a movement between promise and fulfilment. The New Testament testifies to the fulfilment of the promises of God in history. A unity runs through the purpose of the entire Bible.

The Bible is the story of God in history. The Germans have a word

[14]*The Divine Imperative* (Philadelphia: The Westminster Press, 1947), p. 565.

for it, *Heilsgeschichte,* by which they mean the "story of salvation," which treats of a Saviour, a saved people, and the means of salvation. History is seen as the process of divine revelation. All revelation is rooted in life. God was in history first, and all history has moved under his sovereignty.

In the record of special revelation we discover that God has been seeking man. The Bible is a story of the acts of God, what he does in history. The "actuality of history" is the concrete basis for the entire Bible story.[15] God's redemptive acts have value for the worshiper who reads the story in faith. Revelation is God revealing himself, not merely imparting an idea. It is the opening of man's nature to a new dimension of life, the life in God.

The Bible is the treasure in which God's word is kept. The word has been spoken, it has been acted, it has been lived, it has been celebrated, and it has been recorded. Miller says, "In truth we hear the Word of God only when it drives us away from all words back to mystery in which there are no words."[16] In fact, in this personal relationship of true worship, the written Word serves to make known to man the living Word of God. It is a historic witness to God's continuous action in the life of man.

A witness to Jesus Christ.—Against the background of Old Testament history, the New Testament witnesses to the fulfilment of God's purpose in revealing himself in the person of his Son. The writer of Hebrews says, "In many and various ways God spoke of old to our fathers by the prophets; but in these last days he has spoken to us by a Son, whom he appointed the heir of all things, through whom also he created the world" (1:1-2).

The Bible is a witness to the salvation that comes in Christ. The redemptive purpose of God is seen in the story of the incarnation, the life, the death, and the resurrection of Jesus Christ. It is through the Bible that Christ can be known in history. All the church's worship, preaching, and work is based upon it, on what we know through it. The Bible is a revelation concerning redemption that comes by actions rather than by words, by deeds rather than by doctrines.

---

[15]Robinson, *Redemption and Revelation in the Actuality of History* (New York: Harper & Bros., 1942), p. 168.

[16]*Op. cit.,* p. 97.

Goethe said, "The highest cannot be spoken; it can only be acted."

The Bible is more than a book of teachings; it is a witness to a life. It requires more than formal belief in its teachings; it requires union with Christ. The purpose of the Bible is not primarily to get its teachings accepted but rather to lead the soul to living contact with the Redeemer, and thus to an awakening of the whole nature— emotional, intellectual, volitional. For men to bow down to the mere letter of the Scriptures apart from vital faith would be a melancholy defeat of all the Bible stands for.

The Scriptures do not speak *in vacuo,* but in relation to Jesus Christ. The pattern of authority in Christian worship is found in Christ, the living, personal Word of God; in the Holy Spirit, who conveys revelation and witness to its divinity; and in the sacred Scriptures, the document of revelation, the Spirit's instrument in effecting illumination.[17]

A contemporary pastor warns us not to substitute the letter of the law for the life in Christ in our worship as did the Pharisees. Jesus said, "You do not have his word abiding in you, for you do not believe him whom he has sent. You search the scriptures, because you think that in them you have eternal life; and it is they that bear witness to me; yet you refuse to come to me that you may have life" (John 5:38-40). Charles Trentham comments, "Here we see men whose bland worship of Scripture so blinded them that they could not see the light of the glory of God in the face of Jesus Christ; and, refusing to see the light, they twisted the Scriptures to make them compatible with their darkness."[18]

A record of human experience.—The Bible is relevant today in man's worship. It is not only a record of divine or revelation history; it is also a record of human experience in the worship of God. It is a story of man's response to the God who controls history. The vision of the historic Christ presented in the Bible is verified by its correspondence with that knowledge of the living Christ which is given in the experience of Christian men. The Bible

---

[17]See Bernard Ramm, *The Pattern of Religious Authority* (Grand Rapids: Wm. B. Eerdmans Publishing Co., 1959), pp. 36-37.

[18]A published sermon, delivered at First Baptist Church, Knoxville, Tennessee, November 25, 1962.

story presents man in all the stark realism of his wavering life. As a sinner, man stands in need of redemption. In his rebellion he defies God and attempts to carve out a life for himself without God. Made in the image of God he can hear and respond to the voice of God. He has been created with the power to choose, and his redemption is dependent upon his decision to follow the call of God in Christ. The Bible appeals to every condition of man, reminding him of the grace of God revealed in Jesus Christ.

To deny the human element in the Bible is to commit what is known as the "docetic" heresy, the belief that Christ was not really human but only seemed to be human. The Scriptures witness to the real humanity of Jesus Christ. This witness is given through men who know the human situation. Men with frailties and limitations were inspired to record their experiences in the worship of God in Christ.

The glory of the Bible is found in its portrayal of man as he is and its offer of hope of what he may become in Christ. Paul Tournier, writing from his experiences as a practicing psychiatrist and a believer in Christ, says that the Bible is the book of the drama of human life. It shows us man as he is and as we know him, "with all his afflictions, and all his greatness, all his certainties and all his doubts, all his aspirations and all his vileness."[19] Moreover, the Scriptures present the message of grace and what it can do for the man "in Christ."

The Word of the Spirit.—The Bible has rightly been called the "Book of the spirit." There must be inspiration not only in the Scriptures themselves but also in the reader and interpreter of the Scriptures if they are to be heard and received as the Word of life. We receive an understanding of the writers of the Scriptures when we are possessed by the same Spirit who possessed them.

Christian worship is dependent upon the Bible for truth concerning redemption and Christian living. Personal piety is not possible without the testimony to truth provided by the Bible. The Bible as the living Word of God must revitalize and guide our hearing. In the modern world we need to hear the word of God afresh. Man needs

---

[19] *A Doctor's Casebook in the Light of the Bible* (New York: Harper & Bros., 1960), p. 19.

the Bible as a discipline for his own ideas about God. The text he reads retains the power to speak more loudly than his distortions of it. There is always a disturbing note in the Bible, and man takes a risk when he reads it—the risk that God may speak to correct man's errors of judgment.

The Scriptures, then, should determine the content of the church's worship. God's Spirit lives and works in the fellowship of Christians, and this includes their common worship as guided by the truth recorded in the Bible. Perhaps Robertson Smith expressed the conviction of many when he was arraigned for heresy:

If I am asked why I receive Scripture as the Word of God, I answer with all the fathers of the Protestant church: because the Bible is the only record of the redeeming love of God, because in the Bible alone I find God drawing near to man in Christ Jesus and declaring to us, in him, his will for our salvation. And this record I know to be true by the witness of his Spirit in my heart whereby I am assured that none other than God himself is able to speak such words to my soul.[20]

The Church, the People of God

One's doctrine of the church will to a great extent determine the type of worship he follows. For example, the hierarchical or institutional church tends to follow the liturgical pattern adopted by the "established church," whereas the congregational or "gathered church" tends to insist on freedom to plan its own patterns of worship. This idea is delineated rather thoroughly in Horton Davies' discussion of the Anglican as compared with the nonconformist churches in England.[21] In the true sense Christian worship must be understood in the context of the church.

The church as the people of God is as universal as the action of God himself. The estrangement and loneliness of an individual can be overcome only when his participation in the worship of God makes him aware that he belongs to an eternal people. The church

[20]A. M. Hunter, *Introducing the New Testament* (Philadelphia: The Westminster Press, 1946), p. 14.

[21]*Worship and Theology in England: From Watts and Wesley to Maurice, 1690-1850*, pp. 24-25.

is formed in worship, and its vitality is sustained in proportion to the genuineness of its continuing worship. Christian worship occurs only as the people of God respond to his claims upon them.

A local church is a part of the entire body of Christ, a living unit in the kingdom of God's redeemed people. Christ prayed that believers "may all be one" as the Father and the Son are one (John 17:21). If a true ecumenicism is ever realized among the people of God, it must begin in an ecumenical spirit in worship based upon New Testament principles.[22] The church as a living fellowship is prior to the church as a functioning institution. Paul included both ideas in his use of the term *ekklēsia*.[23]

A redemptive fellowship.—The church is different from any other unit of society. It is more than a humanitarian institution concerned with human sentiment and service. It is a particular kind of fellowship. It is a redeemed fellowship (*koinōnia*) of persons created by the Holy Spirit and united under the lordship of Jesus Christ. As a redeemed fellowship, the church must worship. Without worship it is not the church.

God's purpose for the church is redemptive. The church does not exist for its own sake, but for the kingdom of God. It is a part of God's plan in holy history. As a redeemed fellowship, it is also a redeeming fellowship. It exists for witness. The church can fulfil its mission only as it is continually renewed in its relationship to God. This renewal can take place only in worship.

The fellowship of the church is all-inclusive. As a redemptive society it embraces all strata of society. There is no place for snobbishness in the church of Christ. The rich and the poor, the cultured and the unlettered, the elite and the outcast, the white and the colored races—all are included in the fellowship of Jesus Christ. Men of every station and condition may sit down together in the worship of God through Jesus Christ, who has broken down every wall of partition (Eph. 2:14).

---

[22]See William R. Estep, *Baptists and Christian Unity* (Nashville: Broadman Press, 1967).

[23]See the Epistles to the Ephesians and the Colossians for the use of the former and the Epistles to the churches in Corinth, Thessalonica, and others for the use of the latter idea. For a fuller discussion on the nature of the church, see Franklin M. Segler, *A Theology of Church and Ministry*.

Religious faith is social as well as individual, and it finds its full expression only in corporate worship. In the fellowshi of the church's worship the individual faith affirms itself and educates itself. Worship begins with the priesthood of each believer, but it comes to its full and richest realization in the collective priesthood of the church as one.

A living organism.—The church is more than an institution; it is a living organism. In a sense, it is a sort of reenactment of divine incarnation. When Jesus Christ comes into the life of believers, his life becomes incarnate in their life. The church, as the "body of Christ" at worship, is not merely a reminder that he once lived but also a witness to the living presence of the risen Lord. It is a continuation of the life of Christ as he lives in and through the life of his people. The church as a community of the resurrection is the vital, vibrant, and victorious body of the reigning Christ.

Every visible congregation is a representative part of the living body of Christ; it is an outcropping of the kingdom of God. Each local church has this living organic character. Congregational worship insures vitality to the entire body and to individuals severally.

As a worshiping organism the church must always be subject to change. The church is reformed but it is always to be re-formed. As it was created, its life must be in the process of constant renewal and re-creation. In effectual worship the church can be saved from becoming a dead branch. In vital communion it continues to receive its essential life from the vine whose life is eternal (John 15). It is possible for the church to be "reshaped" in Christ. "For my children you are, and I am in travail with you over again until you take the shape of Christ" (Gal. 4:19, NEB[24]).

A worshiping congregation.—Every church must recognize itself as a historic, human institution as well as a divinely created organism. It is involved with truth as well as with spirit. The religion that makes the church is not basically temperamental but evangelical. The church is not primarily dependent upon its cultus or forms of doctrine for its life, but it is dependent upon them for its understanding of itself in worship. It is true that cultus only is a myopic view, but

---

[24] © The Delegates of the Oxford University Press and the Syndics of the Cambridge University Press, 1961.

cultus that leads to Christ is essential.[25] The church as institution must adopt what it considers to be its best means for expressing its beliefs and its worship. It cannot ignore its cultus.

A church can remain alive only as it continually comes to God in worship. In its worship the congregation comes under the judgment of God. Unless it comes repeatedly to confession it cannot remain the witness to God's saving grace. There is a clear scriptural mandate to this effect: "For the time has come for judgment to begin with the household of God" (1 Pet. 4:17). A church without judgment is a church without power. The church must always see itself as a "congregation of sinners" dependent upon the grace of God. Jesus taught his church to pray, "Forgive us our sins; for we also forgive every one that is indebted to us. And . . . deliver us from evil" (Luke 11:4, KJV). As institution the church has not inherited goodness; its essential righteousness is personal and can only be created in humble worship.

The church in history must always be what the early church was after the ascension—a group of redeemed people gathered together to pray and to wait for the coming of the Holy Spirit. The church cannot command or possess the Holy Spirit; it can only wait for him and live by his power. Only as a worshiping congregation can it be the church in history. The church is born today, as it was in the beginning, by a miracle of grace in the hearts of believers. In the midst of all its activities, the church is primarily a worshiping congregation.

A holy priesthood.—In the worshiping congregation the individual Christian finds his highest values. As Dargan affirmed, congregational worship quickens his interest, develops his Christian intelligence, and deepens his spiritual discernment.[26] Furthermore, dynamic worship is the safest and most enduring attraction of the church to those persons outside the church. The worshiping church is a self-transcending community.

The New Testament presents the church as a "holy priesthood."

---

[25]Frederick Herzog, "The Norm and Freedom of Christian Worship," *Worship in Scripture and Tradition,* ed. Massey H. Shepherd, Jr., (New York: Oxford University Press, 1963), p. 98.

[26]*Op. cit.,* p. 560.

Peter exhorts men to come to the "living stone," Jesus Christ, that they may like living stones be built into a spiritual house, a "holy priesthood, to offer spiritual sacrifices to God through Jesus Christ" (1 Pet. 2:5; cf. Rev. 1:6).

The doctrine of the priesthood of believers, suggested by the "holy priesthood" of the church, implies that every member of Christ's body is responsible to worship Christ by offering spiritual sacrifices. This doctrine necessitates participation on the part of the entire congregation. Since all are priests, each individual Christian has the privilege and obligation to worship God for himself and to serve as a priest unto God for his fellowman.

Primitive Christians gave primary emphasis to the preaching of the gospel as a means of bringing salvation. They had a dialogue with the unbelieving world. With the development of "Christian Sacralism," rites were gradually substituted for the preaching of the Word. "In sacramental churches preaching atrophies; in preaching churches the sacraments are secondary."[27] In the Roman Church the act of the sacral rite superseded the essence of the Lord's Supper. Sacramentalism was influenced by the mystery religions. The word *Sacramentum* is the Latin translation for the Greek word *mystērion*. In the mystery religions one partook of deity by ingesting a morsel of a sacrificial victim. The god was said to be infused into the devotee. The Romans practiced this rite in emperor worship. The Emperor Decius attempted to bring about religious uniformity by means of a sacrifice (a mysterium) on an altar.

The doctrine of the priesthood of all believers implies that salvation comes by the faith of the individual presenting himself as an offering to God, and not by the mediating office of the clergy or the mediatorial offerings of the so-called sacraments. The church's worship is personal participation by acts of faith and not by the mere offering of material sacrifices. Only the active faith of the worshiper can activate any outward action or deed so that it becomes a means of God's grace.

God's grace may be manifested in man's experience of worship in various manners. As John A. Mackay suggests, it sometimes "booms

---

[27] See Leonard Verduin, *The Reformers and Their Stepchildren* (Grand Rapids: Wm. B. Eerdmans Publishing Co., 1964.) pp. 135-36.

like the bursting of the sea or like the battering rams at the far Gate in Mansaul, or in a voice that calls 'Why persecutest thou me?' "[28] Or, it may come less dramatically like a still small voice. The manner in which grace operates in worship depends upon the human situation, the state of the soul. From the human point of view communion with God and the reception of his grace depends upon man's faith. Man's positive response to God's grace is faith. Paul declared, "By grace you have been saved through faith" (Eph. 2:8). God has acted by grace; man must respond by faith in worship.

Faith is more than assent to a proposition; it is the commitment of the self to God. It includes openness toward God, decision to accept what God gives, the opening of one's whole being to the incoming of God as the Saviour of life, an attitude of submission and trust in God, and a definite commitment to the will of God in adventurous living.

The priesthood of believers stresses the preeminent importance of personality. However, the doctrine does not imply extreme individualism. An individual can know God in the truest sense only in relation to his fellowman in the church. A man can worship God only as he is rightly related to his fellowman.

---

[28]*God's Order, The Ephesian Letter and This Present Time* (New York: The Macmillan Co., 1953), pp. 103 ff.

5

A Psychology of Worship

What happens when man worships? What kind of experience does he have in worship? What are man's attitudes when he comes to worship? What are man's basic needs to be satisfied? How can the worship experience help to satisfy these needs? These are some of the questions which psychology may help us to answer. Psychology can also aid in the validation of religious experience and in suggesting more effective means of enriching religious experience.

A Person-Centered Experience

Worship is basically a person-centered experience. It is a communion between persons, God and man. This encounter awakens powers and transcendence within us. It is reverently "entering into" a life other than one's own. It is transaction—an actual interchange of energy which involves openness on the part of the worshiper.[1]

Worship involves the whole man and not a mere segment of his personhood. The biblical concept of man presents him as a unitary person. There is no dichotomy in personality, and no dualism in the life of man as is seen in Greek philosophy. "Blessed are those... who seek him with their whole heart" (Psalm 119:2). "With my whole heart I seek thee" (v. 10). Isaiah saw the whole man as a rebel: "The whole head is sick, and the whole heart is faint" (1:5).

Paul prayed, "May the God of peace himself sanctify you wholly; and may your spirit and soul and body be kept sound and blameless" (1 Thess. 5:23). The first and most important commandment implies that man expresses his love toward God with his total being: "You shall love the Lord your God with all your heart, and with all your soul, and with all your mind, and with all your strength" (Mark 12:30).

---

[1] Ross Snyder, "Prayer and Worship Re-examined," *Pastoral Psychology*, XI (March, 1960), 48.

The biblical terms used to designate the various aspects of man's personality are not to be considered independently of one another. *Nous* (the mind), *psyche* (the soul), *pneuma* (the spirit), *soma* (the body), and *kardia* (the heart), all speak of the various aspects of man's total personality. These terms present a unitary concept of man. Worship is experienced by the total person.

Worship is a conscious act in which the worshiper understands God's revelation toward him and in which the worshiper knowingly turns towards God. The worship of God affects the unconscious as well as the conscious aspects of personality. However, communion with God is not an unconscious experience which demands no response on man's part. The gift of faith comes as a conscious understanding of God as he appears in Christ in the midst of historical realities. Our communion with God gains in intensity as we exercise conscious faith in him.

Man responds with various aspects of his total being. Psychologists primarily regard three modes of conscious activity on the part of man—feeling attitude, knowing attitude, and willing attitude. All of these are present in the religious experience and function as a living unity. They are affected by various symbols and actions in worship. The act of worship involves the recognition of an object with which the worshiper is in relation. This is knowledge. Again, the worship experience involves certain emotions in relationship, such as fear and love and trust. This is known as feeling. Genuine worship also involves decision and commitment concretely offered in outward activity, such as sacrifice or service. This is the willing aspect of man's experiencing. According to H. R. Mackintosh all these actions of personality are combined in one vital experience. They are not necessarily successive but are simultaneous and interdependent.[2]

Worship always reaches to the center of the human person. It touches and releases the will. It is more than emotional and intellectual; it involves the will. It determined Paul's will, and his choice determined history.

Man responds with his *senses*. The physical body with its sensory aspects must be considered in worship. Man is reached through

---

[2]*The Christian Apprehension of God* (New York: Harper & Bros., 1929), p. 26.

his physical senses—sight, hearing, smell, taste, touch. By means of sight the worshiper enjoys the beauty of the world, and especially the sanctuary, its architecture, its decorations, and its symbolisms. The sense of hearing enables him to enjoy the musical sounds of voices and instruments. Some churches appeal in their worship to the sense of smell by means of pleasant aromas from burning incense. With his hands the worshiper touches the Bible, the hymnbook, and the offering which he brings. The sense of taste is part of his experience in worship through partaking of the bread and the cup of the Lord's Supper.

Man responds with his *mind.* God created man a thinking being, capable of understanding the truth of God's revelation. Man's knowledge of God is not possible apart from his mental activity. It is important that the various actions in a worship service "make sense" to the worshiper. Karl Heim in *Spirit and Truth* says that worship is a transaction between God and the conscience of man, accomplished "in the light of clear thinking." Paul urged his followers to have the "mind" of Christ Jesus (Phil. 2:5), to "think" on the graces of the Christian life (4:8), and to become transformed by the renewing of their "minds" in worship (Rom. 12:1,2). Jesus declared that we should worship "in spirit and truth" (John 4:24).

Only intelligible public worship is genuine worship. No amount of ritual, however mystical or mysterious, can bring man into meaningful communion with God unless it is understood by the participants. It may even degrade man by the subtle deceit of substituting the outward act for personal communion, as in the case of fertility rites in certain pagan practices, or in the worship of idols.

The argument for intelligibility supports the practice of worship in the language of the people. Much more is experienced in the vernacular than in some ancient, unknown language. It is gratifying to see the Roman Catholic Church moving in the direction of the use of the vernacular in their worship.

Man responds with his *emotions.* In the Bible the "heart" is considered the seat of the emotions. "God is love" (1 John 4:8). Man was created with the capacity to love. "You shall love the Lord your God with all your heart, and with all your soul, and with all your mind" (Matt. 22:37; see also Deut. 6:5).

David Roberts suggests that objectivity has become a fetish in certain religious circles. The validity of belief is thought to be directly proportional to its dispassionateness. He says that this is as bad as the opposite view of equating intensity of feeling with certainty.[3] Actions in public worship occur somewhere between the extremes of abject passivity and unbridled enthusiasm.

Roberts further observes that we do not have to choose between cold objectivity and blind feeling. Neither rational detachment nor fanatical emotionalism will lead to reality. Our emotions can either prevent or implement our search for truth and our willingness to act in the light of it. We must acknowledge that our feelings and unconscious motives, as well as our intellectul processes, play a part in the formulation of our religious beliefs.

Man's emotional attitudes may be conditioned by the atmosphere surrounding him. He is capable of hating as well as loving. He may be led into a mood of hope or a mood of despair. His emotions may be kindled into enthusiasm or lulled into lethargy.

There should be a balance between the intellectual and the emotional. It has been suggested that in worship man needs to intellectualize his emotions and to emotionalize his intellect. Emotions may be given direction and discipline by intelligent worship, and what man knows can be kindled by fervor and compassion. The worshiper should beware of equating his own emotions with the power of the Holy Spirit. The inner motivation should be tested by the teachings of the Bible, by reason, and by prayer in the context of the Christian community.

Man responds with his *will.* In confronting God the worshiping man must make a choice. He must will to commit himself to God's will. God does not have the allegiance of the whole person until man's will is combined with his mind and his emotions in total commitment. The Bible implies that man is free to choose God or to reject him. He can respond in submission and dedication or in rebellion. God presents his invitation, "Come," and leaves man free to decide. Willing discipleship is costly and will tolerate no "cheap grace."

---

[3]*Psychotherapy and a Christian View of Man* (New York: Charles Scribner's Sons, 1951), p. 59.

Man responds on *a superconscious level*. The atmosphere created by the use of music, art, drama, and other symbolic actions in worship adds a dimension to man's experience in communion with God. In the realm of the superconscious God's power works in the spiritual awareness of the worshiper. New insights and inspirations break in upon the person's experience to produce a total impact on the wholeness of being.[4]

This experience has often been expressed, "I just *felt* the presence of God." This awareness may be experienced as the "still small voice," or it may come in cataclysmic force such as Paul's Damascus road experience. This aspect of worship cannot be formalized nor carefully defined theologically. Indeed, man should acknowledge a mysterious beyondness in worship which is accepted by faith and needs not to be explained by creeds and formulas. He simply yields to the moving power of God in a willingness to explore new dimensions of being, which may in turn reveal new dimensions of ministry in God's ever-expanding universe.

Mystery appeals to the imagination of man and often fires the creative aspects of his being. Some Roman Catholics say they prefer the reading of the Bible in Latin rather than in the vernacular because there is more "mystery" present. However, the proper attitude toward the Scriptures being read in the language of the people will make room for this mystery and may even open new vistas as more truth of God's revelation breaks in upon the consciousness. The true meaning of God's revelation for man is that his mystery may be concretely related to man's earthly existence so as to redeem man and the cosmic order. Perhaps this is what Paul meant: "The whole creation has been groaning in travail together until now; and . . . we ourselves . . . groan inwardly as we wait for . . . the redemption of our bodies. . . . If we hope for what we do not see, we wait for it with patience" (Rom. 8:22-25).

An Objective-Subjective Experience

Worship is an objective-subjective experience. It is objective as

---

[4] I am indebted to Edgar N. Jackson for suggesting this aspect of worship in a lecture at Southwestern Baptist Seminary, Fort Worth, Texas, November 3, 1966. See P. A. Sorokin, *The Ways and Power of Love* (Boston: Beacon Press, 1954).

people think primarily about God; it is subjective as they think primarily about themselves. A balance of the two is realized in genuine communion with God.[5]

It is widely observed that subjectivity has been the bane of much Free Church worship. Such worship lacks the higher restraint that can lift the worshipers out of themselves and give a "blazing vision" to reveal to them a better existence beyond themselves.

Worship involves *objective experience*. That is, it has objective content. It is more than man's merely communing with himself or giving primary concern to his own inner feelings and desires. Man's attention is focused first upon God, who comes to man from outside man.

God is objective in his holiness and transcendence and absoluteness. He is not a part of man, nor is he dependent upon man for his own being. In worship man's mind and heart must be directed upward toward God. Man's worship is more than sentiment or emotion. It finds objective reality in God. P. T. Forsyth declared that unless there is within us that which is above us, we shall soon yield to that which is around us. Objectivity can be assured only if we begin to worship for God's glory and not for our own. The objective worth of God is the ground of true worship.

Man's faith comes to rest in Christ, not in his own wistful desires. Worship is a creative encounter and a redemptive act. Subjectivity is an indispensable preliminary to a sense of guilt and the need for purification. Objectivity is an indispensable end to a sense of forgiveness and healing.[6]

As objectivity, worship is directed away from man and toward God. The acts of God in history are primary in man's worship. Man is concerned about the historical facts, the revealed truths, and the person of God as manifested in Jesus Christ. These facts are objective to man. They stand outside man to judge him and to redeem him. Paul E. Johnson says there is room and need for both objective

[5]A. W. Blackwood, "Public Worship," *Twentieth Century Encyclopedia of Religious Knowledge,* II, 1190. See also J. B. Pratt, *The Religious Consciousness: A Psychological Study* (New York: The Macmillan Co., 1920), chaps. 14-15.

[6]Segler, "Worship," *Encyclopedia of Southern Baptists,* ed. Norman W. Cox (Nashville: Broadman Press, 1958), II, 1547.

and subjective aims in worship. Objective worship achieves the best subjective results. If one cannot believe or find objective communion, the problem of worship is indeed baffling.[7]

Christianity must be more than religious sensibility. It must rest on a positive revelation, not on subjective inspiration. The inspiration arises from a revelation. William Temple reminds us that the special quality of authority in revelation "may both stimulate a personal experience responsive to itself and also give to experience a deeper tone, a greater intensity."[8] Worship that fails to confront us with the naked horror of Calvary and the blazing glory of the resurrection has nothing to do with the glorification of the true God.

Worship involves *subjective experience*. In worship the consciousness of God's presence becomes an inner and subjective experience with man. Worship is actually a dialogue in which God and man hold personal communion. But this dialogue is possible only when man recognizes God as standing opposite himself. In the worship of the pietists the action of God tends to be equated with an individual person's conscious apprehension of it. Revelation is not an objective event involving the structures and processes of time, space, and matter so much as a personal and individual experience.

Worship is an experience which takes place within man. It is a dynamic, Person-with-person experience. In his self-examination, man is concerned with his finiteness, his weakness, his guilt, his grief, his brokenness. It is legitimate for man to be concerned about himself so long as this is secondary to his concern about the glorification of God.

Worship involves *Subject-with-subject experience*. In the last analysis, worship is communion, a dialogue between subjects. It is an experience in which God as Subject confronts man as subject. It is an I-Thou dialogue in which two persons consciously commune with one another. Man knows himself in relation to God. Human personality consists in the existence of the "I" in relation to the "Thou." Martin Buber said, "I come into being as over against the Thou; all real life is of the nature of encounter."[9]

---

[7]*The Psychology of Religion* (Nashville: Abingdon Press, 1945), p. 29.
[8]*Nature, Man, and God* (London: Macmillan & Co., Ltd., 1956), p. 331.
[9]See John Baillie, *Our Knowledge of God*, p. 208.

The essence of worship is not a subject-object kind of knowledge, but a subject-subject relationship. Man can never treat God as merely an object of worship. There is danger in speaking of the objectivity of God as a synonym for the reality of God. Kierkegaard protested against this objectivity by emphasizing the subjectivity of God. In his view, God is Infinite Subjectivity.

But God is not a part of our subjectivity. It is perhaps better to speak of his subjecthood. In a secondary sense, God is the object of our knowledge. He is outside of man, standing over against man. God is the knower who confronts us. Man knows him as the "wholly other." In worship, man's knowledge *about* God must become knowledge *of* God. The New Testament has two words for knowledge. *Ginosko* means knowledge about a fact, or objective knowledge. *Epiginosko* is the knowledge of experience such as one exercises in coming to know God. God takes the initiative, and man responds. It is always a "fiercely personal" experience.

In this experience man's personhood is respected by his Creator. As man responds in faith to God's loving call, his nature is transformed. When he submits to the lordship of Christ in worship, he becomes Christ-like. Christ became man in order that man may become like God. Worship is a dynamic experience in which man is re-created by the power of God. As Paul said, "It is the Spirit himself bearing witness with our spirit that we are children of God" (Rom. 8:16).

God meets us, not as one among the many objects of our knowledge, but as another knower by whom both these objects and we ourselves are known. A balance between the objective and the subjective is the ideal. "If objective worship is likely to seem cold, subjective worship is almost sure to be weak."[10] In the combination of the objective source and the subjective experience, certainty and assurance are found.

Man's Basic Needs for Worship

Man has basic needs which can be met in worship. Augustine said, "Thou hast made us for thyself, O God, and our souls are restless

---

[10]Blackwood, *The Fine Art of Public Worship* (Nashville: Abingdon Press, 1939), p. 19.

until they find their rest in thee." In the depths of his nature man has certain conscious needs which must be met. There are hungers of the human heart to be satisfied. These psychological necessities have been approached in various ways. The following categories are another effort at expressing man's conscious needs for worship.

1. The sense of finiteness seeks the infinite. In worship man seeks for completion, for communion with "ultimate being."[11] Sensing his limitations, he goes in search for the rest of himself. The psalmist said,

> O Lord, our Lord,
>   how majestic is thy name in all the earth! . . .
> When I look at thy heavens, the work of thy fingers,
>   the moon and the stars which thou hast established;
> what is man that thou art mindful of him,
>   and the son of man that thou dost care for him?
> Yet thou hast made him little less than God,
>   and dost crown him with glory and honor" (Psalm 8:1-5).

2. The sense of mystery seeks understanding. Man stands in need of knowledge. He approaches God as the source of all knowledge. This act of communion may be spoken of as worshipful problem-solving. Paul exclaimed, "O the depth of the riches and wisdom and knowledge of God! How unsearchable are his judgments and how inscrutable his ways!" (Rom. 11:33). Again he prayed that his fellow Christians might "have power to comprehend with all the saints what is the breadth and length and height and depth, and to know the love of Christ which surpasses knowledge, that you may be filled with all the fulness of God" (Eph. 3:18-19).

3. The sense of insecurity seeks refuge. In an age of uprootedness man realizes his need for refuge and stability. With the psalmist he finds himself saying, "God is our refuge and strength, a very present help in trouble" (46:1).

4. The sense of loneliness seeks companionship with God. In his estrangement and his lostness man feels the need to be loved. Worship is the search for this love which can satisfy his loneliness.

---

[11]Paul Tillich, *The Courage to Be* (New Haven: Yale University Press, 1952).

Job cried, "Oh, that I knew where I might find him, that I might come even to his seat!" (Job 23:3). In genuine worship he comes ultimately to experience personal companionship with God. "I had heard of thee by the hearing of the ear, but now my eye sees thee" (42:5).

5. The sense of human belongingness seeks mutual fellowship with other worshipers. The children of Israel sang a song of ascent going up to the Temple, "I was glad when they said to me, 'let us go to the house of the Lord!'" (Psalm 122:1-2). In worship the early church felt itself to be one body in Christ. Joined and knit together in Christ, each one worked to contribute his part in building up the body in the love of Christ (Eph. 4:1,4-6,16). It is by the grace of God that a congregation is permitted to gather visibly for fellowship in worship.[12]

6. The sense of guilt seeks forgiveness and absolution. In worship the soul is laid bare before God. Man acknowledges his guilt and pleads for cleansing. David cried out, "Have mercy on me, O God, according to thy steadfast love; according to thy abundant mercy blot out my transgressions. . . . Against thee, thee only, have I sinned, and done that which is evil in thy sight. . . . Create in me a clean heart, O God, and put a new and right spirit within me" (Psalms 51:1,4,10). The more real man's sense of guilt, the more necessity there is for confession and dependence upon the atoning grace of God.

7. The sense of anxiety seeks for peace. Anxiety is a normal experience of man in his finiteness.[13] In this deep threat of nonbeing man seeks in worship the courage to become his true self. As emotional tensions build up, man seeks peace from them in the deepest of all emotional experiences—worship. This emotional experience can reach to the depths of man's need for rest and peace. In great distress the psalmist prayed, "As the hart panteth after the water brooks, so panteth my soul after thee, O God" (42:1, KJV). "Why are you cast down, O my soul, and why are you disquieted within me? Hope in God; for I shall again praise him, my help and my God" (v. 11).

---

[12]Dietrich Bonhoeffer, *Life Together* (London: SCM Press, Ltd., n.d.), p. 8.
[13]Wayne Oates, *Anxiety in Christian Experience* (Philadelphia: The Westminster Press, 1955), p. 42.

8. The sense of meaninglessness seeks purpose and fulfilment. The will to meaning is perhaps man's deepest need. In the depths of his soul man realizes that he was created for a purpose. In the midst of life's harassment he affirms, "We know that in everything God works for good with those who love him, who are called according to his purpose" (see Rom. 8:28-30). Perhaps it should be added that the will to meaning finds it deepest significance in the will to worship.

9. The sense of brokenness seeks healing. Man cannot grapple with the enemies of righteousness in a realistic world without becoming broken and bruised. In a broken world he seeks to be made whole. And, as Tournier says, this can happen only as God becomes incarnate in us through the Holy Spirit.[14] Isaiah wrote, "A bruised reed he will not break, and a dimly burning wick he will not quench" (42:3).

10. A sense of grief seeks comfort. Man's innumerable losses leave him with a feeling of emptiness. He grieves over his losses. "Comfort ye . . . my people" (40:1-2). In the worship of the living Lord who overcame all such grief and loss, man hears the words, "Let not your hearts be troubled; believe in God, believe also in me. . . . Peace I leave with you; my peace I give to you; not as the world gives do I give to you. Let not your hearts be troubled, neither let them be afraid" (John 14:1,27).

Another has summarized the psychological needs of man in the area of religious experience as follows: the need to find fulfilment, to make life useful, to find great moments of inspiration, to have real encounter with another person, to know his own identity, and to find superlative significance in a person—Jesus Christ—the ultimate meaning of life.[15] These feelings of need are evidences of the presence of God, sure signs of his address to us.

Attitudes Expressing Worship

There are certain general psychological attitudes of the human spirit expressed in worship. These attitudes have been called emotions

---

[14]*The Whole Person in a Broken World,* trans. John and Hellen Roberstein (New York: Harper & Row, 1964), p. 168.

[15]Gene E. Bartlett, "When Preaching Becomes Real," *Pastoral Psychology,* XIV (October, 1964), 25.

or moods. But such designations seem inadequate. An attitude is more than an emotion or sentiment or mood or atmosphere, although all of these are involved. An attitude includes emotion or feeling, thought or idea, and will or deliberate commitment in the total act of personal consciousness.

W. E. Sangster says that the most appropriate word to use in defining the centrality of personal thought and action is the word "attitude."[16] It implies motivation and purpose and determines decision and action. Sangster says it is prompted by religious and moral motivation and is inclusive of thinking, feeling, and willing. It is akin to Paul's use of the term "mind," when he said, "Let this mind be in you which was also in Christ Jesus" (see Phil. 2: 1-5,KJV). Another kindred word is the word "heart." "As [a man] thinketh in his heart, so is he" (Prov. 23:7, KJV). "With the heart man believeth unto righteousness" (Rom. 10:10, KJV).

Not only does man come to worship with certain attitudes, but worship is also a way of changing the basic attitude so that the thing experienced becomes different and richer in quality. Worship is the chief religious way in which men seek the transformation of attitude (change of heart or way of life) which will usher in a transfigured world. "Of all voluntary acts which shape the attitude of the psycho-physical organism, none can go so deep and none are so effective as worship."[17]

The first attitude of worship is *adoration* expressed in praise. Adoration, a spirit of reverence and awe, is the starting point for all genuine worship. One does not praise him whom he does not adore. To adore is to worship with profound reverence. Evelyn Underhill speaks of adoration as "disinterested delight" in the worship of God.

The Westminster Catechism declared that "the chief end of man is to glorify God and to enjoy him forever." Our most fundamental need and duty is to glorify God. There is a sense in which worship should begin and end in the adoration of God. It is both the beginning and the goal of the life of worship. Man stands in awe at the beauty and splendor and mystery of God. His ways are past tracing

---

[16]*The Secret of the Radiant Life* (New York: Abingdon Press, 1957).

[17]Wieman & Horton, *The Growth of Religion* (New York: Willet-Clark and Co., 1938), p. 391.

out. Although man cannot completely fathom the nature of God, he can respond in adoration to a God great enough to answer all his needs.

Adoration is expressed in praise. The true language of praise is found in the Bible. Such passages as Psalm 103:1, "Bless the Lord, O my soul; and all that is within me, bless his holy name!" or Isaiah's vision of God in the Temple, or the closing chapters of the book of Job, or the prologue to the Gospel according to John, or the lofty passages in the book of Revelation give examples of man's most worthy effort to express his adoration for God. In the early church the true note of worship was struck in the act of adoration: "Worthy art thou, our Lord and God, to receive glory and honor and power, for thou didst create all things, and by thy will they existed and were created" (Rev. 4:11). In worship man stands before God to receive and to acknowledge what God has already provided.

A second attitude in man's worship is *gratitude* expressed in thanksgiving. This is closely akin to the spirit of adoration and perhaps grows out of it. Thanksgiving is occasioned and made possible by God's gracious movement toward us. God's grace expressed through his benevolences creates within us a spirit of gratitude giving rise to thanksgiving, a joyful acceptance of life, a celebration of the gospel. Every Lord's Day is a festival of joyful worship, the thanksgiving (*eucharistia*) of the church.

Bowing in the presence of God, man calls to mind the blessings he has received. He acknowledges God as the source of his blessings, and his heart rises in praise and thanksgiving. The Old Testament contains many songs of worship. "Praise the Lord! O give thanks to the Lord, for he is good; for his steadfast love endures for ever!" (Psalm 106:1). Psalm 107:1-2 repeats the phrase, O give thanks to the Lord, for he is good; for his steadfast love endures for ever!" and then adds, "Let the redeemed of the Lord say so." Again the people sing, "Praise the Lord. I will give thanks to the Lord with my whole heart, in the company of the upright, in the congregation" (111:1).

In the act of counting his blessings, man quite often is brought to the heights of genuine worship. He cannot long languish in sorrow and despair when he realizes how great are God's blessings. Thanksgiving is a celebration of life itself as a gift from God.

At the heart of Christian worship is thanksgiving for God's redemptive love. In Paul's exhortation to the Corinthian Christians to express their gratitude to God, he rises to the heights of worship with the words. "Thanks be to God for his inexpressible gift" (2 Cor. 9:15).

Confession expresses the attitudes of humility and *repentance*. In the presence of the holy God, man recognizes himself a sinner in need of repentance, an attitude which C. S. Lewis characterized as a movement "full stern ahead." Lewis further observed that repentance is not any fun at all, for it is harder than just eating humble pie; it means undergoing a kind of death of the self.[18] True confession is Godward, for man learns genuine humility only in the worship of God in Christ, who experienced the ultimate humiliation in the cross.

In its full-orbed glory, confession includes the acceptance of God's forgiveness. The richness of confession is realized in the assurance of forgiveness. Through John's witness God affirmed this reality: "If we confess our sins, he is faithful and just, and will forgive our sins and cleanse us from all unrighteousness" (1 John 1:9). The worshiper's hunger for restoration to fellowship with God is satisfied in his assurance of forgiveness.

In the presence of an infinite God, man realizes that he is a needy creature and acknowledges his *dependence*. This attitude is expressed in the act of asking God for what man needs. The prayer of petition is the act of asking God to supply the needs of prayer. Jesus taught us to pray, "Give us this day our daily bread; and forgive us our debts" (Matt. 6:11-12).

The prayer of dependence also includes asking for God's blessings on others. This is the prayer of intercession. Jesus' high priestly prayer is the best example of intercession (John 17). Paul urged that "supplications, prayers, intercessions, and thanksgiving be made for all men" (1 Tim. 2:1).

Asking is an act worthy of being included in worship, for God

---

[18]*The Case for Christianity* (New York: The Macmillan Co., 1944), p. 49. Cf. Simone Weil, *Gravity and Grace* (New York: G. P. Putnam's Sons, 1952).

delights to give good things to his children (Luke 11:13). The
essence of worshipful asking is achieved in asking for God himself to enter afresh into the life of the worshiper.

Worship involves also the attitude of *submission* or surrender.
In his struggle with his destined role Jesus himself prayed, "Abba,
Father, all things are possible to thee; remove this cup from me;
yet not what I will, but what thou wilt" (Mark 14:36). And
again at Calvary Jesus worshiped God in the agony of death:
"Father, into thy hands I commit my spirit!" (Luke 23:46).

Every significant worship experience calls for submission and
surrender to the will of God. The encounter in worship is in-
complete if it does not lead to surrender. Genuine surrender is
never with reluctant attitude but always with joy. Jesus agonized
during the encounter, but his final attitude was unreserved surrender. As George Buttrick observes, there was no rebellion in Paul
as he was approaching martyrdom.[19] As he was being "poured
out as a libation on the altar," he saw as his reward a "crown
of righteousness" awarded to "all who have loved his appearing"
(2 Tim. 4:8). Paul's final act was an act of worship.

The experience of worship comes to a climax in the attitude
of *commitment*. Submission is in a sense passive; the worshiper
is acted upon by the sovereign power of God. But commitment
is active; the worshiper wilfully dedicates himself to God.

Isaiah's worship began in adoration with his vision of God's
holiness and glory, proceeded into dialogue with God, and climaxed in his commitment, "Here I am! Send me" (6:1-8). Worship
includes the kind of commitment that knowingly wills to become
involved in the redemptive work of God. God prefers to incline
the will rather than the intellect, for a commitment in faith is
total humility.

---

[19]*God, Pain, and Evil* (Nashville: Abingdon Press, 1966), p. 166.

Part Two

The Means of Expressing Worship

As has been discussed previously, man comes to worship with certain attitudes—adoration, praise, thanksgiving, confession, petition, intercession, and dedication. He uses various means for expressing these attitudes in worship. These different means of expressing worship will be presented in the following discussion. The purpose here is to provide both interpretation and practical suggestions concerning the use of each of these means for expressing worship.

What are the elements in a worship service, and in what order do they come? This question is often asked by those who are seeking guidance in planning and leading worship. The next several chapters will deal with these elements, which include music, prayers, the reading of the Bible, preaching, baptism, the Lord's Supper, the call to worship, the presentation of offerings, public commitment, the reception of new members, the affirmation of faith, and symbols in worship. In a worship service these do not necessarily come in the order in which they will be discussed here. Chapter 13 suggests certain orders of worship—that is, ways in which the various elements may be arranged to fit a general plan.

6

Music and Worship

They cast their crowns before the throne, singing,
"Worthy art thou, our Lord and God,
To receive glory and honor and power."
                                    Revelation 4:11

Since music is the finest of the fine arts and the most universal means for the expression of human attitudes, it should play an important role in public worship. The people of God have given a major place to the use of music in their worship, even from Old Testament times. In the primitive song of Moses (Ex. 15), as well as in the relatively sophisticated music of the Temple, music was sung and frequently accompanied by musical instruments. The music of Israel consisted in songs of praise, thanksgiving, instruction, personal experience, and historical celebration. There were choirs, singers, instrumentalists, teachers, directors, and composers. The book of Psalms constituted the early hymnbook of the Jewish people. About 1050 B.C. David appointed Levites to provide music for the liturgical services (1 Chron. 16:4-7). A later chapter in 1 Chronicles lists the number of offices of the musicians.

At the dedication of Solomon's Temple worship and music were "blended in magnificence." "It was the duty of the trumpeters and singers to make themselves heard in unison in praise and thanksgiving to the Lord, and when the song was raised, with trumpets and cymbals and other musical instruments, in praise to the Lord, 'For he is good, for his steadfast love endures forever,' the house, the house of the Lord, was filled with a cloud, so that the priests could not stand to minister because of the cloud; for the glory of the Lord filled the house of God" (2 Chron. 5:13-14). It is implied that this music brought to the people a sense of the presence of God.

According to Erik Routley, Old Testament music had three outstanding characteristics. First, it was natural and proper to "ecstatic conditions of mind." The psalmist could rejoice in the "singing" of the hills and valleys, and the author of Job rejoiced that the morning stars "sang" at the creation. Second, the music was liturgical. Third, the music had not only power to speak, but also power to act. The influence of music is seen in the story of David as he charmed away Saul's madness by playing on his harp.[1]

Although not a great deal is said in the New Testament about music in worship, it may be fairly assumed that Jewish psalmody became the inheritance of the Christian church. At the birth of Christ the angels broke forth into song. Luke records this song and also those hymns of praise, the Magnificat, the Benedictus, and the Nunc Dimittis.

The singing of a hymn followed the institution of the Lord's Supper (Matt. 26:26-30). Paul and Silas sang praises to God in prison at Philippi. Paul instructed the Christians at Ephesus and Colossae to teach and admonish one another in psalms and hymns and spiritual songs (Eph. 5:19; Col. 3:16). There are many passages in the New Testament regarded as fragments of Christian hymns, such as Ephesians 5:14, 1 Timothy 3:16, Titus 3:4-7, and Revelation 15:3-4.

Dale Moody suggests that the majestic hymn included in John 1:1-5,10-11,14,18 may have been sung by early Christians in the second century. There are more than a score of hymns in 1 Corinthians alone, as may be noted in Moffatt's translation. Romans 5:12-21, 6:3-11, 8:31-38, 13:11-14 may be completed hymns, according to Moody. Certainly Philippians 2:5-11, 1 Peter 3:18-22, 1 Timothy 3:16 and 6:1,2, 2 Timothy 1:9,10 and 2:11-13, Titus 2:11-14 and 3:4-7 are all hymns.[2]

The book of Revelation speaks of the singing of the heavenly hosts. In John's vision it was fitting for the people to worship through music. "And they fell on their faces before the throne

---

[1]*The Church and Music* (London: Gerald Duckworth & Co., Ltd., 1950), pp. 15-17.

[2]*Christ and the Church* (Grand Rapids: Wm. B. Eerdmans Publishing Co., 1963) p. 113.

and worshiped God, saying, 'Amen! Blessing and glory and wisdom and thanksgiving and honor and power and might be to our God for ever and ever! Amen' " (Rev. 7:11,12).

Church Music in History

History presents a convincing witness to the power of music in worship. R. W. Dale said, "Let me write the hymns and the music of the church, and I care very little who writes the theology."[3] In the third century Basil said, "Psalmody is the calm of the soul, the response of the spirit, the arbiter of peace." In the fourth century, Augustine wrote, "When I remember the tears I shed at the psalmody of thy church, in the beginning of my faith; and how, at this time I am moved not with the singing, but with the things sung, when they are sung with a clear voice and modulation most suitable, I acknowledge the great use of the institution." He wrote an elaborate hymn to fortify his people against the Donatists. The opponents of the Reformation did not exaggerate when they said, "Luther has done us more harm by his songs than by his sermons."[4]

During the early Middle Ages music made some progress. "A highly organized body of chant, codified during the papacy of Gregory the Great (590-604), was almost the only worship music of the church for a thousand years."[5]

Until the eleventh century, singing was done in unison. The singing of parts, which arose about that time, led to a number of developments which reached maturity in the music of Palestrina (1525-1594). Around 1600 operatic and instrumental music began to develop. This produced a new type of music in the church, which was harmonically oriented.

During the Reformation Luther sought to restore congregational singing. He saw it as a means of indoctrination as well as a source of joy. Luther declared,

---

[3]*Nine Lectures on Preaching Delivered at Yale, New Haven, Connecticut* (London: Hodder & Stoughton, 1952), p. 271.

[4]T. Harwood Pattison, *Public Worship* (Philadelphia: American Baptist Publication Society, 1900), p. 161.

[5]W. Hines Sims, "Church Music," *Encyclopedia of Southern Baptists,* II, 934.

Music is a fair and lovely gift of God which has often wakened and moved me to the joy of preaching. . . . Music is a gift of God. Music drives away the devil and makes people gay; they forget thereby all wrath, unchastity, arrogance, and the like. Next after theology I give to music the highest place and the greatest honor. I would not exchange what little I know of music for something great. Experience proves that next to the Word of God only music deserves to be extolled as the mistress and governess of the feelings of the human heart. We know that to the devil music is distasteful and sufferable. My heart bubbles up and overflows in response to music, which has so often refreshed me and delivered me from dire plagues.[6]

It is rather strange that Zwingli, who was a trained musician, felt that music had no part in Christian worship, while Calvin believed in the unison singing of psalms but did not approve of instruments.

Metrical versions of the Psalms were sung in English congregations in the seventeenth century. "Although Elizabeth herself detested these public songs which she called 'Geneva jigs', singing in her reign became almost a passion, or orgy, and the Psalms were 'roared aloud' not only in church but in every street."[7] During this century two musical giants appeared, Johann Sebastian Bach (1685-1750) and George Frederick Handel (1685-1759). These developments paved the way for the outstanding hymn writers. Among them were Isaac Watts (1674-1748), Charles Wesley (1708-1788), John Newton (1725-1807), and John Neal (1818-1866). It was the Wesley brothers who popularized Watts's hymns. Among the great hymns which Watts wrote are "O God, Our Help in Ages Past," "High in the Heavens, Eternal God," "When I Survey the Wondrous Cross," and "Before Jehovah's Awful Throne." He has been called the father of English hymnody.

The churches in America patterned their worship services after those in England. From the beginning psalms were sung in the Free Churches. The standard psalm tunes and Americanized English folk tunes were the sources for most of the music in the early churches. The Wesley revivals with the music of Charles

---

[6]Roland Bainton, *Here I Stand* (New York: Abingdon Press, 1950), p. 341.
[7]Albert Edward Bailey, *The Gospel and the Hymns* (New York: Charles Scribner's Sons, 1950), pp. 12-13.

Wesley and other English hymn writers swept away the tradition of psalm singing.

It should be added that America has also made its contribution to music in contemporary worship. Gospel songs are an American contribution. The Puritans and the Pilgrims in New England brought their metrical psalters from England and Holland, using them until they published the Bay Psalm Book in 1640. Among the early American composers were Lowell Mason, who led the movement against the exclusive use of the psalms in New England. He published many hymns and conducted great choruses in the presentation of oratorios.[8]

Music has made great strides in America during the twentieth century. Choral and oratorio societies have come into being. The American Guild of Organists was organized in 1896 with 145 charter members. By 1952 it had grown to 2,000 members, the largest single musical organization in the world and one of the most powerful factors in fostering music of a worthy quality in the churches. Eric Routley writes, "In church music there has been no age so full of surprises and so full of promise as our own."[9]

Today many of the churches are examining again the meaning of worship and the value of music in worship. Universities as well as theological seminaries are giving a great deal of attention to the development of appreciation for church music. Many hymnbooks have been compiled by various denominations during this century. Serious students are giving attention to the relationship of theology and music in worship. An excellent study has been made by Routley.[10]

Our hymns have brought all of us closer together in a spirit of Christian unity. Catholic churches may be found singing hymns written by Free Churchmen, and people in the Free Churches have sung hymns composed by Catholic writers for centuries. For

---

[8]See Luther D. Reed, *Worship: A Study of Corporate Devotion* (Philadelphia: Muhlenberg Press, 1959), p. 175.

[9]*Twentieth Century Church Music* (New York: Oxford University Press, 1964), p. 5.

[10]See *Church Music and Theology* (Philadelphia: Muhlenberg Press, 1959). See also chap. 3 in Horton Davies, *Worship and Theology in England, The Ecumenical Century, 1900-1965.*

example, Bernard of Clairvaux's hymns "Jesus, the Very Thought of Thee" and "Jesus, Thou Joy of Loving Hearts" have long been favorites in devotional worship. Frederick Faber's "Faith of Our Fathers" has aided countless multitudes of Protestant Christians to express the ardor of their faith.

Davies cites Vaughan Williams' contribution to contemporary Christian hymnody. He researched widely into the psalmody of Geneva, the folk songs of Great Britain, the classics of early English hymnody, and the tunes of the French Counter-Reformation, and took from these treasured contributions for his *English Hymnal* and *Songs of Praise*.[11]

Although much improvement has been made in the hymns of the Free Churches, there is yet need for further development. In a critical evaluation Davies says, "The hymnbooks generally show a preference for individualistic piety (the persistence of the first personal pronoun, singular is striking), romanticism in mood (descending to the eroticism of "Still, Still with Thee When Purple Morning Breaketh"), and swooping tunes." These preferences are largely true among Baptists, Congregationalists, Methodists, and, to a limited extent, Presbyterians.[12]

Lovelace and Rice largely agree with him in their evaluation of contemporary church music. They declare that congregational singing in most churches is still at a low ebb. Too many congregations stay with a few "old favorites" without attempting to sing or learn anything new. In this era of activism many of the hymns come in the "how-to" category, which may indicate that a great deal of our church music is guilty of much activity but without real purpose. It is dominated by "emotion and promotion."[13] Hymns and anthems are chosen to please the congregation or to secure a specific emotional response. The church does not fulfil its role merely as an effective organization with a busy program; it must be primarily a living organism. Music in worship must contribute vitality to the organism.

---

[11]*Ibid.*, p. 113.
[12]*Ibid.*, p. 115.
[13]Austin C. Lovelace and William C. Rice, *Music and Worship in the Church* (Nashville: Abingdon Press, 1960), p. 11.

Among the other Free Churches Baptists began to feel the need for a hymnal in their services of worship. In 1850 the *Baptist Psalmody* was compiled by Basil Manly and his son. It contained 1,295 hymns and was a selection of excellent quality. Basil Manly, Jr. was the first professor of biblical interpretation at Southern Baptist Theological Seminary. The publications of other hymnals soon followed.[14] Between the years of 1923 and 1956 eight hymnals were published by the Southern Baptist Convention.

The first hymnal which brought a degree of unanimity in Southern Baptist congregational singing was the *Broadman Hymnal*. It was edited by B. B. McKinney and published by the Baptist Sunday School Board in 1940. Within a decade there was need for a new hymnal. Through the combined work of a committee of thirty-seven, including ministers, musicians, and other denominational leaders, the *Baptist Hymnal* was published in 1956. The general editor was W. Hines Sims, secretary of the Church Music Department. This hymnal, used in most of the Baptist churches of the Southern Baptist Convention, includes both classical hymns and gospel songs. It contains a greater number of outstanding hymns than any other hymnal Southern Baptists have published.

Musical Expression in Worship

Music in itself is neither religious nor irreligious. However, certain of its various forms may be more appropriate for the expression of religious attitudes than other forms. Even the Old Testament writers had an acute sense of the moral force of music.

Edward Dickinson suggests that music may be used to intensify ideas and feelings that are already existent in a prepared and chastened mood, which is an antecedent to worship. In other words, through association music can inspire a prayerful mood and thereby aid in worship.[15]

The purpose of music in worship is to create an awareness of God and a mood for worship, enhance the inner life of man, unite

---

[14]William J. Reynolds, *Hymns of Our Faith* (Nashville: Broadman Press, 1964), pp. xiii-xxiv.

[15]*Music in the History of the Western Church* (New York: Charles Scribner's Sons, p. 397.

the congregation for a worship experience, and express the convictions of the congregation. In other words, music may serve as the bridge that connects man's convictions with his feelings and attitudes.

Music is related to worship in at least three ways. First, music points to the aim or spirit of worship. It is not an end in itself, but should encourage a spirit of reverence in worship. Second, music serves as an aid to worship, recalling fundamental truths and experiences of the writers and sharing these experiences with others. Music may also be an act of worship. For example, when the voice is lifted in praise, the music produced is actually an act of worship.

The importance of hymns in the Free Churches was emphasized in Bernard L. Manning's *The Hymns of Wesley and Watts:* "Hymns are for us dissenters what the liturgy is for the Anglican. They are the framework, the setting, the conventional, the traditional part of divine service as we use it. They are, to adopt the language of the liturgiologists, the dissenting use. . . . We mark times and seasons, celebrate festivals . . . and expound doctrines by hymns."[16]

Certain leaders in different denominations are experimenting with the jazz motif in worship services. The loneliness and estrangement in our generation find expression in jazz and folk singing. Music which expresses real human experience is valid for use in religious worship so long as it does not violate the spirit of Christian worship. For example, the Negro spiritual was a form of folk music which found a valid place in worship, and choir music in the evangelical churches derived its forms from opera. Although these modern expressions may speak out of the depths of human anxiety and need, it is doubtful whether some of them will become a fit vehicle for Christian truth. We should beware of the ready acceptance of popular music which is altogether secular in tone. The Archbishop's Committee reported the following as the general view of the best church musicians today: "Music that is in keeping with the spirit of the liturgy will be characterized by qualities of nobility and restraint, by freedom from sensationalism or mawkishness, and from all suggestions of secularity."[17]

---

[16] Quoted in Davies, *Christian Worship: Its History and Meaning*, p. 96.
[17] Quoted in Routley, *Church Music and Theology*, pp. 63-64.

We should beware also, however, of divorcing so-called religious music from ordinary human experiences and appreciation. As George Hedley says, "To sing worthy texts to worthy settings, and to sing them well, is the immediate objective of music in worship. To sing worthily the praise of God is the ultimate aim."[18]

Music in the service of the church is not at its best when it is trying to be master; but neither is it at its best when it is made a slave. Musicians should serve freely with no thought of attempting to be master. On the other hand, the church should appreciate the service of its musicians and encourage them to give the best of their vocation in leading the church to greater heights of appreciation for good music in worship.

From the beginning of worship God's people have expressed their praise in music through the human voice and through instruments. The voice and instruments are complementary. The church should make the best use of all these.

Instrumental Music

The organ is the primary instrument for accompaniment in worship. In many churches the piano has become more prevalent, although the organ is a better means of producing a worshipful atmosphere. Other instruments may be used to a limited extent in the worship service. Stringed instruments are more fitting for use in worship than brass instruments, although there is a time for the use of the trumpet or other brass instruments.

The organ, piano, and orchestra are used primarily for accompanying congregational singing and choral singing. Besides accompanying vocal music, there are five other ways in which the instrument may be used as an aid in worship.

The prelude.—Prelude music should create an atmosphere and provide an introduction to the remainder of any worship service. A brief period prior to the beginning of the worship may help create an atmosphere for those who come early to the service. It has the effect of calling people to attention as they prepare to meet God in worship.

---

[18]*Christian Worship: Some Meanings and Means* (New York: The Macmillan Co., 1958), p. 126.

The offertory.—Music played during the time when people are dedicating their offerings to God should be appropriate to genuine worship. The selections should suggest to people themes of dedication and commitment.

The interlude.—A good organist can do much to unite the various elements of a worship service by the playing of proper interlude music. Themes that sustain the spirit of worship should be used always.

Meditation music.—During the meditation or silent prayer period appropriate music may aid the congregation. However, some leaders prefer that no music be played during this period of silent prayer.

The postlude.—At the climax of a period of worship it is fitting to have postlude music played by the organist as the congregation retires from the sanctuary.

Choral and Ensemble Music

A trained choir is a great asset in leading the congregation in worship. This is the primary function of the choir. Music by the choir may be interspersed during the service. It is quite fitting to have the choir sing the call to worship or to share in the call to worship with the minister, the minister speaking one line and the choir singing another. It is often helpful to have the choir sing the "Amen" at the conclusion of a prayer. The anthem or other special music by the choir often contributes to the enrichment of the worship experience.

Many larger churches have a graded choir program in which they have children's and youth choirs participating in some of the services of worship. Lovelace and Rice warn against the careless use of junior and children's choirs in the regular worship services. If they do not sing well, their participation may hinder rather than aid worship. A graded choir is valuable in educating the children but may not always contribute to worship.

Other ensemble music and solos often make genuine contributions to worship. Whatever the special music, it should be presented as an act of worship and never as a display of the musician's voice. Only that special music which contributes genuinely to worship should be used.

Congregational Singing

Congregational singing is the primary musical expression in worship. It is an error to think of the choir and the instruments as being primary. Planned worship should provide adequately for the congregation to express itself through singing. All members of the congregation ought to be encouraged to join in song. The singing church is a victorious church.

The Choice of Hymns

In the Free Churches two books have always been considered handbooks of worship, the Bible and the hymnbook. Both should be studied seriously in the planning of worship. The careless choice of hymns may limit the worship experience of a congregation. There are several principles that should guide in the selection of hymns. (1) The leader of worship should know the hymnal well and know how to select the appropriate hymns for a given service. (2) The minister should lead in the selection of hymns or, if the church has a trained music director, assist him in the choice of hymns. In any case, the pastor should assume ultimate responsibility for the appropriate selection of hymns for the service. (3) There ought to be a definite objective in the choice of each hymn. Every hymn should have a specific purpose.

(4) The hymns in any particular service of worship should provide a well-rounded worship experience. There should be hymns of adoration and praise, hymns of devotion and prayer, hymns of affirmation and instruction, and hymns of dedication and commitment. The hymn before the sermon might well be selected on a theme related to the sermon, but the other hymns should be chosen to express particular attitudes in worship. Except for special occasions, all the hymns should not be selected on one theme. This is not psychologically sound because comprehensiveness and variety in the expression of worship are essential. (5) It is good to keep a balance between objective hymns and subjective hymns. There has been a tendency in many of our Free Churches to neglect the great stately hymns for the singing of sentimental, subjective gospel songs. To use only objective hymns is to starve the emotional expression

of experience. On the other hand, to use only subjective gospel songs is to deprive the intellect of the discipline it needs. Objective hymns point more to God, while subjective hymns speak of our experience in personal worship. There is a place for both, and a balance between the two is preferable. For example, "O God Our Help in Ages Past" directs our minds toward God, whereas, "Jesus Is All the World to Me" speaks of the subjective or experiential side of faith. Both are good in their proper places.

Tests for hymns.—There are certain tests which every hymn ought to meet if it is to be most useful in worship. Some hymns and gospel songs are unworthy for use in worship. The following tests will help in the selection of good, usable hymns. (1) Is the content Christian? In other words, is the theology good? Hymns that violate a sound Christian theology ought to be forbidden. In fact, this test should be applied to anthems also. For example, the anthem "My God and I Walk Through the Fields Together" betrays the majesty and holiness of God. To sing that God and I "talk as good friends should and do" is to imply that he is not worthy of worship. (2) Is it worshipful? Does it express Christian feeling? Does it express Christian experience? (3) Is the style lyrical? Does it appeal to the imagination? Can it be followed easily? Does it measure up to good literary form?[19] (4) Is it singable? Can the congregation sing it? A hymn that is appropriate for one congregation may not be suitable for another.

Purpose.—As was previously stated, hymns should be chosen with a particular purpose in view. Every hymn should make a specific contribution to the experience of worship. A worship service should begin with hymns of adoration and praise, hymns whose objective content points to God. It can be disastrous to ask a congregation to begin a worship service with a song such as "Work for the Night Is Coming" when people are already tired as they have come from their week of work. Perhaps they will be ready to sing that hymn when they have first worshiped in praise and devotion and have found some inspiration and comfort for their lives. The hymn of response or commitment should come at the end of the service.

---

[19]For a study of literary form, see Austin C. Lovelace, *The Anatomy of Hymnody* (Nashville: Abingdon Press, 1965).

It will be helpful to people as they worship if each hymn is designated by a modifier, such as adoration, devotion, commitment, and the like. The following suggestions may be helpful in the selection of hymns according to purpose. (1) Some hymns of adoration, praise, and thanksgiving are "Holy, Holy, Holy," "Come, Thou Almighty King," "O for a Thousand Tongues to Sing," "Great Redeemer, We Adore Thee," "Crown Him with Many Crowns," "O God, Our Help in Ages Past," "All Hail the Power Jesus' Name." (2) Hymns of devotion, fellowship, concern, and faith are "Oh, for a Closer Walk," "O Master, Let Me Walk with Thee," "Take Time to Be Holy," "Saviour, Like a Shepherd Lead Us," "My Jesus, I Love Thee," "Sweet Hour of Prayer." (3) Hymns of affirmation, confession, and instruction may be called thematic hymns or hymns chosen according to a particular theme. This type of hymn is usually sung before the sermon and may be related to the theme of the sermon. Some examples are "The Church's One Foundation," "Love Divine, All Loves Excelling," "Majestic Sweetness Sits Enthroned," "When I Survey the Wondrous Cross," and "Jesus Shall Reign Where'er the Sun'." (4) Hymns of dedication, response, commitment, and invitation are usually sung at the conclusion of the worship service. Some examples are "O Jesus, I Have Promised," "Jesus, I My Cross Have Taken," "Have Thine Own Way, Lord," "Just As I Am," "My Faith Looks Up to Thee," "Take My Life, and Let It Be."

Music Leadership

As leader of worship the minister is responsible for the music in a general sense. He will attempt to correlate the entire worship life of the church by giving proper emphasis to the music. He should know good music and hold up a high standard for the music used in the church. The minister is not required to be a trained musician, but he should have a general knowledge of music.[20]

Every minister can be a student of hymnology, which includes not only the history of hymns and hymn writers but also a theology

---

[20]For rudiments of music see James C. McKinney, *The Progressing Music Reader* (Nashville: Convention Press, 1959).

of hymnody.[21] Some ministers have the literary gift and training to write hymns. Many of the best hymns were written by ministers. For example, a good contemporary hymn, "God of Grace and God of Glory" was written by Harry Emerson Fosdick.[22]

The minister is obligated to be acquainted with the graded music program of the church, including the various choirs. He ought to be a constant student of the hymnal. He should understand what his denomination is projecting in the area of music. His major responsibility is to set a good example by singing hymns with the congregation at worship. It is probably true that the level of church music can rise no higher than the minister's estimation of its importance in the life of the church.

The minister of music is directly responsible for the church's music program. He is a specialist in church music and at the same time a minister of the gospel. According to James McKinney, his responsibilities fall in four general areas: performer, teacher, administrator, and spiritual leader.[23] His performance skills include conducting, keyboard, and voice. He will serve as a teacher of voice, speech, theory, and conducting. As administrator of the music program, he will share his skills, methods, and materials for the various age groups in the church. His qualifications include acquaintance with organizational planning, budgets, promotion, keeping of records, the securing of equipment, and other practical matters. As spiritual leader he must have a knowledge of the Bible, of Christian doctrine, and of the total program of his denomination.

The minister and the musician ought to be mutually sympathetic. Both should be aware of their tendencies toward individualism and temperamentalism. They are fellow ministers of the gospel and are responsible to know something about the relationship between theology and music, and should seek to work in harmony as they plan and conduct worship for the glory of God.

---

[21]See Harvey B. Marks, *The Rise and Growth of English Hymnody* (New York: Fleming H. Revell Company, 1937). Also A. E. Bailey, *The Gospel in Hymns: Backgrounds and Interpretations*. Also Reynolds, *op. cit.*

[22]See *Baptist Hymnal*, ed. W. Hines Sims (Nashville: Convention Press, 1956), No. 465.

[23]"Developing Musical Leadership for the Church," chapel message given at Southwestern Baptist Theological Seminary, Fort Worth, Texas, September 13, 1962, pp. 2-4.

The organist (or pianist) also has a vital place in the church's ministry. He or she must be a well-trained person, capable of performing effectively.

The competently trained organist is thoroughly grounded in theory, ear training, harmony, counterpoint, form, canon and fugue, transposition, score reading, composition, improvisation, and musicology. . . . The ability to play by ear should be developed. . . . His education should extend to the art of arranging piano or orchestral scores for the organ. . . . A knowledge of voice and vocal methods should also be a part of the training for every organist whether he directs a choir or not.[24]

The effective organist will understand the relationship between his function and the entire worship service. His task is primarily to accompany and support the other leaders of church worship. A sense of timing is essential in unifying all the elements of a worship service. Making transitions between various elements and providing good preludes, offertories, and postludes can enrich and strengthen a worship service.

The church choir has a threefold task in worship. First, it should lead the congregation in expressing worship through the singing of hymns. Second, it should provide special music which will inspire and enrich the worship experience of the entire congregation. Third, it should lead the entire church in an appreciation of better music and richer worship experiences.

Many contemporary churches have a graded choir program which provides musical training and participation for all age groups. The Music Ministry includes organized choir groups for the purpose of study and development in the knowledge and performance of music for all departments of the church. It is concerned with all age groups old enough to participate. The graded choir program properly conducted will insure the strength of the church's music program for the future. Loren R. Williams declares that "the quality and effectiveness of tomorrow's music ministry in our churches will inevitably be enhanced by the general acceptance of graded choirs

---

[24]Lovelace and Rice, *op. cit.*, p. 73.

and their function as a medium of music training and spiritual guidance."[25]

The music committee of the local church can contribute immeasurably to the success of the church's music program. The music committee is primarily an advisory group working with the minister and the director of music. It should select good leadership and then support the program that is projected. The committee should realize its limitations and not attempt to advise where it is not competent. By assisting the director in recruiting new singers, handling business matters, and educating the congregation, it guides the music program of the church.

The entire church should feel responsible and offer support to the total music program. Each person in the congregation has a particular part to play in the service. The primary responsibility of the congregation is hymn singing. Other responsibilities include the singing of responses, the amens, the doxologies, and even the unique silent sharing of the special music with the choir. The congregation should feel that the choir is expressing praise for them in a public worship service. Members of the congregation should be made to realize the absolute necessity of their participation in the music program of the church.

God deserves only the best music in worship. It is imperative that the leadership of the church seek the highest possible standards for church music, even in the smaller churches. All music selected for worship should contribute to a particular purpose for which the congregation is assembled—namely, to turn hearts and lives toward God.[26]

The level of appreciation for good music can be raised in any congregation. They can be trained to understand the primary purpose of church music. Their knowledge concerning hymnology can be increased. A congregation should not be willing to settle for its present level of knowledge and appreciation of church music. Attitudes should be disciplined in reaching for higher standards.

The level of appreciation will vary among congregations and even

[25]*Graded Choir Hymnbook* (Nashville: Convention Press, 1958), p. 1.

[26]See Martha Reeves Settle, *Music in the Small Churches* (Nashville: The Sunday School Board of the Southern Baptist Convention), p. 24.

among individuals within a given congregation. The leaders responsible for planning worship will therefore be careful in their selection
of hymns to fit the needs of a particular congregation. When selecting
music for public worship, three factors must be kept in mind: first,
it must enable members of the congregation to express themselves
in an idiom with which they are familiar; second, it must be the
best music which they are capable of appreciating; third, it must
assist in turning their minds Godward. William J. Reynolds concludes
that church musicians must continue to work for the day when
every individual in the congregation, with full understanding of what
he is doing and with a full awareness of the Person he is approaching, stands to sing:

> Praise God, from whom all blessings flow;
> Praise Him, all creatures here below;
> Praise Him above, ye heav'nly host;
> Praise Father, Son, and Holy Ghost.[27]

---

[27]*Op. cit.,* p. xxxi.

7

Prayer in Worship

Beloved, we are come together in the presence of almighty God and of the whole company of heaven to offer unto Him through our Lord Jesus Christ our worship and praise and thanksgiving; to make confession of our sins; to pray, as well for others as for ourselves, that we may know more truly the greatness of God's love and show forth in our lives the fruits of His grace; and to ask on behalf of all men such things as their well-being doth require. Wherefore let us kneel in silence, and remember God's presence with us now.

HORTON DAVIES
Christian Worship: Its History and Meaning

Prayer has rightly been called the soul of worship. Many believe that prayers form the most important part of public worship. Throughout history men have worshiped God by calling upon his name in praise and petition. The Bible is filled with examples of private and public prayers. David's prayer as recorded in Psalm 51 is an outstanding example of individual confession. Many of the Psalms mingle praise and petition, showing both a concern for the individual as well as for the national life. Examples are seen in Psalms 60, 79, and 80. One of the outstanding examples of public prayer is Solomon's prayer at the dedication of the Temple. It is an eloquent recitation of God's glory and an earnest plea for his continuing favor upon his people (2 Chron. 6).

The Lord Jesus Christ considered prayer so important that he gave the following as a model prayer for his disciples:

> Our Father who art in heaven,
> Hallowed be thy name.
> Thy kingdom come,
> Thy will be done,
>   On earth as it is in heaven.
> Give us this day our daily bread;

And forgive us our debts,
As we also have forgiven our debtors;
And lead us not into temptation,
But deliver us from evil.[1]

The Model Prayer includes various attitudes essential for worship—adoration, submission, confession, petition, and dedication. The Lord's Prayer has been called the "quintessence of prayer."

There is a definite pattern in this Model Prayer: (1) God's name—who he is, including the essence of his person; (2) God's kingdom—his realm of life, including all his relationships with his people; (3) God's will—what he desires and purposes, including plans, procedures, and methods; (4) man's material needs—his petition for God to supply those needs; (5) man's need for confession of sins—his prayer for guidance in paths of right living and deliverance from evil; (6) man's commitment of all things to God—acknowledgement of his sovereign lordship over all of life. The prayer begins in adoration, as God's name is hallowed, and concludes in doxology, as all things are committed to his purpose and glory.

One of the dynamic characteristics of the early congregation of Christians in Jerusalem was its practice of continuing steadfastly in the prayers (Acts 2:42). The prayers may have been Christian prayers at stated hours, answering to the Jewish prayers, and perhaps replacing the synagogue prayers, as the apostles' teaching had replaced that of the Scribes.[2]

The prayers may have included both new and old as seen in Ephesians 5:19, Colossians 3:16, and James 5:13. The story of the church in Acts indicates the people joined as a congregation in the practice of common prayer. When Peter and John returned from prison, the congregation lifted up their voices together to God and said,

"Sovereign Lord, who didst make the heaven and the earth and the sea and everything in them, who by the mouth of our father David, thy servant, didst say by the Holy Spirit, 'Why did the Gentiles rage, and the peoples imagine vain things?' "

---

[1]Matt. 6:9-13.
[2]*The Expositor's Greek Testament,* ed. W. Robertson Nicoll (New York: Hodder & Stoughton, 1917), II, 95.

And when they had prayed, the place in which they were gathered together was shaken; and they were all filled with the Holy Spirit and spoke the word of God with boldness (Acts 4:24-25,31).

George A. Buttrick observes that corporate prayer is the heart of corporate worship. "The heart of religion is in prayer—the uplifting of human hands, the speaking of human lips, the expecting waiting of human silence—in direct communion with the Eternal."[3] Buttrick adds significantly that prayer must go *through* the order of worship, scripture, symbolism, and sermon, as "light through a window."

Although prayer is an intensely personal matter, it is not individualistic, especially when the Christian joins with the congregation in worship. It becomes then an expression of community, of human solidarity, of spiritual fellowship, within the body of Christ. The church incorporates the community of prayer as a contemporary, worldwide fellowship. For in the church we pray for all kinds of men in every part of the world, and when we pray as members of the body of Christ, we bear witness to our faith that God loves all men and will hear our petitions for all mankind.

There are generally three kinds of prayers used in public worship: (1) fixed or liturgical prayers in which all of the prayers are read in public worship; (2) spontaneous or extemporaneous prayers, which are prayed without planning; and (3) prayers given extemporaneously after preparation. In this third method of praying there is both discipline and freedom, both planning and spontaneity. Many of the Free Churches believe this is the best plan for vital worship.

In liturgical prayers everything is rigidly prescribed; there is no room left for spontaneous promptings of the Holy Spirit. Planned prayer with freedom avoids this particular pitfall. Planned prayer which includes both discipline and freedom enables the minister to gather up and express the desires of the people. But free prayer does not mean freedom to license. In unprepared, spontaneous prayer there is always the danger that the minister may lack discipline in his thoughts; the prayer may be spoiled by unsuitable expressions; it may involve too much repetition; or the minister may inflict his own state of mind upon the congregation.

---

[3]*Prayer* (Nashville: Abingdon-Cokesbury Press, 1942), p. 283.

Carelessness in leading public prayers has often bordered on the ludicrous. A pastor who had forgotten to make an announcement included in the benediction, "Lord, kindly remind the deacons that their meeting set for Monday night has been cancelled." Another error is often made in informing God of what he already knows. One minister began his petition for people who lost their possessions in a flood: "Lord, as thou hast probably heard, many people lost their homes in the recent flood." Using public prayer to retaliate or to condemn other people is a horrible error sometimes practiced by ministers. These weaknesses are proof that more serious attention should be given to leading in public prayer.

Guiding Principles Concerning Public Prayers

The two supreme qualities demanded in public prayers are sincerity and intelligence. Zeal with intelligibility will inspire a congregation to join the leader in prayer. If public prayers are to be most meaningful to a congregation at worship, there are certain guiding principles which ought to be followed in the planning of them.

1. Every prayer should have a specific purpose of its own. A prayer should not deal in vague generalities but come to grips with specific needs. For example, a prayer for forgiveness of sins should specify which sins. When a prayer expresses gratitude for blessings, it should name the blessings. The petition should be concrete and definite. Fosdick said, "Some prayers are a confused jumble of all sorts of requests, meditations, aspirations, and even homilies, which occur to the extempore pray-er."[4] A well-organized prayer can be followed and participated in by each member of the congregation.

2. Every prayer should have good style. The style should be simple, clear, direct, pleasing, and of good literary construction. Perhaps prayers should not be limited to biblical style, but the minister would do well to immerse his mind in the phraseology of the Scriptures, especially those passages which are prayers themselves.

3. The prayer should be addressed to God in the second person.

---

[4]Harry Emerson Fosdick, *A Book of Public Prayers,* (New York: Harper & Bros., 1959), p. 8.

It should be addressed *to* God and not be a discourse *about* God. For example, it is inconsistent to pray, "Our Father, we know that God is concerned about us and will hear our petitions." Here the address is directly to the Father, and the remainder of the statement is a preachment about God.

4. Many leaders in worship prefer the use of the old English forms of the personal pronoun "Thee," "Thou," "Thine," etc. To use "Thee" instead of "you" when speaking to God seems to show reverence to the deity. If this form of the pronoun is used, one must be careful to use the proper verb forms with it. For example, "We know that thou hearest us," not "We know that thou hears us." If one begins by using the classic "Thee," he should be consistent and not change from "Thee" to "you."

5. The delivery of the prayer is important if the congregation is to follow the leader. It should be delivered in a clear voice so that the congregation may hear distinctly. One should avoid a monotone or a so-called preacher voice in public prayers. It is good to keep the voice in a lower register.

6. Wisdom should be observed as to the length of public prayers. A few brief prayers are probably better than one or two long prayers. The congregation will not concentrate too long upon the prayer of the leader. George Whitfield once said of a certain preacher, "He prayed me into a good frame of mind, but he prayed me out of it again by keeping on."[5]

7. Some planning of public prayers seems to be essential if they are to be most effective in leading people to worship in prayer. Some may object to the minister's planning prayers in advance. "Is not prayer a matter of the heart? . . . Yes, prayer is a matter of the heart. But public prayer is a matter of many hearts . . . and involves the mind of the church."[6] Planning and spontaneity, discipline and freedom should be kept in balance.

8. All who are called upon to lead prayers in public worship should be alerted previously lest they be too nervous to collect

[5]Charles H. Spurgeon, *Lectures to His Students*, ed. David Otis Fuller (Grand Rapids: Zondervan Publishing House, 1945), p. 53.

[6]Robert L. Williamson, *Effective Public Prayer* (Nashville: Broadman Press, 1960), p. 9.

their thoughts. Laymen need to study the principles of leading in public prayer if they are to assist the minister. It distracts rather than aids the congregation to have two or more laymen carelessly repeating the same prayers in a given service. Let the layman no less than the minister pray distinctly, with meaning and with fervor.

Types of Prayers As to Purpose

As has been indicated, every prayer should have a definite purpose in a worship service. Unless this principle is followed, there is danger of violating Jesus' command, "Use not vain repetitions, as the heathen do" (Matt. 6:7, KJV). One man asked, "Doesn't God know what we have already prayed earlier in the service without our repeating it to him?" Without definite purpose it is easy for prayers to become mere verbal formalities. Well-worn clichés soon lose their significance and their interest. The following classification of prayers according to purpose may be helpful.

The call to prayer.—A prayer may well be introduced by a call to prayer. The leader may simply say, "Let us pray." He should never begin, "Shall we pray?" or "May we pray?" as if he were asking the congregation's permission. A prayer promise from the Scriptures may be quoted, such as, "Ask, and it will be given you; seek, and you will find; knock, and it will be opened to you" (Luke 11:9). Or, a call to worship may be printed for congregational participation, such as:

Minister: God is our refuge and strength, a very present help in trouble.
Congregation: Therefore we will not fear, though the earth should change, though the mountains shake in the heart of the sea.
Unison: The Lord of hosts is with us; the God of Jacob is our refuge.

The invocation.—The invocation is the opening prayer in which adoration and praise offered to God are prominent. This type of prayer is often called a collect. The purpose is to lead the people to become conscious of God's presence and to open their hearts to receive his blessings. The invocation should be more objective (focusing upon God) than subjective (focusing upon the feelings of the people). The following invocation is an excellent example:

Almighty God, unto whom all hearts be open, all desires known, and to whom no secrets are hid; cleanse the thoughts of our hearts by the inspiration of thy Holy Spirit, that we may perfectly love thee, and worthily magnify thy holy name; through Jesus Christ our Lord.[7]

It will be noticed that the invocation has five parts: (1) address to the Father; (2) a relative clause giving an attribute of God—who he is or some of his promises; (3) a petition, or simple statement of desire; (4) the purpose or objective of the petition; (5) the conclusion, the ground of the prayer, or the ascription.

The pastoral prayer.—This prayer has sometimes been called the main prayer, the morning or evening prayer, or the long prayer of the service. The main prayer usually consists of the following parts. (1) Adoration and thanksgiving may be expressed, unless this has been done already in the invocation. Even then, as God is addressed, there should be the spirit of adoration. (2) Confession follows naturally when people have entered into the presence of God and acknowledged his being worthy of worship. The purpose of this prayer is to lead the congregation to confess their sins to God. (3) Petition is asking God for the things desired. It concerns those who are present in the congregation. (4) Intercession is prayer offered for those beyond the assembled group: absent members of families present, community and national leaders responsible for citizenship, people of other nations, missionaries and other servants' who are serving God in other areas of the world, and other concerns of the congregation. (5) The climax of prayer is reached in submission to the will of God and wilful commitment of our lives to him and his service. (6) Ordinarily, prayers conclude with an ascription to the Trinity or to some member of the Godhead. For example, prayers may conclude "in Jesus' name," "through Jesus Christ our Lord," "for the sake of him who brought redemption and victory to all who believe in his name," or other appropriate ascriptions.

It may be preferable to break the pastoral prayer up into several parts, the leader indicating each brief prayer which is to be prayed by the congregation. For example, after having addressed God and

---

[7]See Morgan Phelps Noyes, *Prayers for Services* (New York: Charles Scribner's Sons, 1934), p. 36.

expressed a spirit of adoration and praise, the leader in worship may pause briefly and say, "Let us now offer our thanks to God for his blessings," and, after a brief pause, lead the congregation in specific thanksgiving. He then would proceed to say, "Let us individually confess our sins to God," and, after a brief pause, lead the congregation in confession. By following this procedure the congregation is enlisted to participate more readily than if the minister simply leads a long prayer without a break from beginning to end.

The silent prayer.—The silent prayer may be a part of the pastoral prayer. Before beginning the long prayer, the pastor may simply suggest that the congregation pause for a brief period of meditation and prayer, and then proceed to lead the congregation in prayer. Or, sometimes it is preferable to have the silent prayer at a different place in the order of worship. It is usually preferred that complete silence reign and that not even soft organ music be played during the silent prayer.

The bidding prayer.—The leader may mention specific concerns and then bid the people to pray for them one at a time. This may be included in the period of silent prayer. It is not necessarily used in every worship service. Many feel that it is an excellent practice for the midweek prayer service.

The litany.—The litany is a form of prayer in which fixed and frequent responses are made by the congregation to brief petitions said by the minister. It is an effective way of encouraging congregational participation. The following is an example of a printed litany. The response is taken from Psalm 123:3.

Minister: Gracious Father, we have neglected to worship thee regularly.
Congregation: Have mercy upon us, O Lord.
Minister: We have been guilty of prejudice toward our fellowman.
Congregation: Have mercy upon us, O Lord.

The litany may be as brief or as lengthy as is desirable.

The offertory prayer.—The offertory prayer is specifically for the dedication of gifts. It may include a brief sentence of thanksgiving for God's gifts to us, a reference to the use of our gifts, and other matters of general stewardship. The dedication of self along with the gift is important. The offertory prayer should be altogether related to those matters in connection with the offering. Again, let it be intelligent planning plus spontaneity in expression.

The benediction.—The benediction is a memorable utterance commending ourselves to God's care and announcing his blessings upon the people. It is an important climax to a service of worship. Andrew W. Blackwood has said that it ought to be like the period at the end of a sentence. It should gather up the attitudes expressed in the worship service and should be offered to God as a commitment of the congregation to go forth into the world to carry out his will. Scriptural benedictions are excellent for use here. In fact, it is difficult to improve upon some of the splendid scriptural benedictions for sending people away in a spirit of worship. The Aaronic benediction has been used down the centuries: "The Lord bless you and keep you: the Lord make his face to shine upon you, and be gracious to you: the Lord lift up his countenance upon you, and give you peace" (Num. 6:24-26).

Paul's conclusion to his Second Epistle to the Corinthians contains another favorite benediction: "The grace of the Lord Jesus Christ and the love of God and the fellowship of the Holy Spirit be with you all" (13:14). Other excellent benedictions are to be found in the following Scripture passages: Ephesians 3:20-21; Hebrews 13:20-21; 1 Peter 5:10-11; Jude 24-25; and Revelation 22:21.

Preparation for Leading in Prayer

The Free Churches do not approve of confining ministers to fixed forms of prayer for public worship. On the other hand, it must not be assumed that one can be most effective in leading a congregation in worship without some kind of preparation. Without preparation he may be guilty of throwing around meaningless terms or even nonsense syllables, as, for example, is usually done in so-called pagan incantations. Where public prayer is undisciplined, corporate worship is in danger of decay. Just as the minister draws from every resource in the preparation of his sermons, so he ought also to draw upon every possible resource in preparation for leading the people in public prayer.

Henry Sloane Coffin has suggested the following qualities which ought to characterize public prayers: comprehensiveness, orderliness, concreteness, objectivity, freshness or relevance, and variety.[8]

Prayer must be absolutely forthright, honest. It demands mental, moral, and religious integrity. Genuine prayer that links the life of men with the purposes of God deserves the best possible in preparation. In view of the importance of leading effectively in public prayers, the following suggestions are offered for leaders in their preparation.

1. *Pray in private.* No person is prepared to lead other people in worship until he has first worshiped God in private. Spurgeon declared that private prayer is the drill ground for public prayer. Jesus taught his disciples to enter into the secret place and talk with God alone. The minister has no right to lead people in public prayer unless he has a private prayer life also. The prayers which he will lead in the presence of the people should first of all be prayed in private.

2. *Consider the needs.* The minister should survey the needs of the congregation as he prepares for prayer. Ultimately the contents of prayer are more important than the techniques or types of prayer. The minister must seek to phrase the desires of his own soul and the people's in such expressions that the people may be caught up into his prayer and pray with him. This calls for deep and sympathetic insight into human need, for sensitive awareness of both individual and social problems, and for faith in God's grace and mercy. And it probably demands as much dedicated and careful preparation as does the preaching of a sermon. If public prayers are to be helpful in worship, they must be relevant to the needs of the people.

3. *Study the prayers of the Bible.* The Bible contains the supreme treasury in the school of prayer. The book of Psalms through the centuries has been the book of devotion which best expresses the universal spirit of prayer. A pastor in a prominent church testifies that the Psalms have meant more to him in preparing to lead people in public worship than perhaps any other piece of literature. The prayers of Jesus exemplify the honesty and intensity with which one must

---

[8]*Op. cit.,* pp. 72 f.

come into the presence of God. The prayers of Paul are also excellent examples for public worship.

4. *Study other prayers.* One's own mind is enriched as he studies the classical prayers which other men have formulated. The minister should become familiar with manuals of public prayer so that he may have the benefit of what others throughout history have learned about leading in public prayer. There are classics in liturgical literature as well as in secular literature. *The Episcopal Book of Common Prayer* is one of the outstanding examples of prayers for public services, both from the viewpoint of the purposes set forth in the prayers and their literary form. One of the best manuals for leaders in Free Churches is Morgan Phelps Noyes's *Prayers for Services: A Manual for Leaders of Worship.* It draws upon many resources and organizes suggested prayers as follows: the call to worship, the prayer of invocation, the prayer of confession, the prayer of thanksgiving, the prayer of petition, the prayer of intercession, the prayer before the sermon, the prayer after the sermon, the prayer after the offering, prayers for special days and seasons, and prayers for special services, including the general service, the marriage service, and the Lord's Supper service. Other good collections of prayers would include Harry Emerson Fosdick's *A Book of Public Prayers,* Roy Pearson's *Hear Our Prayer: Prayers for Public Worship,* John Baillie's *A Diary of Private Prayer,* and Robert N. Rodenmayer's *The Pastor's Prayer Book.*

5. *Outline and write out prayers.* This is not to suggest that the prayers be written to be read publicly. Rather, writing them out will give concreteness and purpose to the prayers. There should be no more objection to writing out one's prayers as a method of preparation than there is to writing out one's sermons. A Baptist pastor who had given very little attention to planning worship became aware of the repetitious nature of his prayers Sunday after Sunday. He decided to plan and write out his prayers. The worship services improved so obviously that many people commented upon it and expressed appreciation for the pastor's leadership in prayer.

6. *Memorize portions of prayers.* It is particularly good to memorize the beginning sentence or two in a prayer. Well-chosen introductory phrases may mean the difference between a helpful prayer

and one which really distracts in worship. It was Alexander Maclaren's practice to memorize introductory phrases in his prayers.

7. *Depend upon the Holy Spirit.* All who worship should cultivate a dependence upon the Holy Spirit in both private and public praying. Paul exhorted the people to pray with the spirit and with the mind also (1 Cor. 14:15). When prayers are planned, the Holy Spirit has more with which to work in leading the congregation in prayer. This will not hinder the spirit of spontaneity in prayer any more than preparation for preaching will hinder spontaneity in one's delivery of the sermon. As H. E. Dana affirmed, "Preparation is as wings, not as weights, to freedom and spirit."[9]

Perhaps many pastors have shared Henry Ward Beecher's feelings about leading in public prayer.

The most sacred function of the Christian ministry is praying. Never in the study, in the most absorbed moments, never in any company, where friends are sweetest and dearest, never in any circumstances in life, is there anything that is to be so touching as when I stand, in ordinary good health, before my congregation to pray for them. Hundreds and thousands of times as I arose to pray and glanced at the congregation, I could not keep back the tears. It seems as if God permitted me to lay my hand upon the very tree of life, and to shake down from it both leaves and fruit for the healing of my people.[10]

[9]*A Manual of Ecclesiology* (Kansas City, Kans.: Central Seminary Press, 1944), p. 339.
[10]*Yale Lectures on Preaching* (2d series; New York: J. B. Ford and Co., 1874), p. 46.

8

Communicating the Word of God

The Bible is central in worship. God communicates his word to man through the use of man's words as vehicles. Since the Bible is a record of the acts of God in history as revealed to man by the Holy Spirit, it is the primary source of the objective content in worship. The Bible presents Jesus Christ as the object of faith in worship.

The writers of the Old Testament story were conscious that God spoke to them. Moses received the Law by the Spirit of God through faith. The prophets heard God speaking to them. For example, Jeremiah said, "The word of the Lord came unto me" (Jer. 1:4). The author of Hebrews testified that "in many and various ways God spoke of old to our fathers by the prophets" (1:1). He goes on to imply that the appearance of the living Word in the person of God's Son verifies the trustworthiness of God's written record. The Bible guides man's thinking in worship and creates the spirit for worship.

Many elements in the order of worship are filled with biblical content. The music, particularly the hymns, communicates biblical truth. Public prayers are often saturated with the spirit and terminology of the Bible. The sermon proclaims the gospel as recorded in the Bible. The public reading of the Bible allows God's Word to speak for itself.

The Reading of the Scriptures

The Free Churches boast, "We are a people of the Book," and yet there is great neglect of the Bible. People fail to read it regularly in private. In many homes the Scriptures are rarely read. Even in public worship services the reading of the Bible is often neglected. When it is read, it is often read carelessly and hurriedly.

The reading of the Scriptures in public worship is highly significant. According to H. E. Dana, we have two models in the Scriptures for us to follow. One is found in Ezra as recorded in Nehemiah 8:5-8: "And Ezra opened the book in the sight of all the people, for he was above all the people; and when he opened it all the people stood. And Ezra blessed the Lord [Jehovah], the great God; and all the people answered, 'Amen, Amen,' lifting up their hands; and they bowed their heads and worshiped the Lord with their faces to the ground." Nehemiah further states that they read in the books distinctly and gave the sense so that the people understood the reading.

The other example is recorded in the fourth chapter of Luke where we have a picture of Jesus "reading in the synagogue the prophetic witness concerning himself while the eyes of all were fastened on him, and men marvelled at the gracious words." Dana further states, "These two model examples not only exalt the reading of the Bible as a channel of the Spirit's power, but demonstrate the supreme value of the content of the portions read and the manner of the reading."[1]

The reading of the Bible is in itself an act of worship—not the worship of the written word but the worship of the living Word to whom the written word gives witness. The influence of the Bible is not merely indirect in worship. Usually some portion of the Scriptures is read aloud, frequently two portions (one from the Old Testament and one from the New Testament) and in some churches three passages are read (one from the Old Testament, one from the Epistles, and one from the Gospels). In the Puritan and nonconformist churches there was always a lengthy reading. They called the brief Anglican "snippets" mere " 'pistling and gospeling.' "[2]

Selecting the Scripture Passage

Careful attention should be given to the proper selection of Scripture passages for use in worship. Some churches have a lectionary suggesting appropriate passages for particular seasons according to the Christian year. Most of the Free Churches, however, do not make use of the lectionary, in which case the minister will need to give,

---

[1]*Op. cit.,* p. 337 f.
[2]Davies, *Worship and Theology in England: From Watts and Wesley to Maurice, 1690-1850,* p. 32.

more serious attention to the selections. Most hymnals contain selections for responsive readings. The following suggestions may aid the minister in the proper selection of Scripture passages.

(1) For the public reading of God's Word select a passage other than the passage from which the sermon is to be delivered. The Bible should be allowed to speak for itself at this place in the worship service. One pastor who is an effective leader in Christian worship asked, "Who is so exalted himself that he feels adequate to pay a tribute to the Bible? Or, who is so frail in his faith that he imagines that the Bible requires any such defense? We have so long substituted debate over the Bible for decisive commitment to the commands of Christ, that we have interposed a strange barrier between ourselves and Christ."[3]

(2) The selection should be in high degree devotional in nature. It ought not only to instruct but to awaken devout feeling. Passages from the Psalms, and certain passages from Isaiah and other prophets, the Gospels, the Epistles, and Revelation abound in devotional spirit.

(3) The passage suggested should be of comparative simplicity in style, language, and imagery. Passages difficult to understand and those which include certain indelicate situations or words usually should be omitted. Poetic and rhythmical passages which appeal to the emotions and the imagination are particularly good for congregational reading.

(4) Familiar passages, which are universally loved, tend to help create a worshipful atmosphere. The choice ought not to be limited, however, to the familiar passages. Many times the lesser known passages have great lessons for the congregation.

(5) The choice of passages should vary between the Old Testament and the New Testament. For example, some leaders feel that if the sermon is to be from a New Testament passage, the passage for public reading may well be selected from the Old Testament.

(6) It is good to use various versions of the Bible in public worship. Perhaps the King James Version, because of its beauty and the people's familiarity with it, is preferred by most congregations. Certain passages, such as Psalm 23, perhaps ought generally to be

---

[3]Trentham, *op. cit.*

read from the King James Version. Other versions quite often make the truth of God's Word more clearly understood. For example, the American Standard Version, the Revised Standard Version, and the New American Standard Version present a more contemporary style of English. There is a freshness in Phillips' translation and in the Centenary translation of the New Testament.

(7) The passage for public reading should be comparatively brief. It should not be so long as to lose the attention of the congregation. The following are examples of good passages for reading in public worship: Psalms 1; 8; 23; 27; 46; 84; 90:1-12; 91; 103:1-17; 104: 1-15; Isaiah 40:1-5,9-11; Matthew 5:1-12; John 1:1-14; Romans 8:28-30,35-39; 12; 1 Corinthians 13; 15:51-58; Hebrews 11 (certain portions); Revelation 5:11-14.

The Art of Reading the Scriptures

Truth, not eloquence, is to be sought in reading the Holy Scriptures; and every part must be read in the spirit in which it was written. For in scripture we ought to seek profit rather than polished diction. We ought not to ask who is speaking, but mark what is said.[4]

To read the Bible well is a rare accomplishment. Good preachers are more numerous than good readers of the Scriptures. R. W. Dale said that he had never heard but one man who read the Bible supremely well, Mr. Dawson of Birmingham. Dale wrote, "It was genuine reading, not dramatic recitation—the dramatic recitation of the Bible is irreverent and offensive."[5]

Dale also suggests that the minister should, by a vigorous imaginative effort, place himself by the very side of the men who wrote the Bible, see what they saw, and feel what they felt.

In his book *Vocal and Literary Interpretation of the Bible,* S. S. Curry reminds us that expression grows naturally and inevitably out of the reader's own grasp of the meaning of that which he communicates to others. He said, "It is not a veneer applied by mechanical rules from without. It expresses the knowledge and emotion

---

[4]Thomas a Kempis, *Imitation of Christ,* trans. Aloysius Croft and Harry F. Bolton, I (Milwaukee: Bruce Publishing Co., 1940), 5.
[5]*Op. cit.,* p. 228.

of him who uses it, as naturally as leaves express the life of a tree."
Curry affirms that the reading of the Scriptures is a peculiar, serious,
and difficult function which demands special study and earnest preparation. He further states that the mode of expression of each
literary form is primarily determined by the spirit that causes it.
The Bible is written in a variety of literary forms which give expression to a variety of spirits, such as the narrative spirit, the didactic
spirit, the lyric spirit, the dramatic spirit, and the epic spirit.[6]

The following brief suggestions on the art of reading the Scriptures
may be helpful. (1) Handle the Bible reverently. Convey the feeling
that it is God's Word. It is a symbol of the living Word speaking to
the hearer. (2) Announce the passage intelligently and distinctly.
One may say, "Let us hear God's word as recorded in the Gospel
according to Matthew, chapter five, verses one through sixteen."
(3) Read the passage interpretively. Emphasize the important words,
especially the verbs and the nouns. Imagine the setting and attempt
to capture the spirit of the writer's experience. Good reading is in
itself exposition.

(4) Read clearly and distinctly so as to be understood. For good
enunciation one must read slowly and deliberately. (5) Read rhyth-
mically, especially when reading poetic passages. Much of the Bible
is written in poetic form and cannot be properly interpreted without
an understanding of poetic rhythm and Hebrew parallelism. For example, Psalm 24 begins, "The earth is the Lord's and the fulness
thereof, the world and those who dwell therein."

(6) Read ordinarily, without interruptions or comment. If some
explanation is needed for a proper understanding of the passage,
give the explanation before you begin reading. Do not preach and
exhort in the midst of reading. Let the Bible speak for itself. (7)
Practice reading aloud to yourself. Become thoroughly acquainted
with the passage, and then read it aloud until you feel that you
thoroughly understand how to communicate its message.

---

[6](Boston: The Expression Co., 1923), p. 3. Curry gives excellent instructions
on the techniques of reading which include rhythmic actions of the mind,
rhythmic modulations of the voice, changes of idea and pitch, inflection, expression of the imagination, sympathetic identification with the congregation,
and movement.

A lesson must be read intelligently and reverently if it is to be a means of worship. Such reading demands careful preparation. Someone has said, "If one reads a passage as though in it he had been confronted by the living God, it will be worshipfully rendered."

There are various ways of reading the Scriptures in public worship. (1) The minister alone may read the passage in the hearing of the congregation. (2) The passage may be read responsively, the minister reading one verse, and the congregation the next verse; or the minister and the choir may read responsively; or the choir and congregation may read the passage responsively. Most hymnbooks have a section of Scripture passages appropriate for responsive reading. (3) The minister may invite the entire congregation to join him in a unison reading of the entire passage.

The congregation should be encouraged to listen to God's Word and to participate in responsive or unison reading. Hearing the Bible read has been called "the listening side of prayer." The minister's attitude and actions can do much toward encouraging audience participation and listening. H. Grady Davis has observed, "When we listen properly our listening also is worship." He further states, "We do not hear only the words of an ancient and venerable book of wisdom. We hear our Maker, our Friend, and Liberator. . . ."[7]

The Preaching of the Word

Through the centuries thousands of ministers have been preaching the gospel week in and week out, "constantly reminding the farmer and the shopkeeper of charity and humility, persuading them to think for a moment about the great issues of life, inducing them to confess their sins." Historian Herbert Butterfield continues, "This has been a phenomenon calculated greatly to alter the quality of life and the very texture of human history; and it has been the standing work of the church throughout the ages—even unto the worst of Popes here was a light that never went out."[8]

---

[7]*Why We Worship* (Philadelphia: Muhlenberg Press, 1961), p. 35. For further study on the public reading of the Scriptures, see Charles Woolbert and S. Nelson, *The Art of Interpretative Speech* (New York: F. S. Crofts & Co., ca. 1934), and Lionel Crocker and Louis M. Eich, *Oral Reading* (2d ed.; Englewood Cliffs, N. J.: Prentice-Hall Inc., 1955).

Primitive Christianity had as its stock and trade the preaching of the gospel. The preaching of the gospel at Pentecost was an innovation. The pre-Christian world had known nothing like it. There was no religious dialogue between those within and those without. Following in this New Testament tradition it has generally been the practice of the Free Churches to make preaching central in the worship service.

There have been two extreme attitudes toward preaching as related to worship. The sacramentalists have often rejected the place of preaching in favor of the sacraments. Martin Luther deplored the loss of preaching in the churches of his time. He declared that the Christian congregation should never assemble except the Word of God be preached. The other extreme view is observed in those who have dismissed the prayer, praise, and Bible reading as the "hors d'oeuvre" to the exposition of the Scriptures in the sermon. So much emphasis has been placed on the sermon that the preciousness of other parts of worship has been obscured. Many people in the Free Churches generally think of the other elements of worship service as mere "preliminaries" to the sermon. You can never make a sermon what it ought to be if you consider it alone. The service that accompanies it, the prayer and the praise, must have their influence upon it.

Although many feel that preaching is more or less outmoded, it is encouraging to see a growing concern for a return to dynamic preaching, even in many of the liturgical churches. At the beginning of this century a minister in a metropolitan pulpit warned that if the pulpit decay, the cause of Christ is lost, and nothing can take the place of preaching. We must agree, however, that there has often been too little emphasis on the other elements of worship and too much emphasis on the sermon.

Preaching should take its place along with the other elements of a worship service. The sermon is important, but it is not the only important part of worship. Too many people refer to Sunday worship as the "preaching service." For example, the Six Point Record

---

[8]Quoted in Davies, *Worship and Theology in England: From Watts and Wesley to Maurice, 1690-1850*, pp. 3-4.

System used in Southern Baptist Sunday Schools still reads, "Attending Preaching, 20%." There is need for a clear understanding of the relationship between preaching and the entire worship service. Hays and Steely believe that the strength of many Baptist churches is directly related to the strength of the preaching they have enjoyed. They warn, however, of the danger that people will think of the worship service as simply a time for "listening" to a sermon.[9] So much stress has been given to preaching in many churches that the sanctuary has been designated the "auditorium."

Perhaps few will quarrel with P. T. Forsyth in his declaration that nothing in the service goes to the root of the gospel like the preaching, and this makes preaching the chief part of our evangelical liturgy. Forsyth believes that it is the part which gives the law to all worship, since the message is what stirs worship and makes it possible.[10]

In order to emphasize the unity of other elements and the sermon in the service of worship, the following propositions are offered.

1. All biblical preaching is contemporary dialogue. The sermon is an offering to God, while, at the same time, the sermon is God's word to man. Expository preaching speaks God's message to man. Preaching is an event in which God acts. All preaching is expository that opens the Scriptures and finds in them that word of God to man which has its focus in the person of Jesus Christ. Only preaching that brings the Scriptures to focus on life in concrete historical life situations can be called expository or biblical preaching. Preaching that just goes "round and round inside the text of Scripture but never comes to focus in the lives of those who are addressed is most unbiblical in character."[11]

Since all worship is encounter with God, it is the purpose of preaching to bring men into a conscious confrontation with their Maker. The preacher speaks to believers to build them *up* as a Christian community, and he speaks to the world to build it *into*

---

[9]Brooks Hays and John E. Steely, *The Baptist Way of Life* (Englewood Cliffs, N. J.: Prentice-Hall Inc., 1963), p. 103.

[10]*Positive Preaching and the Modern Mind* (London: Hodder & Stoughton, 1907), p. 88.

[11]Smart, *The Rebirth of Ministry* (Philadelphia: The Westminster Press, 1960), p. 81.

a Christian community. Heralding the good news may be designated both as prophetic preaching and pastoral preaching.[12] Many effective teachers of preaching indicate that the sermon should meet certain specific objectives as related to the life of the congregation, such as the *ethical objective*—the point at which the converted person touches the life of another person, the *consecrative objective* —which calls people to dedicate to God all the resources under their control, including time, talent, and personality, and the *supportive objective*—which is designed to meet the needs of the people who are enduring great burdens and suffering.[13] We may also compare Roy Pearson's fourfold objective for preaching: "to celebrate the wonderful works of God; to contend for the faith delivered to the saints; to fill the hungry with good things; and to speak to the children of Israel, that they go forward."[14]

The initial object of preaching, of course, is so to present the gospel of God's redeeming grace that unbelieving persons will respond in faith and commit their lives to him as their Saviour and Lord. To preach is to become a part of a dynamic event wherein the living, redeeming God reproduces his act of redemption in a living encounter with men through the preacher.

2. Preaching is the witness of the church to the world. Preaching belongs to the church before it belongs to the individual preacher. It is a part of the commission which the Lord delivered to his church. Herein is a confession of the church's faith.

The church has been designated custodian of preaching. Christ founded a community, a church, whose first charge was the preaching of the gospel. Forsyth calls the preaching of the gospel an *opus operatum,* the central work of the church going forward, the "organized hallelujah of an ordered community."[15]

Preaching the gospel is the business of the church. The preach-

---

[12]For a helpful discussion of pastoral preaching and worship, see C. W. Brister, *Pastoral Care in the Church* (New York: Harper & Row, 1964), pp. 125-30.

[13]See H. C. Brown, Jr., H. G. Clinard, and J. J. Northcutt, *Steps to the Sermon* (Nashville: Broadman Press, 1963), p. 17.

[14]*The Preacher, His Purpose and Practice* (Philadelphia: The Westminster Press, 1963), p. 278.

[15]*Positive Preaching and the Modern Mind,* pp. 88, 105.

er's voice is a representative voice of the entire church. He speaks *for* the church and not merely *to* the church. *With* the church he speaks to the world. The story of the early church tells us that all the followers of Christ were scattered, except the apostles, and they went everywhere "preaching the word" (Acts 8:1,4).

3. Preaching is also the personal witness of the preacher himself. In the individual preacher the everlasting gospel is contemporized, individualized, and actualized. The preacher, redeemed by the grace of God and energized by the Holy Spirit, speaks the things he has seen and heard and experienced. He actually becomes the instrument of Jesus Christ to present his claim to men. Unless the preacher feels the gospel within his own being, it is not likely that others will feel its impact as they hear it from his lips. We are reminded of Phillips Brooks's much quoted definition of preaching as the communication of the truth of God to men through the personal witness of a man. It is truth presented effectively through dedicated personality.

If preaching is to be worshipful and is to contribute to worship generally, thorough preparation of heart and mind is required of the preacher. Such preparation is not confined to the development of a particular sermon but involves the whole personality of the preacher during the whole of his life. Direct preparation goes on in the study while the minister consults commentaries and lexicons on next Sunday's sermon text. The real quality of the sermon depends upon a disciplined spirit and a well-stored mind, a deep knowledge of the people, and a vital experience of the saving power of God in the life of the preacher. The continual cultivation of the minister's own spiritual life requires time for devotional reading of the Bible, the reading of great devotional literature, periods of prayer and meditation, and a sensitivity to the presence of God in the lives of all the people around him.

The acid test of worshipful preaching is the effect it has upon those who hear. There is a close interrelationship between preaching and pastoral work. The preacher must be able to relate theology to life. The primary purpose of preaching is to build up the church and not to glorify the preacher. Effective preaching creates a church in which the people no longer center their attention on the preacher

but have their faith grounded in the revelation of the Scriptures.
The sermon should so present the power of the Word and the
Spirit of God that every member shall know himself called to be
a servant of the Word.

The minister both as leader in worship and as preacher should
be willing to submerge himself in the gospel and be content to be
a representative of the Spirit of God. The time of worship is not
a time for cleverness or excessive levity or the display of oratory
for the sake of exalting the vanity of the preacher. William Cowper
was amazed at the vanity of eighteenth-century parsons:

> What!—will a man play tricks, will he indulge
> A silly fond conceit of his fair form
> And just proportion, fashionable mien,
> And pretty face, in presence of his God?
> Or will he seek to dazzle me with tropes,
> As with a diamond on his lily hand,
> And play his brilliant parts before my eyes,
> When I am hungry for the bread of life?[16]

As James Denny long ago said, no man can give at one and the
same time the impression that he himself is clever and that Jesus
Christ is mighty to save.

Perhaps another suggestion from the eighteenth-century period
may be helpful. Strickland Gough of the Established Church once
wrote to the Dissenters, "I think there are two faults in your manner
of worship, that your prayers are too short and your sermons too
long. The one has too little reverence toward God and the other is
too tedious toward ourselves." He added that God was worshiped for
twenty minutes and the reason of man was titillated for sixty minutes
in the sermon.[17]

The whole point is, the sermon should point toward worship,
not toward the preacher himself.

4. Preaching and the other elements of worship mutually support
each other. They are at their best in a complementary relationship.
Preaching makes a positive contribution to all the other acts of

[16]See Davies, *Worship and Theology in England: From Watts and Wesley
to Maurice, 1690-1850,* p. 71.
[17]*Ibid.,* p. 97.

worship. All the liturgical elements are important in worship. The liturgy needs to be understood by the worshiper in the congregation. Preaching translates all the other elements of worship into the language of the common man. It helps the worshiper relate worship to his life experiences. Preaching is worship's interpreter, the instrument whereby the heart that has "dwelt awhile in heaven is connected with the hands and feet that now must dwell on earth."[18]

Preaching may be regarded as the most highly creative aspect of the minister's office. The emotions and the imagination of the preacher stimulate a like response on the part of the hearer. Inspired preaching makes all the other elements of worship come alive for the congregation.

The sermon is particularly fitted to become the climax of the whole worship service. It may recapitulate the various moods and movements of the service and draw them together as the minds and judgments and wills of the hearers are focused upon the gospel. Commitment, which is the climax of worship, may be challenged by the sermon as it presses for decisions and actions as a proof that the person means what he says and is changed by what he feels.

Preaching is dependent upon the response of the people. The congregation is not simply an audience which remains passive while it is being preached at. The worshiping people are the source of the sermon, for their lives and their needs mold and make the preacher. The preacher realizes that the church is a body of worshipers with whom he shares the insights revealed to him in study and prayer. Actually, the preacher acknowledges the need to allow the congregation the last word after the sermon. The preacher always hopes that the emotions and purposes of the congregation will be expressed in commitment as a result of the appeal made by the sermon. Good worship and good preaching go together. The reverse is also true. Poor preaching and bare worship usually go together.

It is to be hoped that worship will contribute toward better preaching and preaching toward better worship. Participation in the preaching of the gospel and in the other elements of worship provides a shared experience for the minister and the congregation. God has

---

[18]Pearson, *op. cit.*, p. 137.

been at work in the lives of the entire congregation, and the gospel finds witness in the hearts of all present. They recognize and give assent to the gospel when it is preached. The Holy Spirit can work in the common worship experience of the entire congregation. Preachers should trust the Word to produce its own message in the minds of the hearers.

5. Preaching in essence is an act of worship. If worship is a two-way communication between God and man, preaching which brings man into the presence of God surely must be considered an act of worship. The preacher who does not worship while he preaches denies his calling; the church which does not worship while it hears the sermon denies its commission. Preaching that does not express worship is not really preaching; it is only a form of oratory or religious public speech. Worship is a sort of congregational sermon by way of testimony and witnessing, and preaching is but another form of God's part in the dialogue with his people at worship.

So preaching and the other elements of worship belong together as a unity. Worship gives preaching its reason for being, and preaching makes worship relevant.

The Children's Sermon

The communication of the Word of God should be experienced by the entire congregation. Therefore, the children should certainly be included. Since children are the center of interest in the home, as well as in the church, why not have a ministry of the Word for them? Too often worship services are planned with adults mainly in mind, and the children are neglected. Among the earliest instructions which God revealed to his people was the command to love God and keep his words in the heart. This particular passage in Deuteronomy continues, "You shall teach them diligently to your children, and shall talk of them when you sit in your house" (6:7). Jesus himself included the children in his ministry. He said "Let the children come to me, and do not hinder them; for to such belongs the kingdom of heaven. And he laid his hands on them and went away" (Matt. 19:14-15).

One way to include the children in a worship service is to provide a children's sermon for them. Some people object to the children's sermon, but when it has been given a fair opportunity there seems to be little objection. Some denominations have regularly included the children's sermon in the order of worship, while others have not made it a regular practice. Perhaps the following brief discussion may aid those who have the responsibility for planning and leading worship in making more effective the communication of the Word of God in the lives of children.

Values in the children's sermon.—There are certain values in providing the children's sermon as a definite part of the order of worship. (1) It makes the children aware that they are included in the fellowship of the congregation. They are made to believe that they are important as persons. (2) It insures that the children will have one part at least in which they can participate. Certain parts of the worship service are beyond the understanding of the smaller children particularly. (3) It is a means of instruction, an opportunity for "bite-sized" truths to be presented in a brief message. It also becomes a means of training children to participate in the general worship service. (4) It may create interest among the adults as well as among the children, teaching them to listen for illustrations that illumine the main sermon. Quite often adults are helped as much as are the children. (5) It emphasizes family unity by encouraging families to attend public worship service together. Many parents take a more vital interest in the church when they realize that the minister is personally interested in their children.

Some guiding principles.—Perhaps not all ministers or congregations will feel that the children's sermon should be included in their worship service. The decision to include it will depend upon several important factors. (1) The pastor himself should give sober consideration before undertaking the children's sermon. He should make certain that he loves children, that he has ability to communicate on their level, that he will be enthusiastic about it, and that he will be willing to work at making it worthwhile. Some ministers find it easy to communicate with children while others do not have such a gift. Let the minister be certain that he can present it effectively.

(2) The enthusiastic cooperation of the church is necessary for the success of the project. Perhaps it would be wise to give it a

trial run for a few Sundays before definitely adopting it as a regular procedure. (3) There should be a large enough group of children in the congregation to justify it. A certain amount of mass enthusiasm is necessary to make it effective. (4) The response of the children and the adults will determine whether the sermon should be continued as a part of the worship service. The minister should not depend alone upon his own insights but ask other persons to give their opinions concerning the advisability of continuing the children's sermon. (5) The children's sermon should be blended in as a part of the entire order of worship so as not to distract from the spirit of worship. If it cannot be so blended, perhaps it would be advisable not to attempt it. Whatever aids in worship is worthy of being a part of the order of worship, and whatever distracts from worship should be deleted.

Sources for sermon ideas.—The children's sermon will demand creative imagination, study, and detailed planning in advance. The preacher will always be on the lookout for sermon ideas which he may share with the children. Sources for sermons are almost limitless. Historical incidents and epochs, the biographies of outstanding leaders, Bible stories, fables, literature, art, science, nature, school activities, and sports are among the many resources available. For example, Thomas A. Edison's inventing the light bulb strongly teaches the lesson of patient endurance. One pastor told the story of how Gutenburg carelessly knocked some wooden letters into a pot of dye and then placed the letters on some paper to dry. In later years when he became a printer he remembered the incident, and out of his imagination was created movable type for the printing of books. This story suggests to children that we may learn from our mistakes and turn them into victories.

Object lessons are particularly good in presenting the children's sermon. A pastor showed the children a pedometer which he had worn to indicate how far he walked in a day. He then went on to indicate that more important than how far we walk are the places where our feet take us.

Perhaps the first thing a preacher will strive to do is to make the children's sermon interesting. To do this, he must always be on the alert for sermon ideas. He might jot them down in a notebook.

Suggestions as to procedure.—The leader in worship may find himself saying, "If I only knew how to proceed in presenting the children's sermon, I would like to attempt it." The following suggestions may be helpful to leaders in planning and presenting it. (1) Let the preacher never approach the sermon without careful, advance preparation. (2) The children's sermon should be placed at an appropriate point in the order of worship, perhaps following the morning prayer and preceding a hymn. (3) It has been found good to include children from ages six through twelve or grades one through six to participate. It should be limited to these ages. Let this participation be voluntary on the part of all the children and their parents, of course. (4) Give instructions ahead of time as to the procedure which will be followed, what is expected of the children and the parents. Suggest that they sit with their parents toward the front part of the sanctuary but not necessarily on the front rows. (5) The minister may step down from the pulpit as the organ continues to play and say, "Now, the boys and girls ages six through twelve may come forward for the children's sermon." He should direct them to assemble immediately and quietly near the pastor and call for them to look him in the eye and to listen carefully. (6) The minister should firmly and kindly insist upon attention before he begins. Then he should begin with an interesting statement and lead immediately into a story or illustration. (7) The entire period should take only about three or four minutes. As he moves to the climax, he should quickly draw the lesson and then say, "Let us pray about it." A brief prayer pertaining to the lesson should be given. (8) The children will then return and sit with their parents. The congregation will prepare to sing the next hymn and the organ will play while the children return to their seats.

Children like to identify with adults and will learn to do so as they are accepted as a part of the congregation. Some characteristics of children that we must keep in mind in preparing our services and our sermons for them are spontaneity, enthusiasm, optimism, a martial spirit, a challenge to action, and emphasis upon the personal. A warm, personal presentation of biblical truth related practically to life can be a means of leading children into meaningful worship of God.

9

Baptism and the Lord's Supper

Since New Testament times, baptism and the Lord's Supper have been considered central among the many acts and expressions of public worship.[1] In the long history of the Christian church various doctrinal and liturgical viewpoints of them have been held. By some churches these two acts have been called "ordinances," while others have designated them "sacraments." The New Testament does not use either of these terms in referring to these rites of worship. The biblical terms are simply baptism and the Lord's Supper.

Although historically most of the liturgical churches have freely used the term "sacrament," many of the Free Churches object to the use of the term because of its historical connotation. It is generally conceded that the term "sacrament" is valid when interpreted to mean a symbol representing some aspect of God's redemptive revelation. In that sense, all of God's creation is sacramental. But they prefer the term "ordinance" as applied to baptism and the Lord's Supper. There is a danger, of course, that much of the rich significance may be lost from these acts of worship if they are spoken of as "mere ordinances." To be sure, they were commands of Jesus Christ to be practiced by his church throughout the ages. They are more than ordinances; they are acts of worship.

Symbolic Acts As Worship

If baptism and the Lord's Supper are to be meaningful acts of worship, there must be a true understanding of their relation to symbolism. The climate of our time—skepticism, industrialization, scientific realism—tends to reduce all dimensions of life to the pragmatic level and to lose sight of the mystical and supernatural implications of the material. The Free Churches, caught up in this

---

[1] Other ceremonies, such as the wedding, the funeral, dedication services, and others, are also acts of worship in the church. Since these are usually conducted as special services, they will not be discussed here.

spirit of materialism, have tended to speak of the ordinances as "mere symbolism" as opposed to sacramentalism. There is a trend in the modern era back toward a more serious use of symbolism in worship. As Samuel H. Miller says, "Reality can no longer be seriously described or adequately comprehended in non-symbolic terms."[2]

Early Christian worship combined both the inward attitude and the outward symbols representing the gospel as revealed in Jesus Christ. Paul emphasizes both spirit and symbolic acts in his writings. Christians are in a dynamic relationship to Christ, "brought into one body by baptism, in the one Spirit, . . . and that one Holy Spirit was poured out for all of us to drink" (1 Cor. 12:13, NEB). The entire body of Christians shares in the blood and body of Christ. "Because there is one loaf, we, many as we are, are one body; for it is one loaf of which we all partake" (1 Cor. 10:17, NEB). The truth of the gospel is embodied in symbols such as words and objects, and also in ceremonials or actions. Both in Old Testament and New Testament worship the term translated "to worship" emphasizes the physical act of bowing down or prostrating oneself before the presence of the holy and majestic God. Baptism and the Lord's Supper are acts which convey the truth of the gospel. When they are performed as acts of worship, they witness to the gospel of God's grace.

Although the ordinances are symbols of God's revelation, they are not vehicles of God's grace as set forth in the sacramental view. God communicates the truth concerning his grace through the written word, the preached word, and the acted word (such as in baptism and the Lord's Supper); but his grace is effected only by direct personal communion through the Holy Spirit. The "sacramental view" is unworthy to be a vehicle of God's grace. It is also unnecessary and unwise.[3]

None of the historic views—Roman Catholic, Lutheran, Calvinistic, Zwinglian—adequately delineates the dynamic, revelational aspects

---

[2] "Reducing the Reality of the Lord's Supper," *Foundations,* 1-4 (October, 1958), pp. 24-29. See also chapter 11 in this book on "The Use of Symbolism in Worship."

[3] Baker, "Baptist Sacramentalism," *Chapel Messages,* ed. H. C. Brown (Grand Rapids: Baker Book House Co., 1966), p. 25.

of baptism and the Lord's Supper as acts of worship. Zwingli's view that they are "mere symbols" seems to deny the revelational aspect they were intended to convey. In worship a symbol must stand for a present, spiritual reality.

Genuine religion is a faith-relationship and not an exercise in magic. The magical attitude is that the worshiper may strongly influence or even coerce God to do man's will by adhering to proper rituals or invocations. Things in and of themselves have no effectual spiritual power. They must become a part of a relationship in which the human soul is engaged. To assume such power without relating oneself to God's redemptive grace is to attempt magic.

The religious attitude is "not my will but thine be done." God reveals his truth by various media. Man comes to know God in direct, personal relationship through a response of faith based upon the knowledge gained through the media. Baptism and the Lord's Supper are such media of God's revelation. In our full diet of public worship every church needs the two permanent elements appointed by Christ, the preached word and the enacted word, baptism and the Lord's Supper. Although they differ in practice and expression, they are a unity in essential purpose or function, which is the communication of the gospel of redemption in all its incomparable majesty and comfort.

The symbols of water and bread and wine are deeply significant for Christian worship. The reason why these particular symbols and actions, rather than something else, are important in Christian worship is that we did not choose them; they were chosen for us in the context of the acts of God in history. They point to the redemptive action of God in the life and death and resurrection of Jesus Christ. This revelation history is what makes them significant. The rites of baptism and the Lord's Supper are the earliest gospel, for they occurred before the writing of the New Testament.

God uses symbols to communicate to man. All of creation is in a sense symbolical of a deeper meaning, namely, God's sovereignty beyond creation. A symbol points to reality and also serves as a means of communicating ideas and awakening responses. It speaks to the mind and calls forth emotion. It may lead to decisions. A symbol may become effective as a medium of God's grace, not in the sense of magic, but in the area of faith and personal communion with God. The term "mere symbolism" is inadequate to express the meaning of the ordinances because more is present in the experience, such as faith, obedience, commitment, and gratitude.

The Bible is the written word symbolizing and communicating the living Word as incarnated in Jesus Christ. Preaching is the spoken word symbolizing and communicating the living Word—God speaking through persons. Baptism and the Lord's Supper are the acted word symbolizing and communicating the living Word—God speaking through signs. Neither the written word nor the spoken word nor the acted word is an effective medium of God's grace without the faith and commitment of the worshiper. Given the faith-response of the worshiper in personal commitment, each of these media becomes effective in the action of God's grace in the experience of the believer and in the unified experience of the congregation in common worship. The ordinances as acts of worship, performed as a pledge of devotion and loyalty, help to enforce and complete the meaning of worship. In the ordinances the actions and substances are secondary; the persons involved are primary. God speaks through the symbols and actions, and man responds to God through faith. In this dialogue there is personal communion, which is the essence of worship.

There are four ways in which the ordinances speak the gospel. In baptism and the Lord's Supper God speaks in a sign; the performer speaks in the formula (the written word); the believer or candidate speaks in an open act of commitment; the church speaks in the perpetuation of the ordinances as acts of worship.

Biblical Origins

The churches which take biblical authority seriously are concerned primarily with the biblical account of baptism and the Lord's Supper, rather than with tradition.

Origin of Baptism

Baptism was a significant act in the life of the early church. Water was a symbol of divine cleansing in the Old Testament (Ezek. 36:25). Baptism seems to have been a practice among the Essenes and also in the Qumran community.[4] The Jews practiced proselyte baptism. This is seen in the *Didaché,* chapters 1 through 6. John the Baptist practiced a baptism of repentance. Beasley-Murray does not believe that a connection exists between the baptism of John the Baptist and Jewish proselyte baptism. John's baptism inaugurated the new life of the converted, assuring him of forgiveness and cleansing from sin; and it anticipated the messianic baptism with Spirit and fire, giving assurance of a place in the Messiah's kingdom.[5]

The baptism of Jesus is the foundation for Christian baptism. Jesus was baptized of John in the Jordan River (Mark 1:9-12; Matt. 3:13-17; Luke 3:21-23). The purpose of Jesus' baptism was "to fulfil all righteousness" (Matt. 3:15). On Jesus' part it was a deliberate act of self-identification with men. In asking for John's baptism Jesus identified himself with men in four different ways: (1) He identified with men in their search for righteousness. They sought to do God's will, and he fulfilled the will of the Father. (2) He identified with men in their preparation for the coming of the kingdom of God. (3) He identified with men in their search for God. (4) Jesus identified with men in the sin and sorrow of mankind.[6]

The baptism of Jesus was in some sense the fulfilment of the purposes of God for his redemptive work. For Jesus himself, the event of baptism had deep meaning, as was indicated in the voice from heaven, "This is my beloved Son" (Matt. 3:17). It was for Jesus the moment of decision, the moment of assurance, the moment of equipment, and the moment of enlightenment and self-dedication.[7]

The whole context of baptism in the New Testament is a reflection of Christ's own ministry: his own baptism, his special endowment by the Spirit, his life of service, his death, and his resurrection. This is the "pattern" of the gospel story and, consequently, of baptism. The Great Commission of our Lord places baptism in proper relationship to discipleship and teaching (28:18-20). The passage is important both for the authority which it gives to baptism and for linking baptism with the mission of the church in making disciples.

[4]See George R. Beasley-Murray, *op. cit.,* p. 12.
[5]*Ibid.,* p. 39.
[6]See William Barclay, *The Mind of Jesus* (New York: Harper & Bros., 1961), p. 26.
[7]*Ibid.,* pp. 27-29.

Origin of the Lord's Supper

The Lord's Supper, along with baptism, is one of the two ordinances which Jesus gave to his church to be perpetuated throughout history. A common meal shared in a spirit of love, trust, and mutual acceptance has always been an expression of community. The Last Supper of Jesus with his disciples is considered by most scholars to have been a Passover meal. It took place in the evening and extended into the night. Jesus and his disciples reclined together for this last meal, an act practiced in the keeping of the Passover. Jesus took bread and broke it and gave it to his disciples. Then he took a cup of wine and gave it to them, commanding them to drink of it. The Supper concluded with the singing of a hymn, which may have been a portion of Psalms 114 or 115 to 118, the Hallel which closed the Passover meal.[8]

The New Testament contains only a few specific references to the Lord's Supper, but these are very significant. They include Matthew 26:17-30, Mark 14:23-26, Luke 22:14-23, and 1 Corinthians 11: 17-34. There are many other incidental references to meals which the Christians had together, such as Acts 2:42, 46; 20:7, 11; 1 Corinthians 5:17, KJV; 10:3-4, 16-17, 21; and John 6; 15. There are various terms in the New Testament which refer to the Supper, such as "the Lord's Supper" (1 Cor. 11:20), "the cup of the Lord" and "the table of the Lord" (10:21), "the cup of blessing" and "the bread which we break" (v. 16), "the breaking of bread" (Acts 2:42,46; 20:7), "a communion of the blood . . . of the body of Christ" (1 Cor. 10:16, KJV).

The historical facts concerning the institution of the Supper may be summarized as follows: (1) The place was an upper room, probably the home of John Mark. (2) The time was in the evening or night. (3) The Supper was related to the Passover, the Old Covenant and the New Covenant being mentioned. (4) The persons present with Jesus were his disciples. (5) The elements used were bread and wine. (6) Jesus gave thanks to the Father in a spirit of worship. (7) Jesus broke bread and distributed it, then took the cup and passed it among his disciples. (8) Jesus commanded his disciples

---

[8]Higgins, *op. cit.*, pp. 13-21.

to partake of the bread and wine, giving his reasons for their participation, and indicated the act was to be repeated until his return. (9) Following the supper they sang a hymn. (10) Jesus and his disciples went out to the Mount of Olives where he prayed in the Garden of Gethsemane in preparation for the crucifixion.[9]

In the history of the church the Supper has been observed under various designations: Lord's Supper, Eucharist, Communion, and Mass. Some see it as a sacrament in the highest sense. Others look upon it as a symbol and nothing more. Some churches have observed it as a central part of every service of worship. Other churches observe it rarely or neglect it altogether. The term "Lord's Supper," mentioned in 1 Corinthians 11:17-34, may have been a combination of what came to be called the "love feast" (*Agapē,* Jude 12) and the Last Supper.[10] The term "eucharist" is derived from a New Testament word which means a thanksgiving. Mark says that Jesus took bread and blessed it and then gave thanks for the cup (Mark 14:22-23; see also 1 Cor. 11:24). The participles for "giving thanks" *(eucharistēsas)* and "blessing" *(eulogēsas)* are used interchangeably. The term "communion" used by many Christians is based upon Paul's use of the term in 1 Corinthians 10:16 where he speaks of "the communion of the blood of Christ." The Greek word for "communion" is *koinōnia* referring primarily to the unity of the body of Christ. The Lord's Supper was described as a "communion" or *koinōnia* in Acts 2:42. Dale Moody believes that Ephesians 5:18-20 is a liturgical passage referring to the Lord's Supper or Eucharist in Christian worship. This brief celebration is very similar to the details found in 1 Corinthians 11:17-34.[11]

A Theology of the Ordinances

A theology of baptism and the Lord's Supper is essential for their proper observance as acts of worship. They are related to salva-

---

[9] I am indebted to Dr. Curtis Vaughn for a part of this material taken from an unpublished manuscript on "The Biblical View of the Lord's Supper." See also Alfred Edersheim, *The Life and Times of Jesus the Messiah* (Grand Rapids: Wm. B. Eerdmans Publishing Co., n.d.), II, 490-512.

[10] See Oscar Cullmann and F. J. Leenhardt, *Essays on the Lord's Supper,* trans. J. G. Davies (Richmond: John Knox Press, 1958).

[11] *Op. cit.,* p. 112.

tion-history, the kerygma, to Jesus Christ, to the Holy Spirit, and to the Church. They must be considered within a context "at once Christological, ecclesiological, and eschatological" if they are to be given full content and meaning.[12]

They are related to evangelism. As a part of the gospel revelation they persuasively present the offer of God's grace. The church's invitation to fellowship, the individual experience in repentance and faith as a responsible response, a commitment to a new way of life, and nurture and growth in a personal relationship with Christ are all included in a full-orbed evangelism. As James W. McClendon says, "Evangelism need not concentrate on the mere evocation of private experiences. Instead, it can return to its original central business of telling the good news, in the confidence that this gospel will call forth faith whose normal expression within the Christian community will be the response of baptism."[13]

Participation in the Lord's Supper points back and brings fresh experiences to the believer's conscious commitment in the salvation experience.

The ordinances are part of God's revelation of redemptive truth. Just as God reveals himself in the written word (the Bible) and in the spoken word (the witness of a redeemed person), so he reveals himself also in his enacted word through baptism and the Lord's Supper. Since Jesus gave the command to make disciples, "baptizing them in the name of the Father and of the Son and of the Holy Spirit" (Matt. 28:19), we must reason that God speaks in the very act of baptism. H. Wheeler Robinson believed that baptism has spiritual value for worship. Since revelation has objective-subjective aspects, which are united in experience, the event of baptism becomes a worship experience in the commitment of the individual. Baptism is filled with the gospel of Christ; therefore, it is "charged with a new spiritual power." The outer act and the inner experience of forgiveness and faith are closely related. The New Testament never considers them apart.[14] Since Jesus commanded that his fol-

---

[12]See Neville Clark, *An Approach to a Study of the Sacraments* (London: SCM Press, Ltd., 1958), p. 8.

[13]"Baptism as a Performative Sign," article accepted for publication in *Theology Today.*

[14]*Baptist Principles* (London: The Carey Kingsgate Press, 1938), pp. 14-15.

lowers regularly take the bread and the cup as a reminder of his atoning death, we must conclude that in the very act of the eating and drinking God speaks his word. Robinson saw baptism and the Lord's Supper as "acted parables" or dramatic acts in which God speaks his word and the believer identifies himself with Christ.[15]

Since salvation is based upon a personal faith-experience and is not an infusion by a material, sacramental act, infant baptism has no place in Christian theology. Donald M. Baillie goes too far in attributing the benefits of the "sacrament" to the child in "response to the faith of the parents and the church."[16] God does speak to the church through baptism but not without the witness of the individual's faith to the saving gospel. The absence of the practice of infant baptism in the New Testament, together with the clear teaching of salvation by personal faith, prompted Karl Barth and Emil Brunner to denounce infant baptism.[17] The church and the parents have a responsibility to dedicate and train the child, but they cannot act for him in saving faith. Baptism is for believers only.

In recent years serious attention has been given to the theology of Christian baptism. The first World Conference on Faith and Order, meeting in Lausanne in 1927, said of baptism: "We believe that in baptism administered with water in the name of the Father, the Son, and the Holy Spirit, for the remission of sins, we are baptized by the one Spirit into one body." This does not mean that we should ignore the differences in conception, interpretation, and mode which exist among us. It simply reveals that all Christian groups are interested in the meaning of baptism.[18]

The Lord's Supper is an act reaffirming the Christian's eschatolo-

---

[15]*The Life and Faith of the Baptists* (London: The Carey Kingsgate Press, 1946), pp. 77 f.

[16]*The Theology of the Sacraments: and Other Papers* (New York: Charles Scribner's Sons, 1957), p. 83.

[17]See Karl Barth, *The Teaching of the Church Regarding Baptism* (London: SCM Press, Ltd., 1950); Emil Brunner, *The Divine-Human Encounter* (Philadelphia: The Westminster Press, 1944), p. 132.

[18]Several Baptist theologians have given particular attention to the theology of baptism in the last decade. See *Christian Baptism*, ed. A. Gilmore (Philadelphia: The Judson Press, 1959); Neville Clark, *op. cit.*; Payne, *op. cit.*; Beasley-Murray, *op. cit.*; Estep, *The Anabaptist Story*, chap. 9; E. Luther Copeland, "Baptism and the Lord's Supper: A Positive Interpretation," *Review and Expositor*, XLVII (July, 1950), 324-32; McClendon, *op. cit.*

What about Baptism being the door of the Church?

gical hope. It revives his hope each time he participates in it. At the Last Supper Jesus referred to "that day when I drink it new with you in my Father's kingdom" (Matt. 26:29). Paul reminded his fellow Christians that as often as they observed the Lord's Supper they proclaimed the Lord's death (the atoning gospel) "until he comes" (1 Cor. 11:26).

The Lord's Supper has meaning only as it refers to the relationship between Jesus and his followers. Participation in the bread and the wine implies participation in the dying of Jesus. Paul sees a threefold significance in the celebration of the Supper: remembrance of the Christ-event until he comes (vv. 24-26), the presence of Christ in the act of worship, and the eschatological hope of Christ's return. To Paul the Supper was an act of worship, not a mystical act bringing about a union with Christ by compulsive magic.

The Supper represents the continuing presence of the crucified, risen Christ to remind his people of what he promised. When he said, "This is my body and my blood," he implied that the observance with bread and wine would always be a reminder that he is present with his people at worship. The Supper is the Lord's "appointed tryst" with his people.[19] Those who keep this tryst with him can confidently expect that he will assuredly come to meet them. This confidence produces joy and thanksgiving in this act of worship.

Some Practical Considerations

Since baptism and the Lord's Supper are acts of worship, there are several practical matters which deserve serious attention. They ought never to be performed in a perfunctory manner but should be administered in all seriousness so as to aid in worship.

Concerning Baptism

1. The act of baptism should be made a part of a regular worship service and not a mere perfunctory observance. Whether it comes at the beginning or the close of the service, it should be performed in a spirit of reverence.

2. A church is responsible for the administration of baptism. It

---

[19]See Alan Richardson (ed.), *A Theological Wordbook of the Bible* (New York: The Macmillan Co., 1955), p. 257.

What of others other than the Pastor Baptizing?

is commonly held that Jesus gave his commission to his church, a body of baptized believers. The local church is representative of the universal body of Christ and is responsible for the fulfilment of its mission in a particular place.

3. The person to be baptized should be thoroughly instructed as to the meaning of the ordinance and the manner in which it is to be performed. The believer should approach his own baptism in a spirit of commitment and reverence.

4. The equipment for the administration of baptism should be properly prepared. The baptistry should be filled to a depth of approximately forty-two inches and the water warmed to body temperature. Appropriate apparel should be provided for the minister and the candidates. Usually a committee of deacons and their wives will be appointed to take care of this.

5. The minister should perform the ordinance with reverence and dignity. Taking his place in the baptistry, he may read (or have someone else read) an appropriate passage of Scripture pertaining to Christian commitment and then indicate when the candidate should enter the water. He will instruct the candidate to fold his hands on his chest; then, holding firmly the candidate's hands with one of his, he will place the other hand at the base of the candidate's neck. He will then repeat the formula with the following or similar phraseology. He will call the candidate by name and then say, "Upon confession of your faith in Jesus Christ as Saviour and Lord, and in obedience to his command, I baptize you in the name of the Father, and of the Son, and of the Holy Spirit. Amen." He will then lower the candidate slowly into the water until the face is barely covered and then slowly lift the candidate from the water to an upright position. The more slowly and smoothly this is performed, the more it will aid in a spirit of worship.

Concerning the Lord's Supper

If the Lord's Supper is to be observed as an act of worship, it is highly significant that it be observed in the proper manner. Its manner of observance varies according to the customs and traditions of various congregations. In some churches it is observed more frequently than in others. It is observed weekly, monthly, quarterly, and in some instances annually or semiannually. Most of the Free Churches observe it either monthly or quarterly. It should not be observed so often as to make it a perfunctory rite, nor so infrequently as to cause a spirit of neglect.

1. The Lord's Supper, like baptism, should always be observed as a central part of a worship service and not made merely an addendum. In too many instances it has been customary to have a full-length service and then add the Lord's Supper at the end as a sort of afterthought. Such a careless observance is not worthy of this act of worship.

2. The entire order of worship should be so planned as to emphasize the significance of the Lord's Supper. It is appropriate to have it in a regular worship service where the hymns range from adoration and praise to devotion and commitment. Perhaps a full-length sermon is not necessary when the Lord's Supper is observed. A brief meditation in keeping with the spirit of the service is better. In this case the service is kept within the regular time limit. The Scriptures and the sermon theme need not be limited to the biblical passages which are specifically related to the Lord's Supper. Any of the great themes of redemption and the Christian life are appropriate.

3. The administration of the Supper will vary as to procedures in different churches. Many churches proceed about as follows in the observance of the ordinance. (1) In a regular worship service, at the appropriate time, usually following a brief meditation, the minister will take his place behind the Lord's Supper table. (2) Those who assist him, usually the deacons or ushers, will take their places on the front pews if they are not already seated there. The chairman and vice-chairman will take their places at each end of the Lord's Supper table. (3) The minister may read an appropriate Scripture, or make an appropriate remark pertaining to the Lord's Supper.

(4) The minister may or may not break a portion of the bread. He will then have a prayer of thanksgiving and dedication asking God's blessings upon the people as they partake of the bread. (5) The bread trays are then passed to the deacons by the chairman and vice-chairman. The deacons will in turn go to their stations, which

have been previously designated, and proceed to distribute the bread among the congregation. When they have finished, at a given signal they will return to their places at the front of the sanctuary and pass their plates back. The deacons will then be served by the chairman and vice-chairman after which they will be seated on the front pews. The minister may then quote an appropriate Scripture verse such as Romans 12:1: "I appeal to you, therefore, brethren, by the mercies of God, that you present your bodies as a living sacrifice, holy and acceptable to God, which is your spiritual worship," after which he and all the congregation will partake of the bread.

(6) The minister will then quote an appropriate Scripture passage or make an appropriate remark pertaining to the cup as representative of the blood of Christ; then follows a prayer of thanksgiving and dedication, asking God's blessings upon the church as they partake of the cup. Distribution of the cups will then proceed in the manner of the distribution of the bread. When all have been served, the minister will quote an appropriate Scripture verse and then partake of the cup as a signal for the congregation to join him. (7) It is the tradition in most churches to sing a hymn following the observance of the Lord's Supper. A benediction may then be pronounced, and the congregation will retire in a spirit of worship and devotion.

4. George Buttrick makes a practical observation that church members ought to prepare before participating in the Lord's Supper. When we receive the bread and the wine, what should occupy our thoughts and our prayers? The answer depends upon the individual need, but there are some thoughts and prayers in which all members of the church are one:

(1) Our Lord Jesus Christ—God's gift of love and power through him to all mankind.

2) The church—its steady witness in Christ's spirit and our witness through the church by prayer, gift, and service.

(3) Our failures—low aim, ignoble deed, and wasted opportunities; our forgetting that all people belong to God's family; and our share in social wrongs such as race intolerance, economic strife, and war.

(4) Our comrades—those we have hurt and those who have hurt us; our families, friends, employers, servants; the sad and suffering, known and unknown; missionaries, ministers, peacemakers, and a host of those by whom our days are guided.

(5) Our need of strength and joy for daily living in Christ's name. If such thoughts and prayers be ours as we partake of the Lord's Supper, then by faith we shall receive also the power of Christ and the calmness of the dedicated life.[20]

Some Problems in Administration

The ordinances are related particularly to the doctrine of the church. In other words, they were given as commands of Jesus to his church to be perpetuated by his people. The ordinances were given in the context of the body of believers and not primarily to individuals. However, the individual's participation in these acts of worship is first in relation to God and second, to the church.

The functional or practical approach to the administration of the ordinances comes to focus in the local church. It is not limited to a local church, but each church is autonomous and is responsible for the administration of the ordinances according to its understanding of the biblical teachings. Each local church is responsible only to Christ as its head. However, in a secondary sense, each local church is related to all other churches of God's people. The local church is representative of the entire body of Christ and the kingdom of God. Whatever its practice, it must come under the judgment of the Scriptures.

The details of procedure with reference to the ordinances in a local church are not spelled out in the New Testament. The spirit of the observance is clear. There must be loyalty to Jesus Christ and unity in the body of his people. The ordinances must always be interpreted in relation to the person of Christ. The believer is baptized in the name of Jesus Christ, which implies that he is committed to Christ and will be loyal and obedient to him. The observance of the Supper implies that those who partake are related to him and to one another in vital union.

---

[20]*Prayer*, p. 290.

In the New Testament the primary emphasis is given to the experience and relationship of the believer to his Lord and not to the administrator nor to the method of the administration of the ordinances. The administration of the ordinances has been a problem historically, creating divisions among the people of Christ. Methods of administration have varied even within certain denominations. For example, although Baptists have generally agreed on the basic meaning of the two ordinances—immersion of believers, and the Lord's Supper for believers only—they have not always agreed on the authority and methods of the administrator, the church, and on the relationship of the individual to the church. For four hundred years Baptists have varied in their interpretation of church membership as related to baptism and the Lord's Supper. Some have favored a closed or restricted membership, others an open or unrestricted membership. In the sixteenth and seventeenth centuries Baptists in England were divided on these issues. It was not always the Particular versus the General Baptists as regarded the administration of the ordinances.

The report of the Baptist World Alliance meeting in Atlanta, Georgia, 1939, indicates that Baptists still acknowledge these variations: (1) Open membership and open communion after the John Bunyan pattern. (2) Those who would keep both membership and the table for only baptized believers. This was William Kiffin's position. (3) Those who feel the table should be open and that membership should be closed. This was Robert Hall's position in early Baptist life.[21] Payne observed that in the New Testament the case for believer's baptism is clear. The exact relationship of the right to the membership of the church is not always clear.

While Baptists have generally agreed on the immersion of believers only, they have not always agreed on what constitutes valid or proper immersion. Generally speaking, there are three viewpoints concerning the validity of immersion. (1) Some churches accept into their membership without rebaptism persons who have been immersed on profession of their faith into the membership of non-Baptist Churches, provided that at the time of his baptism the

---

[21]See Payne, *op. cit.*, pp. 88-89.

individual held the same doctrinal concept of baptism in relation to salvation that Baptists generally hold. (2) Some churches receive into their membership without rebaptism persons who have been baptized into the fellowship of a church of another Baptist general body. (3) Other churches require rebaptism of persons who come from any church outside their own denominational affiliation. They hold that the administrator is "alien" theologically and is not authorized by the proper authority. Thus they call this "alien immersion." W. W. Barnes observed that those who reject alien immersion have never come to agreement among themselves as to "how alien must an alien immersion be in order to be alien."[22]

The majority of Baptists are in accord with other Christians on the basic doctrines governing the observance of the Lord's Supper. Most denominations agree that the Supper should be restricted to those who have made a Christian profession and have been properly baptized into the fellowship of God's people. Because Baptists have had a strict doctrine concerning baptism, some of them have been very restrictive in the observance of the Lord's Supper. There have generally been three points of view relative to the Lord's Supper, sometimes referred to as open communion, closed innercommunion, and closed intracommunion.[23] Some Baptist churches practice open communion, inviting all individual Christians who feel themselves to be qualified to participate at the Lord's table. Other Baptist churches practice closed innercommunion, inviting only those who hold membership in other Baptist churches to participate with them. Still other churches practice closed intracommunion, holding that only persons who are members of a particular local church may participate in the Lord's Supper when it is administered by that church.

Robert A. Baker observes that it is impossible to estimate what proportion of Southern Baptists hold to these views or to some similar position. It is the practice of many of the churches to make no statement as to the qualifications of individuals for participation when the Lord's Supper is observed. When the elements are passed to all who are present, each person must decide for himself.

---

[22]"Alien Immersion," *Encyclopedia of Southern Baptists*, I, 32.
[23]Baker, "Requisites to the Lord's Supper," *Encyclopedia of Southern Baptists*, II, 794-95.

Throughout the nineteenth century it was customary for Baptist general bodies to observe the Lord's Supper when they came together. Certain state conventions and associations in annual meeting regularly observed the Lord's Supper. Although certain associations and state conventions have made "alien immersion" and "closed communion" a test of fellowship among the churches, the Southern Baptist Convention has never done so. As late as the 1966 session of the Convention the president so ruled openly.

The most extreme views on alien immersion and closed communion are a modern innovation in Baptist history. They arose in what is known as the movement of Landmarkism dating from about 1850 under the leadership of J. R. Graves.[24] These views do not represent the historic Baptist position concerning baptism and the Lord's Supper. Every church is autonomous and independent and must be accorded the right to determine its own doctrines and practices. L. L. Gwaltney states, "Whatever the churches do about such doctrines should by no means enter into the fellowship of the Baptists. Such doctrines should no more affect the fellowship of the Baptists than differences of opinion on the millennium question."[25] He reminds Baptists that one of their cardinal doctrines is the right of private interpretation of the Scriptures and that God's kingdom is not circumscribed by the members of any one church nor by all of the churches combined.

In perpetuating baptism and the Lord's Supper, worship is primary; procedures are secondary. Worship is the *esse* of the church; ordinances and ceremonies are the *bene esse* of the church. Therefore, problems in administering the ordinances should not be allowed to hinder the spirit of worship. The local church as a responsible institution is autonomous, but it does not exist in isolation from other Christian bodies. To place the institution above the living fellowship is idolatry. The local church is representative of the larger body of Christ. There is a place for the denomination, but to place any given denom-

---

[24]See W. Morgan Patterson, "Landmarkism," *Encyclopedia of Southern Baptists*, II, 757. See also Barnes, *History of the Southern Baptist Convention* (Nashville: Broadman Press, 1954), p. 100.

[25]*The World's Greatest Decade: The Times and the Baptists* (Birmingham, Ala.: Birmingham Printing Co., 1947), p. 128.

ination above the body of all believers is presumption and idolatry.

Those who ignore the basic doctrines of the New Testament in relation to the administration of baptism and the Lord's Supper are guilty of disrupting the unity of Christ's people; and those who ignore the spirit of faith and worship by giving priority to detailed methods and procedures in perpetuating the ordinances are also guilty of disrupting the fellowship of Christ's body. Let each church be firm where the New Testament is clear and specific, and let all be charitable and flexible where the New Testament is not clear. Jesus prayed that

They may all be one; even as thou, Father, art in me, and I in thee, that they also may be in us, so that the world may believe that thou hast sent me. The glory which thou hast given me I have given to them, that they may be one even as we are one, I in them and thou in me, that they may become perfectly one, so that the world may know that thou hast sent me and hast loved them even as thou hast loved me (John 17:21-23).

10

Other Acts of Worship

The Lord is in his holy temple;
Let all the earth keep silence before him.
Habakkuk 2:20

Great is the Lord, and greatly to be praised;
he is to be feared above all gods.
Honor and majesty are before him;
strength and beauty are in his sanctuary.
Psalm 96:4,6

This chapter will discuss several elements of worship that do not require individual chapter treatments.

The Call to Worship

The call to worship is an appropriate way to begin a worship service. It calls a congregation to give attention to the primary objective for which the church is assembled, to "stand at attention" before God. The first words and movements of the leader will often determine the spirit of the entire worship service.

Purpose.—The purpose of the call to worship is (1) to direct the minds of the congregation toward God, (2) to remove distractions from the attention of the congregation, (3) to call for participation of the congregation in all that transpires, (4) to call for a unity of all the people assembled, (5) and to create the proper attitude or atmosphere for worship. It may be compared with the call of an army officer, "Attention!"

Nature.—The call to worship may be (1) a passage of Scripture, such as Psalm 100:2,4-5 (KJV): "Serve the Lord with gladness: come before his presence with singing. . . . Enter into his gates with thanksgiving, and into his courts with praise: be thankful unto him, and bless his name. For the Lord is good; his mercy is everlasting; and his truth endureth to all generations." (2) It may be a stanza of a hymn or some appropriate poem.

(3) The minister may prepare an appropriately worded invitation for the people to unite in worship. In this case the leader should give careful attention to the composition of the call to worship.

Presentation.—The call to worship may be presented in various ways. (1) The minister may step forth to proclaim it alone. (2) The minister and congregation may give it jointly:

Minister: I will bless the Lord at all times;
Congregation: His praise shall continually be in my mouth.
Minister: O magnify the Lord with me,
Congregation: And let us exalt his name together (Psalm 34:1,3).

(3) The minister and choir may give it jointly, the minister speaking a line and the choir singing a line alternately. (4) The choir may sing the entire call to worship, such as "O Worship the Lord" by Robert C. McCutchan. The call to worship should be presented in a reverent spirit, whatever the nature of the selection and whatever the manner of presenting it.[1]

The Offering of Gifts

The offering of gifts has been a universal practice in the long history of man's worship. In many instances the motivation was prompted by superstitious fear, and offerings were made to placate angry gods. In Christian worship the offering of gifts is an expression of gratitude and appreciation to God. This concept of worship is found both in the Old and New Testaments. The psalmist sang, "Bring an offering and come into his courts!" (96:8); the writer of Hebrews exhorted his fellow Christians, "Through him let us continually offer up a sacrifice of praise to God. . . . Do not neglect to do good and to share what you have, for such sacrifices are pleasing to God" (13:15-16).

Protestant worship has often neglected the act of giving. An outsider observing Protestant worship might report, "At a certain point in the service, money was collected." The church certainly needs money but the raising of money to support the church should not dominate the motivation in giving. Some churches make a practice

---

[1]For other suggestions for use of the call to worship, see Noyes, *op. cit.*

of collecting their gifts for the budget through the Sunday School classes. This tends to detach the act of giving from the main worship service of the church. It is entirely possible that by this method churches may have raised more money and made bookkeeping simpler, but it may have taken away the seriousness of making an offering as an act of worship.

Since worship is dialogue, with upward movement, as well as downward movement, the offering of gifts should be considered seriously. Winward reminds us that Christianity is a " worldly religion, not a dualistic philosophy. We are not Gnostics, Manichaeans, or Christian Scientists.[2] The offering of gifts is a symbol of sacrifice. It is a positive act which symbolizes as inner attitude of homage. In an hour of physical need King David asked for a drink from the well at Bethlehem. Men risked their lives to bring him a drink. But he would not drink it; it was too precious, and "He poured it out to the Lord" (2 Sam. 23:16). Worship needs the spirit of sacrifice, and yet "the spiritual sacrifice without concrete embodiment lacks at least one element of costliness, and is out of touch with the here and now realities of human life.[3] The offering of money in the offering plate is no less an act of worship than are the offerings of hymns and prayers.

A theology of giving.—There is a sound theological basis for offering gifts as an act of worship to God. In the Old Testament, sacrifice was the essential act of external worship. In the very act of sacrifice a personal union with God was achieved, for God accepted the offering and also the worshiper who made the sacrifice. Paul refers to this act of sacrifice: "Are not those who eat the sacrifices partners in the altar?" (1 Cor. 10:18).

Proper motivations grow out of a Christian theology of giving as an act of worship. Christian giving is prompted by a grace relationship, not by a legalistic fear. Grace is above law as Calvary is higher than Sinai.

The following theological principles are basic to giving as an act of worship. (1) In Christian worship, making an offering is a symbolic act representing the giving of the self. Paul commended the Christians in the churches of Macedonia for their generosity. The real value

---

[2] *Op. cit.,* p. 27.
[3] *Underhill, op. cit.,* p. 48.

of their giving is attested by the fact that "first they gave themselves to the Lord," and their sacrificial giving attested their sincerity (2 Cor. 8:5).

(2) Unselfish sharing is proof of our love for our fellowman. All true benevolent giving is based upon love. John challenged his fellow Christians to share this world's goods with the brother in need: "Little children, let us not love in word or speech but in deed and in truth" (1 John 3:18).

(3) Generous giving expresses our missionary zeal. All world missionary enterprises are dependent upon the gifts of God's people. Indeed, "How are they to hear without a preacher? And how can men preach unless they are sent?" (Rom. 10:14-15).

(4) Worshipful giving is proof of our gratitude to God for his gifts, especially the gift of grace in Christ. The motivation for Christian giving is based primarily upon gratitude rather than upon law. Paul's appeal to the Corinthian Christians to share their material goods with the needy people of Macedonia concludes with a paean of praise, "Thanks be to God for his inexpressible gift!" (2 Cor. 9:15).

(5) Worshipful giving is a quality of life. Paul speaks of it as a grace, listing it alongside faith, utterance, knowledge, earnestness, and love. He exhorted, "See that you excel in this gracious work also" (2 Cor. 8:7).

Procedure in giving.—Since giving is an act of worship, the manner of presenting gifts in worship is significant. A disciplined approach toward the presentation of gifts will prevent an attitude of carelessness and indifference.

(1) A proper motivation for giving may be inspired by the use of an offertory sentence preceding the presentation of gifts. A brief statement or a Scripture verse concerning the meaning of our giving may be used to prepare people's minds and hearts for presenting their gifts. Second Corinthians 8:9 is a good example: "You know the grace of our Lord Jesus Christ, that though he was rich, yet for your sake he became poor, so that by his poverty you might become rich." (2) All members of the congregation should be encouraged to participate in the act of making an offering. Every member of the family should have the privilege of placing his own gifts in the offering plates. Proper motivation for giving may be thus enforced in

developing the character of children particularly. (3) Appropriate offertory music, either instrumental or vocal, may aid in this act of worship.

(4) The offerings of the people should be gathered in an orderly and dignified manner by the ushers. A spirit of seriousness and reverence on their part will aid people in their worship. (5) The presentations of the offerings at the altar is the climax of this act of worship. A well-worded prayer dedicating the gifts may imply God's acceptance and serve as a symbol of communion between him and the worshipers. A hymn response or a congregational "Amen" may be used, if desired, at the conclusion of the prayer of dedication.

The Affirmation of Faith

An affirmation or confession of faith may be used effectively in public worship. The Apostles' Creed has been used traditionally in many Protestant churches. Many of the Free Churches reject the use of a fixed creed. In many instances, however, they have made effective use of their own brief confessions or affirmations of faith in the planned order of worship.

The affirmation of faith is a confessional statement in which the congregation participates. A brief contemporary affirmation may be more meaningful than the Apostles' Creed. The affirmation should be read by the congregation standing at attention before the God of truth. Such an affirmation of faith may help to keep worship alive in dialogue with the living God.

To be sure, men do not find their inspiration primarily in statements of faith. Their highest inspiration comes as a result of revelation, not of theology. Religions commit suicide when they find their inspiration in their dogmas. The value of confessions of faith is that they tend to elicit the experience which the dogma seeks to formulate. The revelation offered to us in worship is not mere information but Christ himself. The affirmation of faith calls forth our personal devotion to Christ. "Let the redeemed of the Lord say so" (Psalm 107:2).

An affirmation of faith may sometimes be presented in the form of a litany, a statement to be read responsively. At other times it may be read in unison. The following litany is an example.

Reaffirming Our Common Faith

Leader: In the living God our Father, maker and sustainer of the universe, who in Jesus Christ has perfectly revealed himself and his redeeming love to men,

Response: We reaffirm our faith.

Leader: In Jesus Christ our Lord, God's only Son, who for our salvation came to earth in human flesh, lived a sinless life, died for our sins, and rose again in accordance with the Scriptures,

Response: We reaffirm our faith.

Leader: In the blessed Holy Spirit, revealer of truth, convicter of sinners, and ever-present helper of all who believe,

Response: We reaffirm our faith.

Leader: In God's eternal purpose of grace, whereby, through the gospel of Jesus Christ, redemption, forgiveness, reconciliation, and the gift of eternal life are accomplished in the experience of every believer,

Response: We reaffirm our faith.

Leader: In the power and authority of the Scriptures as God-breathed writings which are able to make men wise unto salvation and equip God's servants for every good work,

Response: We reaffirm our faith.

Leader: In the church, the body of Christ, fellowship of the redeemed, set apart for worship and witness, teaching and ministry, in the midst of an unbelieving, lost, and suffering world,

Response: We reaffirm our faith.

Leader: In the surpassing worth, immediate urgency, and certain victory of the kingdom of God,

Response: We reaffirm our faith.[4]

It is appropriate for present day churches to write their own affirmations of faith in the forms of contemporary language, as is done here.[5]

---

[4]This litany was used May 30, 1966, in a brief chapel service during a conference of seminary and Baptist Sunday School Board personnel. For particular service in the local church, perhaps a briefer affirmation concentrating on a certain theme would be preferred.

[5]For a detailed study of the Apostles' Creed see George Hedley, *The Symbol of the Faith* (New York: The Macmillan Co., 1948). Also see William L. Lumpkin, *Baptist Confessions of Faith. The Inter-Church Hymnal,* edited by A. W. Palmer of the Congregationalist tradition, includes twenty-five "Confessions of Faith," ancient and modern, in the section on "Aids to Worship."

Most of the Free Churches provide opportunity for the individual to make a public commitment of himself when he desires to do so. In response to the acts of worship, particularly to preaching, an invitation is extended to persons who wish to commit themselves publicly. While a hymn of dedication or invitation is sung, they present themselves to God in the presence of the congregation. The invitation is extended to nonmembers who desire to confess their faith in Jesus Christ in response to a conversion experience, or to persons coming from another church by transfer of membership. Other motives for public commitment include response to the call of God to a life vocation, and a rededication of life asking the church's forgiveness and prayers for past errors.

The Reception of New Members

The presentation of the individual for membership in a church deserves to be taken seriously. He is enlisting in the service of Christ, and his initiation should be worthy of both the lordship of Christ and the sincere commitment of the individual. This ought to be a memorable occasion in the experience of each individual.

Churches vary in their methods of receiving new members. Some of them invite individuals to present themselves following the sermon as the hymn of dedication or invitation is sung. Upon the individual's request he is received by letter from another church, upon confession of faith as a candidate for baptism, or upon a statement that he has been a member of a church of "like faith and order" but for some acceptable reason is now unable to receive a letter of recommendation from a former church.

Many churches immediately receive new members by a vote of the congregation. Some churches request them to meet with a membership committee who will hear their personal witness and later recommend them for membership. Other churches have a "waiting period" during which the candidates attend a class of instruction.

Whatever the time of their reception, the ceremony should be performed in seriousness and with dignity. The pastor may ask the candidates to stand facing the congregation, then read their names, giving the essential facts about them. Then they may be asked to confess their faith in Christ and their allegiance to his church. This may be done in the form of questions asked by the minister or by the reading of an affirmation prepared by the church. The congregation may then stand with the candidates and sing a hymn of commitment such as "Jesus, I My Cross Have Taken." The pastor may follow this with a prayer of dedication and the benediction, after which members of the congregation may file by and welcome the new members with a hand of fellowship. Let this brief ceremony be characterized by reverence, discipline, creativity, and a spirit of joy. It should be neither dull nor overdramatic, but rather dignified and worshipful.

The Congregational "Amen"

It might be good to restore the use of the congregational "Amen" to public worship. It was evidently used in Old Testament worship. Moses' directions for worship included, "And all the people shall say 'Amen' " (Deut. 27:14-26; see also 1 Chron. 16:36 and Psalm 106:48).

The Hebrew "Amen" has the force of strong affirmation or assent, usually to something spoken by another. The early Christians used it in their worship as an expression of the entire congregation in assent to praise. Paul refers to the people's "Amen" of thanksgiving (1 Cor. 14:16). It is also used in an exalted passage of worship in the book of Revelation (5:6-14). In the second century Justin Martyr wrote: "Then we all rise together and pray, and . . . bread and wine are brought, and the president in like manner offers prayer and thanksgiving, according to his ability, and the people assent, saying, 'Amen.' " The term was used later in the liturgy by the priest or the choir alone. During the Reformation Luther interpreted the "Amen" as an expression of "firm and hearty belief, and its use was restored to the congregation in a number of cases."[6]

The "Amen" may be expressed by the congregation or sung by the choir at the end of a prayer, or following the reading of a Scripture passage, or at the end of a hymn, even if it is not encouraged as an emphasis in response to some part of the sermon. The punctuation of the worship service by frequent "Amens" by certain enthusiastic

---

[6]*The New Schaff-Herzog Encyclopedia of Religious Knowledge,* I, 501.

individuals should be discouraged. It is unbecoming for the individual to call attention to himself by frequent use of the term.

The Miscellaneous Period

Must there be a period for announcements or informal comments during a worship service? If so, where is the best place in the order of service for it? How shall such necessary informalities be handled? Leaders in worship are not unanimous in their answers to these questions. Perhaps all agree that this can be a distracting part of a worship service. On the back cover of one printed order of worship these three columns were listed: "Brotherhood Bylines," "Sisterhood Sidelines," "Temple Teen Talk." Most routine announcements should be presented on the back of the bulletin rather than as a part of the order of worship. Oral reports on attendance should be omitted.

It seems necessary to have some kind of informal period during the order of worship. It may be designated "The Minister's Greeting," "Recognitions," "Welcome to Guests," "Informal Period," or some such term. A cordial welcome to guests on behalf of the congregation is in order. They should not be singled out as individuals nor their names called publicly before the congregation. Their attention may be called to visitor's cards in the pew racks which they may fill in.

Only major items in the church's program should be mentioned in the service of worship, and they should be presented in such manner as not to distract from the spirit of worship. There may be no *best* time to take care of this miscellaneous period. It is not good to begin a service of worship with it, nor is it good at the conclusion of the service which should be the spiritual climax in worship. Perhaps a good time is rather early in the service following the call to worship, an invocation, a hymn, the Scripture reading, and the morning prayer. This seems to be the time for a natural break when people have had an opportunity to enter well into the experience of worship. The pastor should give much attention in the preparation of the brief remarks which he will present. Dull phrases repeated each Lord's Day are not appropriate. He should seek fresh and creative ways of making this period seem natural in the order of worship.

11

The Use of Symbols

As the hart panteth after the water brooks,
So panteth my soul after thee, O God. . . .
Deep calleth unto deep at the noise of thy waterfalls:
All thy waves and thy billows are gone over me.

Psalm 42:1,7, ASV

The poet Tennyson in "The Higher Pantheism" expressed what every sincere worshiper has discovered, namely, that man can experience direct communion with God:

> Speak to him, Thou, for he hears,
> And spirit with Spirit can meet—
> Closer is he than breathing,
> And nearer than hands and feet.

And yet it is obvious that man's knowledge is first mediated to him through certain tangible media. Man is not pure spirit; he is embodied spirit. The *total* man is involved in his relationships to God and the universe. That is why we may speak of embodied worship. All of history is a story of the relation between the outward and the inward. The eternal God reveals himself to us through outward forms. Even his highest revelation through Jesus Christ comes in the incarnation, a person embodied in the physical. Inner devotion requires outward expression in words and deeds, in personal and social activity. In the body, then, our communion with God and with other persons takes place by some bodily means of communication. Material symbols represent "an invisible transaction between God and man, a shared communion of worship."[1]

The word "symbol" is derived from the Greek verb *symballo,* to compare, hence to conjecture or infer. The noun *symbalon* takes its

---

[1] L. Harold deWolf, *A Theology of the Living Church* (New York: Harper & Row, 1960), p. 340.

meaning as a sign by which one knows or infers something. Edwyn Bevan in *Symbolism and Belief* has defined a symbol as "something presented to the senses which stands for something else." Symbolism in worship is that use of outward objects and actions which stand for some inner religious meaning.

Beauty is not its own excuse for being. Rather, beauty in nature points to the good and the true in the nature of God. Back of the particular expression of beauty in the physical universe is a general reality of beauty, or the ideal which the object suggests.[2] A sense of feeling for the beautiful, the good, the true, is a part of man's natural experience.

Evelyn Underhill says that a symbol is a significant image which helps the worshiping soul to apprehend spiritual reality. Generally speaking, "Symbols represent and suggest, while 'sacraments' work."[3] Obviously, many will disagree with her definition of sacrament. Nothing is in and of itself a sacrament in the usual sense of the term.

Von Ogden Vogt observes that symbols bridge the gap between the sensory and the spiritual. Symbols are aids to attention, and attention is primary to worship. A symbol is only something that helps man to keep his attention upon God. Objects are symbols, useful in worship because they represent certain facts, ideas, or feelings.

The Old Testament recognizes beauty and order in the universe and attributes these qualities to God who created them. God created the earth and the forms within it and saw that "it was very good" (Gen. 1:31). The expression "good" conveys the idea of excellence, that which is pleasing, or that which is fitting. Man's sense of the aesthetic is a part of the "image of God" in which he was made. God ordered that the design and appointments of the tabernacle and the Temple be beautiful, for they were "holy places" where God promised to meet his people. The "holy garments" prescribed for Aaron, the first high priest of Israel, were "for glory and for beauty" (Ex. 28:2).

The early Christians recognized the value of symbolism, using it freely in the catacombs. For example, the symbol of a fish was a

---

[2]For a full treatment of aesthetics see Benedetto Croce, *Aesthetic: A Science of Expression and General Linguistic,* trans. Douglas Aimslie (New York: The Noonday Press, 1962).

[3]*Op. cit.,* pp. 42-43.

password among the faithful. The five letters in the Greek word for fish are the initials for "Jesus Christ, God's Son, Saviour." Although the use of symbolism was carried to an extreme and was abused in the Middle Ages, symbols properly used are acknowledged to have value in worship. Paul Tillich in modern day, however, questions the use of symbols which have to be interpreted. To use them as mere decoration without functional necessity would be dishonest and repellent.[4] Symbols grow out of the life and thought of human culture and must be related to the particular period in which they are used.

F. W. Dillistone insists that man's supreme need at this time is to become related to powerful and meaningful symbols. They are essential for proper communication between man and man. Most of the great realities are not accessible to us without symbols. Symbolism is the very texture of human life.

God and the world are beyond our sensible experience and cannot be conceived except by means of symbols. The eternal Word of God is expressed in the written words of the Bible which are symbols. J. Allen Kay says, "We are not pure spirit, but are embodied in flesh and blood, and our life is inseparably connected with matter, time, and place. This means that we can only express the spiritual reality of our thought and feeling by material things and by actions in space and time.[5]

The Value of Symbolism in Worship

Symbols are concrete methods for calling man away from himself to God. Man acknowledges the presence of God by using symbols. In worship symbols have a twofold direction, an ascending and a descending action. They are agents for God to show himself to us, and they are agents by which we express ourselves to God.

Man must always remember that Christian symbols do not compel God's presence. He remains free, for he is God. They can be used, however, to acknowledge that God has acted in history and that he is continuously present in history. Symbols point beyond themselves

---

[4] See Albert Christ-Janer and Mary Mix Foley (eds.), *Modern Church Architecture* (New York: McGraw-Hill Book Co., 1957), p. 125.

[5] *The Nature of Christian Worship* (London: The Upworth Press, 1953), p. 66.

to a greater reality. Tillich says, "They point to the ultimate reality inplied in the religious act, to what concerns us ultimately."[6]

Symbols are valuable for the purpose of communication. They may be used to re-create the thought or feeling which originally gave them birth. They often describe more accurately than words such concepts as God, Christ, salvation, atonement, eternity, and so on. Symbols begin with man where he is and take him to the great mysteries of God, even to that which "it is not lawful for man to utter." For example, the descriptions of heaven as presented in John's book of Revelation point to something greater than the object pictures presented.

For the kindling of the senses man usually requires something tangible, touchable, visible. To reject symbolism in religion leads to a false dualism of life, a separation of the "spiritual" from the "material" or "physical." In the biblical context the spiritual life as a whole is discovered through the physical life; it rises from the "fires of sensibility."[7] Spirituality is the desired end, and the physical symbol is the necessary means.

Paul Elmen believes that symbolism expressed in the arts can aid the church in maintaining a "newness within oldness," the retention of its ancient truths by means of contemporary expression. He feels that even the "absurdity" of man's existence expressed by the modern artist may point man to his only hope—God who creates *ex nihil* and communicates himself to man in the form of revelation. He cites Albert Camus' observation: "The absurd is sin without God."

Some Dangers of Symbolism in Worship

The tendency in the Free Churches to play down the value and use of symbolism stems mainly from the dangers and abuses of symbolism observed in the history of the church. When the Reformers broke with Rome, they smashed the sculpture on the churches, destroyed the stained glass, and dethroned the "Virgin." In their repudiation of all these sensuous manifestations of the old faith, they found them-

---

[6]Quoted in *Symbolism in Religion and Literature,* ed. Rollo May (New York: George Braziller, Inc., 1960), p. 77.

[7]Vogt, *Art and Religion* (Boston: Beacon Press, 1960), p. 52.

selves at last worshiping "in a meeting house as prosaic as a drygoods box."[8]

Today, many evangelical churches, including the Baptists, are introducing symbolism back into their worship. The proper and limited use of symbolism will aid in worship, but there are some grave dangers involved which ought to be noted.

(1) Symbols are always in danger of being taken for the thing symbolized. Instead of being aids to worship, they become objects of worship. (2) Once symbols lose their meaning, they tend to become mere superstitions. To use them as mere decoration is unworthy of the Christian faith. (3) Symbols may convey no ethical suggestions. They may simply become a fascinating study. (4) Symbols may be entirely detached from personal fellowship with God. One may become absorbed in symbolic meanings without having an experience of personal relation to God. (5) In the final analysis, the real value of symbols depends on the contents in mind. The mind of the worshipers must be filled with the right Christian content in order to make the proper use of symbols in Christian worship. There is the constant danger that false concepts may creep into the mind of the worshiper.

Although symbols are powerful, they are also inadequate in themselves. They cannot take the place of reality nor express truth fully. A symbol should never be treated as if it contained God, for then it becomes an idol. For example, when the "sign of the cross" is thought to contain power and protection against evil, it becomes an idol and a hindrance to the worship of the crucified, risen Lord.

Even though the use of symbols in worship is dangerous, man's hunger for beauty is a God-given desire. Vogt suggests that when there is demand for stern measures, it may be denied or suppressed; when the desire for beauty tends to dominate or usurp experience, it is feared; in healthy, normal life it should be satisfied.[9] In religious symbolism, properly used and controlled, the sense of beauty rises to its highest level and is most fully satisfied.

---

[8]Albert Edward Bailey, *Art and Character* (New York: Abingdon Press, 1938), p. 32.
[9]*Art and Religion*, p. 135.

Symbols Suitable for Christian Worship

All Free Churches have made some use of symbolism in their worship. Today theologians, poets, novelists, dramatists, and a certain school of philosophy acknowledge the penetrating and illuminating power of symbols. The arts are being rediscovered as a means of inspiration and teaching. Music, art and color, drama, and poetry may all be used as a means of expressing worship and as aids in directing the mind in worship. Our worship is directed toward God, but it provides also for God's action toward men in this present age. We cannot say when this confrontation will take place; we can only set the stage.[10]

All the arts depend on what they suggest, as well as on what they represent. Claude Phillips says, "The sublime in art is the power to suggest, to evoke round the thing represented, luminous circles, that grow vaster and vaster still. . . to lay bare the canopy of heaven above the head of the gazer or the abysses of hell beneath his feet."[11]

Worshipers in Free Churches need to become aware of the meaning of the symbolism which they use. A more thorough understanding of its meaning can enrich the experience of worship and aid in that person-to-person experience which reaches beyond the objects used as symbols. The following are suggested as symbols that may be usefully employed as aids in Christian worship.

Language.—The most obvious symbol in Protestant worship is that of language. H. Wheeler Robinson reminds us that words in themselves mean nothing until they are referred to life. "Life is continually moving beyond vocabulary which was evolved to describe it, continually putting new wine into old wineskins."[12] Word signs are never capable of permanent definition. They have to be interpreted in the light of their historical setting. Our use of language in regard to the eternal realm appears to be symbolic in two ways: the word is a mere symbol of some experience; that experience is the symbol of something beyond itself. The symbols of time are taken up into

---

[10]Louise H. Curry and Chester M. Wetzel, *Worship Services Using the Arts* (Philadelphia: The Westminster Press, 1966), p. 13.

[11]Quoted in H. Wheeler Robinson, *Redemption and Revelation*, p. 46.

[12]*Ibid.*, p. 43.

the language of eternity, the language of divine activity—that language of God which is a revelation because it is first a redemption

In religion symbolic language is often used to express realities which otherwise cannot be expressed. Donald M. Baillie mentions many spatial metaphors which point to spiritual realities: "When we say: 'The Lord is in his holy temple,' or 'Lift up your hearts' . . . or 'Come down, O Love divine,' or 'Feed me with food divine,' we are using spatial and material metaphors, 'up' and 'down' and 'come' and 'feed.' "[13] The writers of Scripture used anthropomorphic terms to express divine, eternal realities. The Bible symbolizes truth beyond the words it contains. The written words are symbolical of the living Word.

Robinson suggests that of all the arts, poetry comes nearest, in combined effect, to the adequate expression of unseen spiritual reality. As compared with painting, architecture, and music, poetry makes much more primary demand on the reader or hearer, and the printed page is far more removed from life than the outline and color of the canvas, carved stone, and painted glass on the building, in directing the sensuous excitation of the sympathy. In spite of the limitations of language, the articulation of poetic language, the unlimited range of imaginative portrayal, and the greater scope of its descriptive power make poetry supreme in the representation of spiritual reality.[14]

Church architecture.—The church building itself symbolizes a congregation which assembles within its walls to worship. The building is not the church, but it does symbolize the church which makes use of it. As Stafford indicates, one can worship God in a barn or a hall or any other structure completely devoid of Christian symbolism or churchly character, but under such conditions there is great need for discipline of the spirit. Secular and paganizing influences must be overcome, and the symbolism of the building may point away from the distracting influences of the world to a life of personal communion with God who is higher than man.[15]

It is encouraging to note that the Free Churches in recent years

---

[13]*The Theology of the Sacraments: And Other Papers*, p. 51.

[14]*Redemption and Revelation*, p. 47.

[15]Thomas Albert Stafford, *Christian Symbolism in the Evangelical Churches* (New York: Abingdon-Cokesbury Press, 1952), p. 104.

have been erecting buildings designed to achieve a mood in which an individual may find it easier to have a worship experience rather than a setting where the activity of the church is predominant.[16] Free Churches are beginning to construct buildings compatible with their own theology of worship rather than simply following the extremely liturgical tradition which uses designs emphasizing a priestly and sacramental religion.

Contemporary designs should express the transcendence and immanence of God at the same time. Walter L. Nathan pleads for the use of contemporary materials and styles in church architecture. He insists on honesty and simplicity, for a "work of art must make demands upon the viewer" and must speak to the whole person.[17] Modern architecture presents the opportunity of showing the power of God through its symbolism. At the same time the sanctuary should be so constructed as to emphasize the fellowship of the congregation. The arrangement of space and pews should be such as to bring the congregation close together.

The cross.—The cross is probably the most universal symbol of Christianity. It is a reminder of the redemptive work of God through the offering of his Son, Jesus Christ. The corrupt use of this symbol becomes obvious in the crucifix where the body of our Lord is still on the cross. The empty cross is a reminder of an act which was completed and which is symbolized in the resurrection triumph of Christ over death.

The Bible.—The open Bible is symbolical of the acts of God in history. It contains the written word which points to the living Word. The open Bible should always be in view of the congregation. Some churches make a practice of displaying the open Bible on the Lord's Supper table. Others argue that the proper place for it is on the pulpit.

In some Free Churches an officer of the church brings the Bible in and places it on the pulpit, opening it at the desired place and arranging the bookmark properly as a signal for the morning worship

---

[16]John Knox Shear (ed.), *Religious Building for Today* (New York: F. W. Dodge Co., 1957), p. 4.

[17]*Art and the Message of the Church* (Philadelphia: The Westminster Press, 1961), p. 163.

to begin. In the majority of churches, however, at the appropriate time the minister steps up to the pulpit and opens the Bible for the public reading of God's Word. In both instances the dramatic action calls attention to the significance of God's Word in worship.

The pulpit.—The pulpit symbolizes the centrality of the Word of God. From there the Word is proclaimed. Therefore, it seems appropriate for the pulpit to be in the center rather than at one side. The Lord's Supper table, the pulpit with the open Bible, and the baptistry all symbolize the gospel, and thus it is appropriate for them to be in the center of the building facing the congregation. Some leaders, however, believe that the divided chancel with the pulpit on one side and the lectern on the other is still a valid arrangement for Free Church worship.

Certain leaders in Free Church worship object to the center aisle, arguing that it points to the empty place where once the altar stood as the "holiest place" in Roman Catholic worship. However, the altar has been replaced by the Lord's Supper table, the pulpit, and the baptistry. Therefore, the center aisle may symbolize the free accessibility of the gospel and a welcome invitation for the acceptance of Christ symbolized in the preaching of the Word.

The baptistry.—The baptistry is a visible symbol of the commitment of the believer to Jesus Christ as Lord. It symbolizes his death to sin and his resurrection to a new life. The baptistry has particular significance for churches that believe in the immersion of believers only. It symbolizes responsible decision to follow Christ. Located at the front of the sanctuary, back of the pulpit, and in line with the Lord's Supper table, the baptistry is a constant reminder of the death, burial, and resurrection of Jesus Christ.

The Lord's Supper Table.—The Lord's Supper table should be located in front of the pulpit on the same level as the congregation. This emphasizes the fellowship of believers and a sense of common unity of the entire congregation. The design of the table should be simple without heavy decoration. It should be shaped to look like a table and not like an altar.

Dramatic action.—From Old Testament times drama has been the handmaiden of worship. Bodily actions are symbolic of man's inner attitude in worship. Standing to show praise and adoration toward God, the bowing of the knee or head to show humility and an attitude of prayer, gestures of the hand to acknowledge the majesty of God, and other actions all have symbolic significance in expressing attitudes of worship. The processionals of the choir and minister, the new convert walking down the aisle, and the common handshake as a greeting of fellowship all symbolize the various aspects of worship. The dramatic play also has been used to communicate the truth of the Christian gospel through the centuries.[18]

The visual arts.—The church may well be given the credit for the development of the visual arts. The dedicated Christian artist may capture on canvas religious attitudes the average person is incapable of capturing. Thus, the artist shares his convictions and ideals with those who view his art.

Pictures have been used effectively to portray Christian truth and to challenge the worshiper to heroic action. Holman Hunt's *Light of the World,* Hermann Clementz's *The Rich Young Ruler,* and Heinrich Hofmann's *Christ in Gethsemane* all capture great themes involved in Christian worship.

Stained glass may have a powerful influence upon the emotions of the worshiper. Bailey suggests that it arouses the feeling associated with worship—awe, reverence, and aspiration. These, in turn, lead to insight, idealization, and the will to do and to be.[19] One church, semi-Gothic in design, contains two impressive and meaningful stained-glass windows. Back of the baptistry and immediately in view of the congregation a window symbolizes Christ with outstretched arms suggesting his invitation, "Come unto me." At the rear of the sanctuary, facing the congregation as they go forth from worship into the world, is a rose window symbolizing the theme, "Go ye into all the world." Doubtless, the entire Christian world would acclaim Michelangelo's paintings on the ceiling of the Sistine Chapel as the best of symbolism inspiring worship.

Sculpture as a part of the building itself is acceptable in the Free Churches. However, many object to the use of sculpture standing alone because it suggests idols and idol worship. Still others

---

[18]For a perceptive discussion of symbolic action, see Lawrence Abt, *Acting Out* (New York: Grune & Stratton, Inc., 1966).

[19]*Art and Character,* p. 293.

would insist that such work as Thorvaldsen's *Christus,* standing in a church in Copenhagen, has had powerful influence in the lives of many worshipers. Michelangelo's *David* in Florence conveys an idealism in the character of the Old Testament man of God which serves to remind the beholder of the God of Abraham, Moses, and David.

Light and color are among the primary elements in the expression of beauty. Von Ogden Vogt reminds us that the same color in nature that moves men to praise can be used inside the church for the same purpose.[20] In the more liturgical churches, various colors are used throughout the year to symbolize events of the Christian faith. This much emphasis is probably not acceptable in some of the Free Churches, but valid use can be made of color and light in aiding people to worship.[21]

All symbols should contain two elements if they are to be useful in worship; namely, beauty to inspire the senses, and form which points to some Christian truth. God created man with a sense of aesthetic appreciation. Since beauty has come from the hand of God, it should be used to point to the God of truth and beauty.

Perhaps we find it difficult to worship in these days because the artist in us has been crowded to the wall by the scientist. Sperry affirms, "The critical frame of mind which is content when it has dissected, analyzed, described, and catalogued the Christian life may be put down as the gravest liability of contemporary Protestant worship."[22]

It must be remembered that symbolism should be used sparingly and in good taste. Symbols which are mere embellishments are always superfluous and really evil.[23] The quantity of symbols can never be an adequate substitute for a few well chosen symbols which convey deep meaning.

---

[20]*Modern Worship,* p. 110.

[21]For a more detailed study of the meaning of various Christian symbols, see Hedley, *Christian Worship: Some Meanings and Means,* p. 53.

[22]*Op. cit.,* p. 232.

[23]Douglas Horton, *The Meaning of Worship* (New York: Harper & Bros., 1959), p. 36.

Part Three

Planning and Conducting Worship

Worship consists of our words and actions, the outward expression of our homage and adoration, when we are assembled in the presence of God. These words and actions are governed by two things: our *knowledge of the God whom we worship*, and the *human resources we are able to bring to the worship*. Christian worship is distinct from all other worship because it is *directed* to the *God and Father of our Lord Jesus Christ*. Its development is unique because the *Holy Spirit* has been with and in the church to counsel and to guide it since the Day of Pentecost.

W. D. MAXWELL
An Outline of Christian Worship

12

Form and Freedom in Worship

Honor and majesty are before him;
Strength and beauty are in his sanctuary.
Worship the Lord in holy array!

Psalm 96:6,9

When you meet for worship, each of you contributes a hymn, some instruction, a revelation, an ecstatic utterance, or the interpretation of such an utterance. All of these must aim at one thing; to build up the church. . . . For the God who inspires them is not a God of disorder but of peace. . . . Let all be done decently and in order.

1 Corinthians 14:26,33,40, NEB

The Bible nowhere prescribes an exact order of worship, but always it acknowledges some essential form for the expression of worship. The Old Testament gives more emphasis to forms and ceremonies; the New Testament stresses more the spirit and freedom of worship but does not reject essential forms and actions. In John's classic story of Jesus' conversation with the woman of Samaria concerning worship, Jesus epitomized the reality of worship: "God is spirit, and those who worship him must worship in spirit and truth" (John 4:24). The "truth" is the content and must be embodied in some communicable form; the "spirit" is the attitude of the worshiper. The two are combined in a unitary experience. Herzog notes that since the norm of the liturgy is not set forth in the Bible, we cannot speak of the "shape of the liturgy" in certain terms. The shape of the outward form is always evolving, and "we must always worship in tentative patterns."[1]

In the previous discussion concerning worship in the Old Testament, it was noted that specific instructions were given as to the particular purpose of the various psalms in worship—"for thanksgiving," "for repentance," and so on. The Bible assumes that intelligent direction

---

[1]*Op. cit.,* p. 120.

is essential for meaningful public worship. Obviously this principle has not always been observed. For example, the elaborate Roman Catholic ritual, when conducted in the Latin language, has seldom been adequately understood by the congregation. Too often the priests have been talking to themselves. Then, the worship practices of the "nonliturgical" or Free Church groups have often been so spontaneous and unplanned that the congregation has not understood the specific aims of certain elements in the service. Here also the leaders of worship have been talking to themselves, even when they had something meaningful to say. In such practices leaders have been either presumptuous or naïve in their approach to worship.

Freedom was one of the outstanding characteristics of the spirit of Jesus. He was not a traditionalist but a revolutionary. He refused to put the new wine of the gospel into old wineskins of tradition. He probably primarily used extempore prayer, appropriate to the occasion. In 1 Corinthians we have a description of early charismatic, pentecostal worship with a minimum of order and a maximum of freedom. However, we must not overdraw this contrast. Christian worship was grounded in a dual tradition—the Jewish synagogue and the upper room. There were both order and freedom, and the two are complementary. Jesus obviously acknowledged and used the forms necessary to communicate with and to lead his fellowmen in the worship of the Father.

In the practice of public worship it is not a question of either form or freedom, but both. Form and freedom combine to aid genuine worship. Order without spontaneity becomes dull and lifeless; spontaneity without order becomes subjectivity and license. Worship in the Bible includes both cultus or order and freedom of spirit. God created a universe of order and set man in its midst with the ability to relate himself to an orderly universe. Therefore, man must always proceed with an orderly or ordered freedom.

Objections to form and dignity in worship are sometimes due to our own mental laziness or to spiritual evasion. We dread the encounter with God which the discipline of ordered worship demands. It is more comfortable to follow our own impulses and to soothe our feelings with a humanistic subjectivism. But if the trumpet gives an uncertain and indefinable sound, the soldier will not be prepared.

Gene Bartlett points out two hindrances to a mature approach to worship in the Free Churches: a deep-rooted suspicion of "formalism" and the fear that the emphasis upon worship will result in a corresponding de-emphasis on preaching.[2] Let us not assume that spontaneity and order are incompatible and that we must choose one or the other. Both are required, for spontaneity without order becomes excess and even chaos, and order without spontaneity becomes compulsive ritual and even magic and superstition. Stephen F. Winward, a Baptist minister in Great Britain, observed, "The liturgy is the place of encounter between Lord and church, the vehicle of divine revelation and human response. It is worship ordered so as on the one hand to declare the whole gospel, and on the other hand to enable the people to make an adequate response."[3]

Liberty and liturgy, freedom and form are "twin pillars" of worship. There is always tension between freedom and tradition, spontaneity and order, the extempore and the liturgical, the charismatic and the formal, the prophetic and the sacramental. These should be kept joined and in proper balance. We must beware of championing a false antithesis between form and freedom. It is a tragic mistake to set spontaneity and order, freedom and tradition in opposition. We need both in our contemporary effort at creative, relevant worship.

We of the Free Churches often misinterpret our freedom. It is not simply release from law but a positive challenge to some new and commanding principle. It is not negative but positive. Freedom does not imply formlessness but the mastery of form. True freedom makes use of form rather than becoming a slave to formlessness. The Christian is not privileged in his worship to make a fetish of his freedom. It is to be a responsible freedom.

The ideal, as in the early church, is an ordered service with which congregations are so familiar that they may easily participate, one which allows liberty for the spirit to suggest—through local and worldwide current events and through the particular needs of the people—the content of the forms.[4] It is often the thoughts and

---

[2]"Worship: The Ordered Proclamation of the Gospel," *Review and Expositor*, LXII, No. 3 (Summer, 1965), p. 276.

[3]*Op. cit.*, p. 277.

[4]Coffin, *op. cit.*, p. 37.

motives behind the forms and not the forms themselves that are erroneous. Perhaps the content and ideas need to be changed rather than the forms themselves.

Certainly, formality can endanger the human spirit. However, a swing to informality also poses its threats. J. P. Allen has reminded us that "as paralyzing as formalism is to the freshness of creative worship, the reaction is possibly worse if praise and preaching degenerate to noisy, pious talk about Jesus."[5] This minister goes on to affirm that we do not necessarily have to choose between form or warmth, ritual or reality. He cites the Old Testament passage which calls God's people to "worship the Lord in holy array" (Psalm 29:2). The picture conveyed here is of an army standing at attention, resplendent in full regalia and drawn in strict regimentation. We are to stand in order before God like an army stands ready to obey the orders of its commander.

Since worship is one of the primary purposes of the organized church, the church has a responsibility for providing the place, the media of communication, the leaders, and helpful symbols as aids in worship. There is always the peril of drawing attention to the precise forms and the material objects until the mind of the worshiper is actually distracted from God himself. This danger, however, ought not to prevent our using forms and objects in the proper manner.

Even the Society of Friends, seeking to gain inner light by direct revelation from God, still have their own ritual in ruling out all fixed forms and symbolical objects. The silence of the Quaker meeting became a ritual in its own right, and the very absence of symbols was a symbol of intense significance.[6] The average Protestant church, even while declaring its hatred of ritual, has usually developed a ritual of its own, which probably is less beautiful and less effective. Hedley observes that every Protestant minister, however "anti-liturgical" he may think himself, has his own ritual phrases with which he passes from one part of the service to another; and the less he is conscious of them, the more likely he is to use them without variation. B. B. McKinney, former professor of church music at Southwestern Baptist Theological Seminary, once declared that Baptists

---

[5]*Reality in Worship* (Nashville: Convention Press, 1965), p. 75.
[6]See Hedley, *op. cit.*, p. 7.

may not be ritualists, but they usually are "rutualists." If they do not plan some order or ritual, they usually drift into a rut which they follow as slavishly as the more liturgical churches follow their liturgies.

The Values of Form

Form is necessary to convey witness and meaning to the acts of God's redemption—the incarnation, the life of Jesus Christ, the cross, and the resurrection. Men communicate through forms or ceremonies. While we are spiritual, like God, we are also something else. We have a material or physical nature. We need outward expression to communicate with the world and with one another. Spiritual worship must have its externals, although they must always be subordinate to the spiritual in worship.

The Free Churches have always insisted upon a certain amount of spontaneity in worship, and they will continue to do so. However, there is a necessity for order and form in all worship. The dread of formality and ritualism must not cause people to repudiate all form in worship. In Reform circles the dread of superstition became itself a superstition.

God who is spirit has revealed himself through the material world. Man who is made in the personal or spiritual image of God is also flesh. He has a material body and lives in a material world. Worship is related to the spiritual and the material. Therefore, it must be "embodied" or symbolized in material forms that point to and express spiritual values and relationships.

It is never a choice between forms and no form, but between good forms and bad. What makes forms good? Truth, intelligibility, taste, coherence, and style. Whatever speaks to the total man and aids him in his communication with God is good form. The following values may be found in an order or a plan of worship.

1. It is psychologically sound. People form and use habits in all the activities of life. This is also true in worship. There is value in following a fixed order of worship. The law of familiarity and tradition aids the worshiper in his inmost feelings. People do not like too much variety in their order of worship. Rather, they like for variety to come in the content of the familiar order.

2. It gives intelligent direction and purpose to the act of worship. The minds of the people are thus directed toward God and are provided interpretation concerning all aspects of the service. Whatever turns the mind toward God is an aid to worship.

3. Good form leads the congregation into a unity of participation. All minds unite in praise and prayer and giving to God.

4. It gives concrete expression to the inward attitudes. The ceremonial acts enforce the thoughts and feelings and seal the will in dedication.

5. It insures that the objective content of worship will be valid. The minds of the congregation are directed toward God and his provision of redemption. Faith can no more dispense with worship than sincere worship can dispense with faith. "Formal worship is the body of religion, as faith is its soul, and it is the body that prescribes the limits within which the soul shall develop, and imparts to it some at least of its qualities."[7]

6. An order of worship provides a discipline for the worshiper. Too often people approach the worship service with a careless, or even indifferent attitude. If ever one is to stand at attention and discipline himself in the presence of another, it is before God.

Evelyn Underhill says that habit and attention must cooperate in the life of worship. Habit tends to routine and spiritual red tape, the vice of the institutionalists; attention is apt to care for nothing but the experience of the moment, and ignore the needs of a stable practice, the vice of the individualists. "Habit is a ritualist. Attention is a pietist. But it is the combination of order and spontaneity working together freely within the liturgy and not in defiance of it, which is the mark of genuine spiritual maturity."[8]

These may be called the traditional and existential approaches to worship. The traditional and institutional is basic to good norm; the existential and spontaneous is basic to vitality. Habit and custom are strongly felt in religious worship; this can be improved in any church. On the other hand, a congregation can become so accustomed to variety and change that even this becomes a fetish, and a diversion to order and stability is resisted.

---

[7]H. Wheeler Robinson, *Redemption and Revelation*, p. 103.
[8]*Op. cit.*, p. 27 f.

Factors Determining the Order of Worship

As was indicated in the chapter on "A Theology of Worship," a church's theology greatly influences its manner of worship. The closer the Christian group has adhered to the Scriptures, the less elaborate have been their forms of worship. The more man depends on his own works for salvation, the more elaborate his ceremonies and rituals become. A theology built upon sacerdotalism and sacramentalism tends toward a more formal and fixed liturgy. Churches which believe in salvation by grace alone, effected by the faith of the believer, will feel less necessity for a fixed and formal liturgy.

Then, orders of worship usually follow the traditional patterns of a given church or denomination. These patterns may be good or bad. Tradition should be honored but it ought not to limit a congregation in its endeavor toward a more creative approach to public worship.

Aesthetic and cultural tastes also help to determine the forms of worship. Some congregations desire the more elaborate and artistic forms, whereas others prefer simpler and fewer aesthetic forms.

Furthermore, the emotional level of a congregation often dictates the amount of subjective material and spontaneous response used in worship. Certain groups of people will insist upon a high emotional intensity and more outward emotional expressions to satisfy their desires in worship. People who are more disciplined in their emotions will desire a more objective and formal approach to worship. The diversity of worship services in the American churches can be explained in the light of historical, sociological, and theological considerations. Every denomination should reexamine its historical foundations from time to time and "repair the defects in the light of the objective Word of God."[9] Services of worship will differ not only from culture to culture but also from one subculture to another.

Based upon these factors, types of liturgy have developed into three general patterns: (1) the liturgical, as seen in the Roman Catholic, the Episcopal, and the Lutheran churches, for example; (2) the nonliturgical, in which there is no planned order (the-

---

[9]Bernard Schalm, *The Church at Worship* (Grand Rapids: Baker Book House, 1962), p. 10.

oretically at least), such as is desired by the Quakers and other evangelical groups; (3) the free or planned order of worship, such as is followed in a majority of the Protestant churches. They have no fixed order of worship, but they do plan the order of worship, allowing for a certain amount of freedom and spontaneity. Douglas Horton observes that worship often surprises the human mind, coming not in the "decent Episcopal session, but with sudden Anabaptist spontaneity."[10]

Within Christendom worship ranges all the way from the ritualistic pomp of the Catholic mass to the unadorned silence of the Quaker meeting. But underneath all this diversity of forms is a similarity pointing to the glory and ultimate mystery of the invisible Lord. In an age of pragmatism and rationalism, reverence and mystery need an emphasis which ceremony and form tend to give.

A visitor gave his impressions of certain worship services carelessly conducted:

People who would hiss a play which was so ill planned that the order of the acts and scenes was of no importance, or would throw into the wastebasket a novel which was so utterly without form that Chapter 3 and Chapter 16 are interchangeable, still pathetically go to church on Sunday morning to take part in a disorderly medley of music, hymnsinging, scripture reading, praying, and the sermon . . . . Many church services today are a quaint mixture of concert, lecture, and prayer meeting.[11]

Principles Governing Form

Since some form in worship is a necessity, there are certain practical principles which should govern the order of worship.

1. The order of Christian worship should never contain anything contrary to biblical truth. For example, in Exodus God commanded, "You shall not make yourself a graven image. . . . You shall not bow down to them or serve them" (20:4,5). The most effective way to avoid an erroneous view of Christian worship in terms of cultus is to relate its origin to Jesus Christ.

[10]*Op. cit.,* p. 18.
[11]Donald Macleod, *Word and Sacrament: A Preface to Preaching and Worship* (Englewood Cliffs, N. J.: Prentice-Hall, Inc., 1960), p. 119 f.

2. An order of worship should be in keeping with good historical tradition. The churches in the past have given us a heritage which cannot be ignored without serious impoverishment.

3. A good order will be intelligible to the particular congregation and will make the gospel relevant to present life situations. Only when it is conducted in the language people understand can it be most meaningful to them.

4. Every experience of public worship should have a definite purpose or objective in view. In order to be meaningful, every element in an order of worship should have a definite purpose.

5. A good order of worship must have unity. "Unity is not primarily that of a single idea, but the coordination of all parts of the service pointing to the same objective. It must not be a collection of unrelated items strung together."[12]

6. Public worship, like a story or a drama, must have movement or progress. In the use of praise and prayer and the reading of God's Word, the attention and feeling of the congregation must be moving and not standing still.

7. Good form in worship necessitates alternation—contrasting moods and movements, silence and expression, standing and sitting, spoken words and music, and participation by the minister and the congregation.

From the foregoing discussion, it can be seen that the order of worship has movements like a symphony or acts in a play. The movements of praise and prayer, listening and responding to the Word of God, offering and receiving—all move together toward a grand climax in bringing glory to God and in doing his will.

So long as the church bids men to the worship of God and provides a simple, credible vehicle for worship, it need not question its place, mission, and influence in the world. If it loses faith in the act of worship, is thoughtless in the ordering of worship, and careless in the conduct of worship, it need not look to its avocations to save it. It is dead at its heart, and no chafing of the extremities, producing what Carlyle called "quaint galvanic sprawlings" will bring back the life that has left it.[13]

---

[12]Coffin, *op. cit.*, p. 44.
[13]Sperry, *op. cit.*, p. 168.

Planning the Order of Worship

Dr. George Buttrick, for twenty-seven years pastor of the Madison Avenue Presbyterian Church, New York City, told a class in pastoral theology at Harvard University that he always spent approximately three hours per week planning the morning worship service. This time was calculated apart from the time spent in preparing the sermon. In other words, it included the selection of hymns, the preparation of prayers, and all the other elements of the worship service. The class appreciated his careful attention to this planning when they worshiped under his leadership in Harvard Chapel.

One of the explanations for much ineffective worship in our churches is the lack of serious planning on the part of leaders. This carelessness in planning may be due to the following facts: some leaders in worship have closed minds on the subject; their knowledge of the dynamics of participation may be limited; their poor theologizing about worship sets it apart as being irrelevant.[1]

The entire church has a large responsibility concerning public worship. The church determines the liturgy, the hymnal, the plan and appointments of the church building, and the general program for the Christian year. However, the church looks to its minister for leadership in planning worship. Throughout the history of the Christian church, the bishop or minister has been considered responsible for planning and leading worship. Even the Free Churches in America are giving more attention to the training of ministers for leadership in worship. For example, the six seminaries of the Southern Baptist Convention all offer elective courses in worship for ministers in training, and one of them includes a required course in its curriculum. Southern Baptists and some other denominations are yet giving too little emphasis to training ministers for leadership in worship.

---

[1]See Editorial, *Pastoral Pschology,* September, 1964.

Some Guiding Principles

Planning a worship service should include all that will enrich and aid worship and exclude all that will impoverish or hinder true worship. Perhaps the following suggestions may serve as guidelines in planning worship.

1. Specific persons must accept the responsibility for planning worship. This responsibility should be taken seriously and carried forward with discipline. Ordinarily, the pastor or senior minister is primarily responsible for planning the order of worship. He should plan the design for each service of worship, keeping in mind the theme which will be emphasized in all the elements. He should give attention to every detail of the order, especially the call to worship, the prayers, the hymns, and the Scripture selections.

In the larger church other persons will probably assist the pastor in planning the order of worship. The minister of music and the pastor should work together in the selection of appropriate hymns for worship. The assistant pastor, the minister of education, the organist, and other staff members may be invited to study the order of worship and make creative suggestions. A church committee on worship can add strength to the creative planning of the order of worship. From time to time the congregation may be invited to make suggestions for the improvement of worship in order to meet the variety of needs which people in the congregation have.

2. Plenty of time should be devoted to planning an effective order of worship. If we spent one tenth as much time planning the "devotional parts" of worship as is devoted to the sermon, worship would more often be a glowing experience for the leader and those who are led. Certain hours should be set aside every week for the study of the worship service and enough time allowed for a thorough job to be done. Furthermore, worship should be planned far enough in advance for the musicians to have time to select appropriate music and to rehearse in preparation for the worship service. Long-range planning will be needed, particularly for the special programs of music to be provided by the choir.

3. The order of worship should be suited for a given congregation. Someone has suggested that it ought to be "tailor-made" for a particu-

lar church. There are times when members or families in the congregation have had experiences which call for a certain kind of
worship experience, especially in times of grief and tragedy. Those
who plan worship should beware, however, of neglecting the needs
of the congregation as a whole which will call for a well-rounded
order of worship.

4. The minister should have a definite purpose in mind as he plans
the order of worship. Micklem suggests that he should seek to bring
the congregation to a new point of view or decision.[2] To this end he
will select the hymns, prayers, Scriptures, and sermon, weaving them
all into a harmonious whole with a view to leading the congregation
into a well-rounded worship experience.

5. Although no one season is more important than another, many
churches find it helpful to plan their worship according to the calendar
of the Christian year. Every day is the "day which the Lord hath
made." All time is holy, and every day is a day for worshiping God.
However, the observance of certain days and seasons may keep the
church reminded that God who has acted in history is continuously
acting in the lives of his people. "Worship must not degenerate into
a single tune played on one string."[3]

Most of the Free Churches follow the Christian calendar to some
extent in planning their worship. Worship and preaching are often
planned to emphasize the Advent season, which focuses upon the
Messianic expectation; Christmastide, which stresses the Nativity and
the Incarnation; the Lenten season, which emphasizes the suffering
and death of Jesus and the consequent repentance and confession
which it prompts; Eastertide, which is the season of the resurrection
and ascension of our living Lord; and Pentecost, which comes fifty
days after Easter and stresses the doctrine of the Holy Spirit and
his empowerment of the church.[4]

---

[2]Nathaniel Micklem (ed.), *Christian Worship: Studies in Its History and
Meaning* (London: Oxford University Press, 1936), p. 201.

[3]William R. McNutt, *Worship in the Churches.* (Philadelphia: Judson Press,
1941), p. 245.

[4]For a fuller presentation of the use of the Christian year in planning
worship, see John E. Skoglund, *Worship in the Free Churches* (Valley Forge,
Pa.: Judson Press, 1965), p. 137 ff.; also Hedley, *Christian Worship: Some
Meanings and Means,* p. 72 ff.

6. A certain amount of variety in the order of worship will keep the attention of people and stimulate their concern in worship. In general, it is wise to conserve the overall design of the service with which a congregation is familiar. Ordinarily the variety should come in the alteration of parts of the service within the general structure without radically changing the main structure. To surprise a congregation with a radically new and unexpected order of worship evokes wonder at what is happening. This prevents them from focusing their attention upon God.

7. The use of manuals and other aids can assist leaders in planning worship. For example, handbooks of prayers, hymns, and manuals on order of worship prepared by many denominations may stimulate the thinking and provide enrichment materials for those who plan worship. The use of such materials may prevent leaders in the Free Churches from a narrow and individualistic approach to the order of worship.[5]

8. A printed or mimeographed order of worship can aid a congregation in worship. This visual aid is particularly helpful in directing the attention to the particular objectives of the various elements in worship. This should be made as attractive as possible.

9. It is often advisable for the evening service to differ somewhat from the morning worship service. The morning service usually is more closely structured and is given more dignity, and the evening service is more flexible and provides for more freedom. The morning service is more objective in emphasis and the evening service more subjective. This variety in the kinds of worship services provides a balance for the emotional experiences of the congregation, as well as for the different perspectives which various people have.

10. Planning for worship includes the preparation of the building and facilities. The house of worship should be made attractive. Cleanliness is a mark of Christian concern for God's house. Jesus said, "This is my Father's house." Everything should be in order—the pulpit cleared of extraneous bulletins and extra materials, hymnbooks in the pew racks, musical instruments in inconspicuous locations, the choir arranged so as to assist in praise and not for concert or

---

[5]See the Bibliography on "Resources for Planning Worship" appearing toward the end of this book, pp. 221 ff.

display, and appropriate flowers and other symbols appointed so
as to beautify the sanctuary. The temperature and ventilation of the
building should be properly controlled to make the place of worship
reasonably comfortable. Simple beauty induces reverence.

11. Creativity in planning is essential for vital worship. Neither
slavish dependence upon resource materials which others have provided, nor the naïve presumptuousness that no previous thought or
planning is necessary for a public worship service is valid. Meaningful
planning for worship will make good use of literary resources created
by others in the heritage of the churches, and it will call forth the
best creative thinking and praying in the present. Vital worship costs
in concern and imagination and work; for the worship of God is
dialogue, and dialogue calls for involvement in the gospel of redemption. The Holy Spirit desires to work creatively in the minds of those
involved in planning worship, and he will inspire and guide as
vitally in the planning as he will in the actual experience of worship.

Suggested Patterns of Worship

Various suggested patterns may be helpful in planning an order of
worship. A good summary has been stated in the Methodist church's
The Book of Worship for Church and Home: "There is a fourfold
aspect of an order of worship. Four attitudes of the devout worshippers
are presented in ascending movements—adoration, confession, affirmation, and dedication. These imply the divinely descending movements of vision, pardon, illumination, and fruition." The following
general patterns for worship have been suggested by various writers.
Von Ogden Vogt presents five stages in the "natural progress of the
soul in worship": (1) presentation—a vision of God as one offers
himself for worship; (2) penitence—a sense of humility in the divine
presence which induces contrition, confession, and an appeal for
pardon; (3) exaltation—which follows the consciousness of pardon
expressed in praise; (4) illumination—the soul receives light before
setting forth upon the path of life anew; (5) dedication or consecration—given a new sense of God, of pardon, of rejoicing, and, having
been taught where the pathway of life lies, the soul in truest
consecration enlists for further service.[6]

---

[6]*Modern Worship*, p. 153 f.

Seidenspinner speaks of three movements in worship: (1) adoration of God; (2) communion with God; and (3) dedication to God. He feels the unity of the service should be like a symphony.[7]

Sperry suggests the following pattern in *Reality of Worship*: (1) vision of reality; (2) contrasting human situation; (3) new comprehension; and (4) dedication.

Edgar S. Brightman in *Religious Values* gives a similar outline: (1) contemplation; (2) revelation; (3) communion; (4) fruition.

Based upon the foregoing principles and the suggested patterns for an order of worship, a fourfold summary is suggested as an outline for worship: (1) adoration and praise; (2) confession, petition, and intercession; (3) affirmation and the proclamation of the Word; (4) submission and dedication to take the gospel into the world according to God's will. These four attitudes or movements suggest four major divisions of the order of worship according to purpose. The various elements or means of expressing worship—call to worship, hymns, prayers, the reading of the Scriptures, offerings, and so on—may be appropriately arranged under these divisions.

Two suggested orders of worship are here presented: the first, an elaborate order for the large church; the second, a simpler form for the smaller church.

MORNING WORSHIP

10:50 A.M.

WE PRAISE THEE, O GOD

Sacred Organ Music, "Sortie" — Wm. J. Marsh

Processional Hymn No. 50,

"God Is Love, His Mercy Brightens" — Stuttgart

Call to Worship

Minister—Behold, what manner of love the Father hath bestowed upon us, that we should be called the sons of God.

Congregation—If we love one another, God dwelleth in us, and his love is perfected in us.

Minister—There is no fear in love; but perfect love casteth out fear; because fear hath torment. He that feareth is not made perfect in love.

---

[7]Clarence Seidenspinner, *Form and Freedom in Christian Worship* (Chicago: Willet-Clark & Co., 1941), p. 186 ff.

Congregation—We love him, because he first loved us.
Prayer of Thanksgiving and Invocation
Gloria Patri

***

WE CALL UPON THEE

Pastor's Paragraph
Reading of the Word of God—Matthew 6:25-33
Call to Prayer, "Hear Our Prayer, O Heavenly Father"   Chopin
Silent Meditation
Pastoral Prayer and Choral Amen

***

WE MAGNIFY THY HOLY NAME

Children's Sermon
Hymn of Affirmation No. 255,
   "O for a Faith That Will Not Shrink"   Arlington
Offertory, "Chorale"   Wm. J. Marsh
Offertory Response, Hymn No. 535,
   "We Give Thee But Thine Own"   St. Andrew
Offertory Prayer
Anthem, "Hear My Cry, O God"   Kopyloff
Sermon, "Dangerous Words—Tomorrow"   Minister

WE HEAR THY CALL

Hymn of Invitation No. 257,
   "My Faith Looks Up to Thee"   Olivet
Reception of New Members
Benediction
Choral Response and Organ Dismissal

*** Ushers will assist with seating at these periods.

Other headings that may be used to designate this fourfold outline for the order of worship are here suggested. The various elements of worship—the hymns, prayers, sermon, and so on—are to be filled in under these headings in a manner similar to the order of service given above. Several of these are based upon actual passages of Scripture. By using the imagination those who plan the order of worship will be able to think of other thought-provoking headings for the program.

1. SEEK YE THE LORD

***

CALL YE UPON HIM

***

KEEP HIS COMMAND-
MENTS

***

THAT YOUR DAYS MAY
BE LONG

2. THE GLORY OF GOD

***

THE WORD OF GOD

***

THE NAME OF GOD

***

THE CALL OF GOD

3. THE PRAISE OF GOD

***

THE HEARING OF THE
WORD

***

THE PROCLAMATION OF
THE GOSPEL

***

THE RESPONSE OF FAITH

4. I SAW THE LORD HIGH
AND LIFTED UP

***

WOE IS ME, FOR I AM
UNDONE

***

WHOM SHALL I SEND

***

HERE AM I, SEND ME

5. WORSHIP IN PRAISE

***

WORSHIP IN PRAYER

***

WORSHIP IN AFFIRMA-
TION

***

WORSHIP IN DEDICA-
TION

6. ADORATION

***

COMMUNION

***

INSTRUCTION

***

DEDICATION

7. ENTER INTO HIS COURTS
WITH PRAISE

***

SEEK YE THE LORD
WHILE HE MAY BE
FOUND

***

THY WORD IS A LAMP
UNTO MY FEET

***

PRESENT YOUR BODIES
A LIVING SACRIFICE

8. FATHER, GLORIFY THY
SON

***

KEEP THEM FROM THE
EVIL ONE

***

SANCTIFY THEM IN THE
TRUTH

***

I HAVE SENT THEM INTO
THE WORLD

Leaders of worship in some small churches will realize that the order of worship above may be too elaborate. A trained choir is not always available. If an order seems too elaborate, it may become a hindrance to some congregations. The foregoing principles and suggested outlines can be simplified and abbreviated to fit the smaller congregation.

Churches, large or small, even within a given denomination, will vary to some degree in their use of orders of worship. The following is an example of a simpler order which may be used by either large or small. It is suggested that general headings still be used to indicate the purpose of the various elements in the order of service.

MORNING WORSHIP

WORSHIP IN PRAISE

Prelude: "My Jesus, I Love Thee'   arr. Thompson
Call To Worship: "Surely the Lord is in this place.
                 This is none other than the house
                 of God, and this is the gate of
                 heaven."
Hymn of Adoration: No. 20, "O Worship the King"   Haydn
Invocation

WORSHIP IN PRAYER

Welcome to Guests
The Reading of God's Word (Responsive Reading No. 504)
Morning Prayer
Hymn of Devotion: No. 344, "Saviour, Like A Shepherd Lead
   Us"   Bradbury

WORSHIP IN WITNESS

Hymn Anthem: "Fairest Lord Jesus"   arr. R. S. Willis
             —The Choir
Offertory: "O, God Be Merciful To Me"   Bach
Dedication of Offering
Hymn of Affirmation: No. 382, "I Love Thy Kingdom, Lord"
                                                     Williams
Sermon: "Christ's Glorious Church"   Pastor

WORSHIP IN COMMITMENT

Hymn of Dedication: No. 360, "Jesus Calls Us"   W. H. Jude
Reception of Members
Benediction
Postlude: "Glorious Things of Thee Are Spoken"   Haydn

Perhaps it should be reaffirmed that no fixed liturgy is implied here. However, the suggested use of definite and intelligible orders of worship should not be taken lightly. They can be used as an aid for people to enter into the presence of God and have a well-rounded experience of worship. Regardless of the order of service, "It is absolutely essential that the act of worship should be open towards God, that God may intervene in his saving power."[8] The spirit of worship is the primary concern and should never be dominated by the form in which it is expressed. Let the form be an aid to the spirit of man as he approaches God and responds to the gospel of grace by faith and active dedication.

---

[8]Von Allmen, *op. cit.*, p. 288.

14

Leading Worship

And the twenty-four elders, and the four living creatures fell down and worshiped God who is seated on the throne, saying, "Amen. Hallelujah!" And from the throne came a voice crying, "Praise our God all you his servants, you who fear him, small and great." Then I heard what seemed to be the voice of a great multitude, like the sound of many waters and like the sound of mighty thunderpeals, crying, "Hallelujah! for the Lord our God the Almighty reigns. Let us rejoice and exult and give him the glory."

Revelation 19:4-7

Public worship consists not only of content or form but also of actions or ceremonial. Actually, worship is an act, the presentation of ourselves and our substance to God in praise, thanksgiving, and dedication. In a sense all worship is drama. This does not mean that those who lead and participate attempt to be dramatic. It simply means that all that is done is carried forward in action which is similar to an unfolding drama. Therefore, all the acts of worship are significant because they imply the attitudes underlying them.

This is particularly significant in the case of the leader in worship. Second only in importance to the form of the service is the method of conducting it. It should be remembered that worship is offered to God, hence demands dignity, reverence, and our very best in preparation, leadership, and participation. This means that there should be no attempt to provide "atmosphere" through the use of theatrical techniques. Above all else, the spirit of worship should be genuine. Many churches are busy seeking to create a "folksy" attitude in the worship service. They feel more comfortable with the emphasis on the human dimension, for it is a "dreadful" experience to face God.

But we can't produce worship by seeking to bring God down to our level. Rather, we must seek to come up to his level of dialogue, which demands the attitudes of humble dependence, awe and adoration, confession and affirmation. The Lord says, "My ways are higher than your ways and my thoughts than your thoughts" (Isa. 55:9). The church must approach worship seriously and with a dignity which dialogue with God deserves.

Although it is less painful and costly to take a subjective approach to worship, it is doubtful whether such an approach will reach the spiritual depth needed for radical, transforming worship. A constant awareness that God stands above and outside of man as judge will keep man serious in his attention to all the ceremonials of worship.

Luther D. Reed warns against fussy and meaningless practices which cannot satisfy men who are seeking reality. He insists that the mechanics of worship be unobtrusive and that the details must not attract attention to themselves. They must never introduce a false focus or deaden the devotional spirit by the weight of the machinery.[1] The best ceremonial is that which expresses the content of worship most clearly and naturally. There are at least four factors which ought to determine all ceremonial actions: purity, significance, simplicity, and restraint. The emphasis upon the audio-visual in mass communication today demands that leadership in all the ceremonial actions of public worship be of high quality.

The Leader of Worship

The actual experience of worship depends upon three things—the worshiper himself, the Holy Spirit's power, and the human leadership provided in the order and conduct of worship. In the functional sense, leadership is a necessity in the church. Although there is no distinction between the so-called clergy and laity, the congregation selects from its midst leaders who are qualified to point the direction and to call the congregation to a unified effort in all its acts of worship and ministry.[2]

Ordinarily the pastor is the primary leader in worship. In many churches other staff members and sometimes laymen, share in the leadership. All this discussion applies to them also. The leader in

---

[1] *Op. cit.,* p. 320.
[2] For a more detailed study of leadership, see Segler, *Theology of Church and Ministry,* p. 57 ff.

worship is both prophet and priest. The prophet contends for change and vitality; the priest seeks stability and instruction. The prophet speaks forth the ideal and eternal truth of God; the priest comes to God in behalf of man's temporal and partial grasp of truth and reality. These elements are always in tension in the work of the minister, and both affect his approach to leading in worship. As the pastor leads in worship, he is not acting for himself alone but for and with the congregation. The minister is not only the transmitter of the things of the people through Christ to God and the things of God through Christ to the people; he is also one of the company of transmitters. He is a member of a line. He acts not merely as an individual but as one of a team.[3]

It is hoped that contemporary worship may become a powerful force for bringing in the day of brotherhood. Pastors will have to lead their people into creative and cooperative quests if this is to become a fact. Ralph C. Raughley, Jr. feels that most of our worship is "fundamentally dull, inglorious, irrelevant, and lacking in adequate abrasives."[4] Leading people into creative worship is a major task, and "a tinkering with existing liturgies, a little sopping up of drippy sentimentalism, or a little tacking on of choice selections here and there will not do."[5]

The leaders' spirit.—Charles Haddon Spurgeon once said that the man who guides others into the presence of the King must have journeyed far into the King's country and often looked upon his face. It is an awesome thing to come into the presence of God. The leader must commit himself anew for each particular occasion. His private prayer period is supremely important. Perhaps he will wish to kneel in the study for another moment of dedication just before he enters the sanctuary. The leader should subordinate himself and exalt God as the objective of worship. The spirit of the leader should be characterized by seriousness, reverence, joy, disciplined enthusiasm, hope, expectancy, and humility. All of these are dependent upon the grace of God through the Holy Spirit.

---

[3]Horton, *op. cit.,* p. 101.
[4]*New Frontiers of Christianity* (New York: Association Press, 1962),p. 128.
[5]*Ibid.*

The leader's appearance.—The leader should be properly dressed when he enters the pulpit to conduct worship. No general custom prevails in the Free Churches, but good taste dictates that a minister's dress be such as not to distract. The discipline of worship demands moderation in dress. In the Free Churches ministers have usually worn the same style of clothing as that worn by the laity—namely, street dress. The business suit should be in good taste and contemporary in style. Dark suits—black, blue, grey, or brown (in that order)—are preferred. Dark accessories to match should be carefully selected.

In some of the Free Churches the minister's robe is acceptable, or even preferred. A black academic robe is acceptable. It is strange that in America our churches accept robes for choirs, rejecting the minister's robe, whereas in Great Britain the churches accept the minister's robe but object to robing the choir. The main objection to the clerical robe is that it tends to make a distinction between the minister and the congregation. One argument in favor of the robe is that it tends to make the minister less conspicuous by concealing his own personal dress.

Whatever the minister's attire, it should always be clean and freshly pressed. A lack of good taste here is considered by many persons a lack of good manners, or even a lack of consideration for the congregation, who usually give a great deal of attention to dress and appearance.

The leader's deportment.—One's bearing before a congregation is highly important. It is not fitting for a man to rush into the pulpit, or "balloon" into it, or sneak into it. It is not becoming for a man to sprawl across his pulpit desk or stand with his hands in his pockets or loll about. The minister's appearance should give the impression that he has come from the audience chambers of heaven with a message from God, and that he has a sense of ambassadorial status.[6]

Decorum should indicate sincerity, **not** pretense. For example, in seventeenth-century England the clergyman might have worn his hunting clothes and spurs beneath his cassock and Genevan gown as

---

[6]W. E. Sangster, *The Approach to Preaching* (Philadelphia: The Westminster Press, 1952), pp. 58-59.

he raced through the service in his eagerness to get to the social diversions of the day. Simply to appear decent and well-mannered is not sufficient. As Davies said, "Even a corpse has dignity, and anglican decorum sometimes seemed next door to death."[7]

Principles of Leadership

Since Christian worship is never a solitary undertaking but is organic in character, it is important that certain principles be observed in order to enlist the widest participation in worship. Leaders of worship will keep in mind that the corporate life of worship is central in all that is done and said. The following principles are suggested as guidelines for leading in worship.

1. There should be complete preparation in the details of the service. The leader must know exactly what he is to do step by step. He should see that all items are in order: the Bible, the hymnal, the order of worship, the sermon notes (if he uses notes), and all other notes pertaining to the details of conducting the service.

2. Proper mental preparation will lead to poise and a calm self-confidence. It will assist the leader in mastering his fears and timidities. If he is to lead others in worship he must be free from self-conscious attitudes that call attention to himself. He cannot give in to depression, personal fears, and doubts. A consciousness that he is God's leader will go far toward making his leadership effective.

3. The leader should seek personal rapport with the congregation. As he seeks to identify with the congregation he should be constantly aware that his own emotions are communicated. Actually, the congregation absorbs the "feeling tones" of the leader.[8] It is possible for the leader to communicate one message verbally and an entirely different message emotionally.

4. A positive attitude is essential in leading others in worship. An attitude of firmness and moderate discipline will inspire confidence on the part of the congregation. Words should be well chosen so as to avoid awkward expressions. In calling the people to prayer or to

---

[7] *Worship and Theology in England: From Watts and Wesley to Maurice, 1690-1850*, p. 75.

[8] James T. Hall, "Measuring the Communication Feeling During Worship," *Pastoral Psychology* (October, 1963), pp. 50 ff.

participation in music the leader should be positive in his expressions. For example, "Let us pray" is better than "Shall we pray?" or "May we pray?"

5. The leader should speak in a natural tone of voice, never using the perfunctory tones of the "professional clergyman." The voice communicates either honesty or pretense, and the modern congregation, accustomed to hearing voices on radio and television, can instantly unmask the phony personality. The conversational tone is usually preferred in contemporary communication.

6. Let the minister be punctual, never beginning a service late, nor allowing any part of the service to drag or to consume more than its appropriate amount of time. People's habits condition them psychologically so that they are distracted and irritated when the timing is poor. Worship services should be completed within the appointed time, usually not over an hour. Rarely will people give their undivided attention past twelve o'clock on Sunday mornings. Of course, the exceptions will be services on special occasions or services in which a visitation of God's power leads the people to wait upon his Spirit.

7. Personal eccentricities and distracting idiosyncracies of a leader are annoying and become a hindrance to worship. Almost everyone is subject to one kind or another—a halt in speech, a facial expression, peculiar bodily movements, adjusting the glasses, playing with the handkerchief—and should be constantly on the alert to overcome them. Should one have a natural and unavoidable handicap, let him avoid a self-conscious attitude about it, and the people will accept it graciously.

8. The spirit of a leader is contagious. Therefore, a leader of worship should reflect a spirit of optimism and hope and enthusiasm, and never a spirit of pessimism or a sense of indifference or failure. Spiritual zeal may kindle enthusiasm, but enthusiasm is not a substitute for a zeal for God. Worship is always an occasion of joy and hope. God has promised to meet his people when they approach him in worship. Why should a leader ever doubt that fact? Every service should be approached with a spirit of expectancy. The difference between a militant church and a dead one can often be attributed to the spirit of the minister who leads in worship.

9. One of the privileges of the leader in worship is that of partic-ipating in worship with the congregation. The minister should wor-ship *before* and *while* he leads others. He should sing the hymns with the congregation and show his interest and concern for every part of the service. People will follow a leader who shows his genuine interest in them by cooperating with them in their acts of worship.

10. The minister should freely give of himself at all times. Un-selfishness in the worship service speaks of his wider concern for persons and may encourage people to come to him at other times for counsel and support. At the conclusion of the service the pastor may wish to take his position at one of the doors or in the foyer so that people may come by to see him. Let him not encourage the people to believe that he expects their praise for his sermon. Rather, they should sense that he is making himself available to them in warm, personal relationships.

11. Should laymen be enlisted to assist in the conduct of worship, such as leading in prayer and reading the Scriptures? That all depends. Theologically, there is no distinction between "clergy" and "laity." Practically and functionally, however, the Bible and tradition teach that members should function according to their gifts and training.

If the motive for enlisting laymen is to involve the congregation as a whole in more meaningful worship, it may well be done; but, if it is done to exalt certain personalities, or simply to pass the honors around, it will distract from worship. One pastor says, "To empha-size the fact that worship is a congregational experience, we use a responsive call to worship and responsive Scripture readings. A dif-ferent layman leads in these and sometimes in the invocation or in the offertory prayer."

If laymen are to assist in conducting the service, they should be instructed regarding the purpose of each element and the best manner in which it may be done. They should be enlisted far enough in ad-vance to give them time to prepare thoroughly. Due to the numerous problems involved, many pastors feel that it is best for trained leader-ship to conduct most of the planned worship services. Informal ser-vices, such as the prayer meeting, and other group meetings provide opportunity for wide participation, even to voluntary leading in prayers and giving personal testimonies.

Laymen generally do have a major part in the worship services, such as looking after the building and facilities—the lighting, the ventilation, the public-address system, and the like. One man is usually designated to supervise such matters.

Ushering is an important function in the conduct of worship. The usher is the host in the Lord's house and should set an example for all other members in the worship service. His main purpose is to make it easier for people to worship God. This ministry demands reverence, dignity, patience, courtesy, tact, and discipline on the part of the usher. The responsibilities include greeting the people, seating them, distributing the order of worship, receiving the offerings, and handling minor emergencies. If this is to be done effectively it will demand organization—training in the techniques and skills in "congregational engineering."[9]

12. The choir has a major task in leading worship. Their appearance and decorum, as well as their spirit of cooperation, can aid or distract the congregation. They should work closely with the minister in all parts of the service. A noticeably wandering mind, a roving eye, or a wriggling body in the choir loft can interfere with the close communication that should exist between the minister and the congregation. Choir members should give careful attention to getting into and out of the choir area as well as to their deportment during the service. Good manners demand a spirit of reverence, cooperation, and self-discipline at all times.

Congregational Participation

"You are a chosen race, a royal priesthood, a holy nation, God's own people, that you may declare the wonderful deeds of him who called you out of darkness into his marvelous light" (1 Peter 2:9).

In medieval worship the clergy had a kind of monopoly over worship. Because the liturgy was performed in Latin and the people could not understand it, they ceased to be active participants and became spectators in worship. The sanctuary was a "sort of stage for a

---

[9]Further helpful discussions on ushering include the following: Church Ushers Association, *Principles of Church Ushering* (New York: Church Ushers Association of New York, 1951); Willis O. Garrett, *Church Usher's Manual* (Philadelphia: Judson Press, 1924).

mystery drama which they watched, to which they contributed little except the necessary fees to keep it going."[10] They seldom participated in the Lord's Supper more than once a year. Doubtless, many of them paid their fees and attended services to escape purgatory.

This description may well be applied to contemporary worship in many instances. Too often the congregation listens too much and participates too little. The sermon is listened to. The prayers are listened to. The anthem is listened to. They do not participate enough. Of what value is freedom without participation? It is dishonest to boast of a freedom which is not honored and exercised.

The doctrine of the priesthood of all believers does not mean that every man is his own priest merely, but that every man is priest to every other man. And this necessitates community. This means that all members of the congregation, as a "royal priesthood," have a responsibility in public worship. Like our High Priest who offered himself as a sacrifice for his people, they too must offer themselves to God and to their fellowmen. In this case they offer "spiritual sacrifices acceptable to God through Jesus Christ" (1 Peter 2:5).

The obligation of the individual to worship has a threefold basis theologically: (1) he is to give to God the glory and honor due unto his name; (2) he is to witness to the spiritual needs of society; (3) he is to receive for himself the "unsearchable riches of Christ."[11] As a part of the church he is God's representative to the world in his generation.

The congregation's part in worship is a responsive action. The individual worshiper is obligated to cooperate in this response. This responsive action is expressed in the music, the prayers, the offerings, the responsive reading of the Scriptures, and in listening to God's Word as it is preached. These responses may be both audible and visible, or they may be silent and unseen, except as God observes the inner man. Congregations need training in good manners and in principles of participation.

Just as leaders prepare for public worship, so must the congrega-

---

[10]Shepherd, *The Worship of the Church* (Greenwich, Conn.: The Seabury Press, 1952), p. 84.

[11]John G. McKenzie, *Psychology, Psychotherapy, and Evangelism* (London: George Allen & Unwin, Ltd., 1940), p. 228.

tion be prepared before entering the sanctuary. Such preparation includes the preparation of the body, which is the "temple of the Holy Spirit" (1 Cor. 6:19). This calls for sufficient rest for the Lord's Day and a relaxed state so that the mind dominates the sensory feelings of the body. A second essential is a prepared attitude, which can be realized through the exercise of private devotion. Each member should not only expect to *receive* something from public worship, but should also *bring* something to public worship. Regular family worship also helps prepare individuals for public worship.

If one is to participate, certain principles must be followed. (1) Regular and punctual attendance is essential. This will call for determination and dedication. Public worship demands action, and the individual can prove his sincere devotion to Christ and his church by being present in body. One is not likely to pray "just anywhere" unless he definitely prays "somewhere." (2) The worshiper must approach worship with a spirit of reverence—respect for the house of worship, for the day of worship, and for the leader of worship, as well as reverence for God and his Word.

(3) To be a good follower is as essential as to be a good leader. The individual must wilfully cooperate with the leaders and unite with his fellow members in singing praise to God, in praying to God, and in every act of worship included in the planned order. This should be viewed both as a privilege and a duty. (4) Every member should remain to the end of the service. It is neither good religion nor good etiquette to distract others by rushing for the exit. (5) The period of brief fellowship as the congregation is leaving provides an opportunity for friendly greeting. Greeting strangers and making them feel welcome is part of a worship service.

If we are to grow in worship, we must cultivate a spirit of expectation. Growing as a Christian depends upon growing in the art and discipline of worship. The mind must engage all its powers in the exercise of imagination and creativity in order for worship to achieve its greatest potential. We must "expect a blessing" and then respond to the requirements if we are to receive a blessing. The "fruits of worship"—guidance, comfort, and inspiration—will come as a result of the higher action of giving glory and honor to God through the giving of ourselves to him.

As Kierkegaard pointed out, the leader and the congregation should not think of themselves as actors but as servants and responders.[12] The stage is eternity, and the listener stands before God who speaks. Our response to his revelation is judged by his Spirit, and we are rewarded as he will, for the Spirit moves where he will. The Holy Spirit moves in the hearts of God's people according to the preparation he finds in the place of worship.

---

[12]Soren J. Kierkegaard, *Purity of Heart,* trans. Douglas Steere (New York: Harper & Bros., 1938), p. 163 ff.

15

Worship and Church Renewal

The church stands always in need of renewal and revitalization. It must be forever building, for it is forever decaying within and being attacked without. Thinking people inside and outside the church today are calling for church renewal. One historian characterized the ancient church as a dynamic, the medieval church as a mutation, and the modern church as a mere survival.

Theologians, both conservative and radical, are joining in the challenge. Many are critical and pessimistic, while others see signs of hope on the horizon. A pastor of a "conventional" church writes, "In the hour of the church's institutional success, its spiritual failure is being exposed." But he goes on to affirm that there is a Divinity that shapes our ends, that molds us into the shape of Christ.[1]

Sociologists and journalists on a wide scale portray the "secularization" of the church.[2] Secularism has been defined as the living of life as though God were dead, as though he did not exist. Henry Sloane Coffin, Jr., chaplain of Yale University, may be correct. "We churchmen have never had attendance so high and influence so low," he said.

Church and society are in crucial tension today. The church faces the challenge of the new morality, the secularization of life, the body-conscious attitude, existential theology, knowledge explosion, new communication media, the ecumenical movement, liturgical renewal, racial and minority group struggle, and the crisis mentality of our society produced by gigantic world problems. The church must take account of this revolution and seek new ways of communication

---

[1]Robert A. Raines, *Reshaping the Christian Life* (New York: Harper & Row, 1964), pp. 3,13.

[2]See, for example, Peter L. Berger, *Noise of Solemn Assemblies* (Garden City, N. Y.: Doubleday and Co., 1961); Harvey Cox, *The Secular City* (New York: The Macmillan Co., 1965); Pierre Berton, *The Comfortable Pew* (Philadelphia: J. B. Lippincott Co., 1965); Mark Gibbs and T. Ralph Morton, *God's Frozen People* (Philadelphia: The Westminster Press, 1964).

with the contemporary world. It must not, however, turn to the world for its norms of basic life and character. In its apology to the "secular man," it has sometimes been guilty of drawing its norms from the world and feeding them back to the world.

Genuine worship in the church is the secret of renewal. It is only in worship that the community is edified. If it does not take place in the church it does not take place anywhere. Renewal is not an end in itself but a result of sincere worship. Vatican Council II declared: "The liturgy is the outstanding means by which the faithful can express their lives, and manifest to others the mystery of Christ and the real nature of the true church." The Documents acknowledge that the liturgy "does not exhaust the entire activity of the church. . . . Nevertheless the liturgy is the summit toward which the activity of the church is directed; at the same time it is the fountain from which all her power flows."[3] The Free Churches would doubtless reverse this order. Worship is certainly the source of the church's power, but the summit is reached in the life and ministry of the church for which worship prepares the faithful. Life and ministry are an extension of worship.

Church renewal is not the same thing as liturgical renewal. The liturgical renewal movement is primarily concerned with a reformation of the liturgy with a "profound interest in the origins and meanings of the church's historic forms and practices of worship, and a concern for their relevance to the problems of our contemporary world."[4] Church renewal is concerned with the revival of spiritual vitality in the lives of God's people.

The thesis of this chapter is that true worship will bring new life in the church. In a sense, it is a discussion of the objectives and the results of worship. As the branches must be vitally connected with the vine, so must the church itself be vitally related to the source of its life, the living Christ. There is need for constant renewal of a sense of God's presence and power.

Renewal demands sound theology. As Joseph Sittler has said, since

---

[3]*The Documents of Vatican II,* ed. Walter M. Abbott (New York: Guild Press [Angelus Books], 1966), pp. 137, 142.

[4]Shepherd, *The Liturgy and the Christian Faith* (Greenwich: The Seabury Press, 1966), p. 1.

man is multiphasic, and since worship is the multiphasic witness of
the church to the presence and power of God, liturgical renewal must
relate to man's basic impoverishment. Effort at church renewal will
end in failure if it attempts to use the liturgical movement "to lubri-
cate temperamental dispositions toward ceremonial scrupulosity, ritual prissiness, or the multitude of marginal ritual cosmetics to reduce
to banality a profound need of man."[5] God's power to transform
man's basic nature must be truly acknowledged if the church is to
realize renewal.

The spirit of worship may be lost while the form remains. This is
true in both liturgical and free types of worship. On the other hand,
the vital spirit of true religion may be experienced in both liturgical
and free patterns of worship. The church is primarily concerned with
motivation. Without the motivation prompted by the love of God and
vitalized by his spirit, the programs and activities of the church tend
to enervate the very life of God's people.

Worship is the fountainhead of all the ministries of the church—
indeed, the "life of the church." If this fountain grows stale from
disuse or becomes clogged from foreign pollutions, the life of the
church will ebb and its ministries diminish or cease altogether. This is
why there must be a revival of worship before there can be church
renewal. A plea for a serious restudy and effort at realistic worship
is not necessarily a plea for more form or more embellishment of art
and symbolism, but a more intelligent use of resource materials
and principles with a view to combining form and content with
spirit. What is needed is a real encounter in fellowship with God. It
may be true that many churches are seeking to escape this real encounter by taking refuge in the liturgy.

J. S. Whale issued an appropriate warning. Instead of putting off
our shoes from our feet, because the place whereon we stand is holy
ground, we are taking nice photographs of the burning bush from
suitable angles. We are chanting about theories of atonement with
our feet on the mantelpiece, instead of kneeling down before the
wounds of Christ. Whale goes on to say that, apart from worship,
Christianity is no more than archaeology, a museum piece for anti-

---

[5]Shepherd, *Worship in Scripture and Tradition*, p. 8.

quarians. In the worship of the church the Christian religion is given to us in all its meaning. "The church lives, not on ideas about God, but on God's grace itself, mediated by his spirit in corporate worship."[6]

A Conscious Relationship with God

The first step toward renewal in the church is the consciousness of a personal relationship with God. This can come about only in worship. If the first duty of man is to glorify God, the first privilege of man is to learn to enjoy him in personal communion. Worship is not primarily utilitarian. God is worshiped for his own sake, and true worship results in the glory of God. God is always seeking man's fellowship. Augustine realized this as he prayed,

Too late loved I thee, O thou beauty of ancient days, Yet ever new! Too late loved I thee! And behold, Thou wert within, and I abroad, and there I searched for thee; deformed I, plunging amid those fair forms, which thou hast made. Thou wert with me, but I was not with thee . . . thou touchest me, and I burned for thy peace.

A new awareness of the transcendent holiness of God and the acceptance of his cleansing grace will bring renewal. The church needs to recall Isaiah's deep consciousness of God in the commanding vision in the Temple, or Paul's Damascus road experience as he heard the voice of the Lord and was blinded by the light of the Lord's outshining holiness, or the early church assembled in the breaking of bread and in prayers, waiting for God, as they suddenly became aware of his presence manifested in the tongues of fire. New experiences in worship bring new revelations of God and his kingdom and new perspectives on life.

Confrontation with the holy God brings judgment. It is impossible for a man to confront Calvary or the resurrection without being challenged to the depth of his personhood. Unless he faces the cross honestly, his own religiosity and respectability and even his so-called mental health might be threatened. The honest man goes to worship because he is guilty. He has a bad conscience which is always with

---

[6]*Christian Doctrine* (Cambridge: The Cambridge University Press, 1952), p. 152.

him; it is chronic. But God's judgment also brings cleansing and forgiveness to him. "The blood of Jesus his Son cleanses us from all sin" (1 John 1:7). God's judgment and forgiveness are creative, prompting in man positive cooperation with God. As James Stewart has said, in true forgiveness, the judgment itself will seem transformed. "It is not the remission of a penalty; it is the restoration of a relationship."[7]

Forgiveness brings renewal. It produces holiness of character in man. To receive God's cleansing power is to obtain the likeness of his character. Charles Trentham says, "Christo-centric worship causes the character of the man of Nazareth to pass creatively before us until we long to be like him. As our longing passes into prayer, God's power works regeneratingly within us, and we are made whole."[8]

Building Up the Church

The church is built up and unified in worship. Where there is no worship, there is no unity. Man seeks fellowship with his fellowman in one way or another. The common worship of one Lord assures that fellowship and unity. Paul said, "There is one body and one spirit, . . . one Lord, one faith, one baptism, one God and Father of us all, who is above all and through all and in all" (Eph. 4:4-6). Unity in worship builds up the body of Christ.

Individual Christians mutually strengthen one another in worship. Even the physical presence of other Christians is a source of joy and strength to the believer. Man was created in the form of a physical body, and the Son of God appeared in a body and was raised in a body. The church is composed of persons who acknowledge their dependence upon one another. Each contributes something to his fellow members, for worship is cumulative. As the church comes for worship week by week one new experience builds upon previous experiences until one Lord's Day the dynamic of God's presence surges forth in revival.

In worship the church experiences forgiveness and thus becomes a forgiving community. Confession of one's sins in the presence of a

---

[7]*A Faith to Proclaim* (New York: Charles Scribner's Sons, 1953), p. 63.
[8]"Some Theological Bases of Worship," *The Review and Expositor*, LXII, No. 3 (Summer, 1965), 271.

brother is the profoundest kind of humiliation. Confession hurts and cuts a man down. It is a dreadful blow to his pride. Bonhoeffer observed, "In the presence of a psychiatrist I can only be a sick man; in the presence of a Christian brother I can dare to be a sinner."[9] Let a man beware of making a pious profession as a pretense for confession. Worship is costly just as discipleship is costly. Worship is a part of discipleship. Indeed, there is no place in worship for "cheap grace."

Christian Nurture for the Individual

One of the purposes of worship is the edification of the individual. It is wrong to base the necessity of worship on its usefulness, but it is equally wrong not to keep in mind the usefulness of worship for the individual worshiper. In fact, the key to the building up of the body of Christ is the building up of the individual Christian. Church renewal can come only through personal renewal.

Christian nurture has its foundation in public worship, which is the fountainhead for all other areas of Christian nurture in the church. The Sunday School, the training units, the service groups, and other educational organizations find their inspiration in worship. In these smaller groups worship is also provided as a means of edifying the individual. Education is "built into every experience of a worshiping congregation." There must also be education for worship.[10]

Edification means the building up of the individual—the mind through instruction, perception, and discernment; the emotions through the energizing of interpersonal relationship; the conscience through the sensitizing power of God's spirit; and the will in its motivation to action. Edification does not mean merely peace of mind but a preparation for battle. The chief nature of the new life in Christ is warfare and struggle. To grow in grace does not mean that we progressively root out sin in our lives. It means that we are progressively more aware of sin's subtleties, progressively more conscious of God's love and forgiveness, progressively bolder and less apprehensive as we live more fully by his power and grace.

---

[9]*Op. cit.*, p. 109.

[10]See Randolph C. Miller, *Christian Nurture and the Church* (New York: Charles Scribner's Sons, 1961), chap. 7.

Worship has healing power for the individual worshiper. Man finds his wholeness in proper relationship to God. This Jesus taught and demonstrated in his miracles of healing. Man becomes a new creature in Christ. The psalmist prayed, "Create in me a clean heart, O God; and renew a right spirit within me" (Psalm 51:10, KJV). The Christian finds peace and assurance in proportion to his wholeness in Christ. Man's physical and psychological needs find in worship a creative dynamic which produces wholeness in human relationships.

Man is seeking to be a free person, but he feels bound by his finiteness and his weaknesses. In worship our true selves are handed back to us. The individual matures only as he finds edification in the worship of God. Paul said that Christ frees us in order that we may be free to grow in the life of the Spirit. The fruits of the Spirit —love, joy, peace, patience, kindness, goodness, faithfulness, gentleness, self-control—are realized only when men walk with Christ. The individual finds his highest achievement in public worship. William Temple said, "Throughout our growth as Christians, worship is a duty; as we advance, it becomes a delight; and at all times a true act of worship is the fulfillment—for a moment—of the true destiny of our being."[11]

Personal edification involves ethical and moral responsibility. Worship results in the commitment of the self, which includes one's abilities, his possessions, and his opportunities. The doctrine of Paul's union with Christ was "the sheet-anchor of his ethics." Along with the motive to seek the mind of Christ is God's gift of power for living. Paul said, "I am ready for anything through the strength of him who lives within me" (Phil. 4:13, Phillips[12]).

The Church in the World

The church that finds God in common worship will also take God into the common life. In the broadest sense, worship is the glorifying of God in the common life. In too many instances worship has been used as mere escapism. Then worship ceases to be inspirational and

---

[11]*William Temple's Teachings,* ed. A. E. Baker (Philadelphia: The Westminster Press, 1951), p. 107.

[12]From *The New Testament in Modern English,* © J. B. Phillips, 1958. Used with permission of The Macmillan Company.

redemptive. Worship is a life dedicated to God, not a fugitive hour in a week devoted to unscrupulous business. The renewed emphasis on the laity (people of God) provides a new challenge for the church at worship to become the church in the world, as I have discussed more fully in *The Christian Layman.*

In the worshiping church the line of impact for Christ is from pulpit to pew to pavement. The Christian life is not the following of a set of rules but is a dynamic engagement—a way of buying and selling, of paying taxes, of relating to sexual behavior, of treating one's neighbor, of sharing with the poor, of relating to the moral outcast, of giving support to political leaders. The worship of the church is the stimulus to the Christian life in the world. God is as interested in the mill as in the minister and in the counting house as in the cathedral.

Church renewal comes when the church makes itself relevant to man's world. Many of the elements of worship—the body, the voice, the ear, the eye, the hands, food, water, song, prayer, and the affirmation of belief—are also the "materials of social and cultural action."[13] Although the primary object of worship is God and the primary object of social and cultural action is man, the two find their goal in the unified action of a genuine dialogue between God and man. The practical denial of God's claim in our lives is perhaps more serious than our intellectual doubts and denials. We come nearer to obliterating the recognition of God that exists in the bottom of our hearts by denying God in our deeds than we can by denying him with the top of our minds. He who sincerely worships God with his mouth will also serve God with his hands.

Worship is related to Christian vocation. For the church there can be no dichotomy of worship and work. As Luther said, to pray is to work, and to work is to pray. Every revelation of God is a call to vocation. Man is religious not only when he prays; his work is religiously done, his recreation religiously enjoyed, and his food and drink religiously received. He does his duty religiously, "for duty to him is the stern daughter of the voice of God."[14]

---

[13]See Richard M. Spielmann, *History of Christian Worship* (New York: The Seabury Press, 1966), p. 162.

[14]Temple, *Nature, Man and God,* p. 334.

The God who forgives his people as they worship in the church demands that they carry this same spirit of justice into the world. For the Christian the whole world becomes a temple, and in every part of the earth—shoe shop, factory, mines, and scientist's laboratory—time flows into eternity. The church which seeks to do its duty toward God will also perform its duties toward the world. The world may be unholy anywhere, in the church or outside of it, and at any place it may be the throne of grace where God meets his creation and finds it responsive to his will.

In worship the church sees itself as a unique form of human society. Fellowship with Christ produces in the church a new solidarity with all other communities—the nations, races, tongues, and peoples who constitute the world.[15] The church in serious dialogue with God will also seek relevant dialogue with the world. To worship with the primary purpose of building up the institution is idolatry. But for the church to be preoccupied and satisfied with its own esoteric experiences in worship is worse than idolatry; it is hypocrisy.

The church at worship remembers Jesus Christ as present in the "world of the flesh." A new meeting with the incarnate, living Christ will bring a new awareness of the church's involvement in the world. W. H. Auden has captured this truth in his Christmas oratorio, *For the Time Being*. Because Christ came into the world in human flesh, the world has been given a new significance:

> Remembering the stable where for once in our lives
> Everything became a you and nothing an It
>   gives significant meaning to the stable.
>   In the meantime
> there are bills to be paid, machines to be kept in repair,
> Irregular verbs to learn, the Time Being to redeem
> From insignificance. . . .
>
> He is the life.
> Love him in the world of the flesh;
> And at your marriage all its occasions shall dance for joy.[16]

---

[15]Paul S. Minear, *Horizons of Christian Community* (St. Louis: The Bethany Press, 1959), p. 125.

[16]Quoted by Robert McAfee Brown, *The Spirit of Protestantism* (New York: Oxford University Press, 1961), p. 117.

Augustine, writing about the City of God and the sinful, doomed City of the World, observed,

"These men you may see today thronging the churches with us, tomorrow will be crowding the theaters with the Godless. But we have the less reason to despair of the reclamation even of such persons, if among our most declared enemies there are now some, unknown to themselves, who are destined to become our friends. In truth, these two cities are entangled together in this world, and intermixed until the Last Judgment effects their separation."

The restoration of meaning in contemporary life can come only if the church carries meaning out into the world. Whatever glory may be ours must be encountered in the place where we find ourselves now in the world. If the conscience of the world is to be affected it must come through the God-consciousness of the church in the world. Business and politics and production and communication will become righteous only as the people of God live righteously in these various areas of the common life.

Motivation for Service

The church's motivation for service will be found in the inspiration of its worship. There is a certain rhythm in the Christian life which moves from the experience of worship to the valley of service. "One must rise to the mount of transfiguration and then return to the valley of everyday living . . . to remain on the mountain top is to become sterile. To stay too long in the valley is to become exhausted of the spiritual."[17]

As has been pointed out earlier, the biblical word *leitourgia,* translated "worship," actually means service. We speak of worship as going to church, and service as going out into action in the world. Our worship of God is part of his service, and our service a part of his worship.

The church finds its ministry by sharing the ministry of Christ which it discovers in its worship. Jesus said, "Whoever would be great among you must be your servant . . . even as the Son of man came not to be served but to serve, and to give his life as a ransom

---

[17]Allen, *op. cit.,* p. 112.

for many" (Matt. 20:26-28). The church does not exist for its own comfortable enjoyment of worship; it is redeemed for ministry. It does not exist as a pure fellowship in a vacuum. It is created within an empirical context for a concrete purpose. In worship man comes to feel the same compassion and desire to serve that Christ feels. The church has a concern for people in their current condition, not in the ideal or the abstract but in the raw, concrete situation.

The church is motivated to minister not only to its own members but also to those on the outside. One of God's ministers who understands worship in its deeper implications has stated it perceptively:

> While there is a lower class
> I am in it.
> While there is a criminal element
> I am of it.
> While there is a man in jail
> I am not free.[18]

In the context of worship the church becomes a ministering fellowship. Its people serve as a healing community in the world. The care of souls is the responsibility of the entire church. All the laity find renewal for ministry in worship.[19]

The dynamic experience of worship is a creative force breaking out of bounds so far as institution and tradition are concerned. The church is compelled to find new ways of ministering to a new world condition. Worship brings new and fresh experiences of the Holy Spirit, making the church aware of new opportunities for sharing the good news of Jesus Christ. The church must not become static with no place for creative deviation. As one critic has expressed it:

> All our fathers have been churchmen
> Nineteen hundréd years or so
> And to every new suggestion
> They always answered "No."[20]

---

[18]Howard Thurman, *The Inward Journey* (New York: Harper & Bros., 1961), p. 101 f.

[19]For a more thorough discussion see C. W. Brister, *op. cit.*, chap. 4.

[20]Horton, *op cit.*, p. 90.

Evangelism and Missions

Evangelism must find its source in worship if it is to be genuine evangelism. It is a heresy to separate worship from evangelism. C. E. Autrey places worship and evangelism in the same context. He defines the church as a "body of believers in Christ banded together by covenant for worship, Bible study, prayer, fellowship, service, and world evangelization."[21]

In an era when the tides of evangelism ebb and the fires of zeal burn low, the hope for renewal may be found in worship. Organizations and campaigns and human activities are essential in God's work, but they alone cannot bring a revival of evangelism. It is the week-by-week experience of worship which keeps the church renewed for sharing the gospel. The burning heart is a result of fellowship in the presence of the living Christ. Because of what had happened in her own life as she had talked with Jesus, the woman of Sychar rushed eagerly to others with the invitation, "Come see a man" who told me about my life and who brought new life into my existence. Her motive was sharing the good news. This is always the motive for evangelism.

Salvation does not come through pastors, or through evangelists, or through the "priesthood of believers," but through God's "sheer grace." This treasure is a free gift and cannot be earned by any ecclesiastical form or action. Any demand for man to guarantee this gift by his own efforts is sheer humanism based upon presumption. In dialogue with Christ the church catches a vision of the world of unbelievers. Believers hear Christ saying, "Lift up your eyes, and see how the fields are already white for harvest" (John 4:35).

The common experience of God's power felt in worship will attract lost persons to church services. In the fellowship of God's church the presence of God is felt as judgment for the sinner. Such an atmosphere brings him to a spirit of repentance. Thus, worship creates the atmosphere in which the unbeliever is encouraged to acknowledge Christ as Saviour and Lord in public commitment. Worship also encourages the new Christian to enter into the fellowship of the church. As Arthur C. Archibald says, "The New Testament knows nothing

---

[21]*Basic Evangelism* (Grand Rapids: Zondervan Publishing House, 1959), p. 51.

of evangelism apart from the church. Everything goes out from the churches and draws back into the churches."[22]

Worship is tridimensional. It brings the worshipers close to Christ in the context of congregational fellowship; it extends into all the activities of the life of the community; and it carries the relationships of God to man and man to man, which are knit together in Christ, to the boundaries of the world. When the church truly worships, it cannot but become missionary and evangelistic. A missionary of Christ is one who lets his own convictions be known, approaches other faiths as systems of conviction held by honored friends, and depends upon God (not upon his own power in any form) for any conversions that may take place. There is no better means of preparing the church for life in this horizontal dimension than honest, open-souled, sensitively responsive, corporate Christian worship; in that fellowship one develops towards one's neighbor the same depth of concern expressed in the love of Christ for the world.[23]

Seeking Christian Unity

True worship in the church will move toward the goal of Christian unity among the people of God. The conscious worship of the living Christ tends to unite all people who worship him and to elicit the yearning for all to be one as Christ and the Father are one. True ecumenicism can be realized in true worship. Christian unity is a "dynamic and living thing" which may be realized only in a spirit of humility and worship. Baptists, among others, hold that it is possible to achieve a spirit of unity within a diversity of institutions if Christ is worshiped and served as the head of his church.[24] This spirit of unity is first realized in the local congregation and then reaches out to embrace all who acknowledge Christ as Saviour and Lord. All Christians should be willing to join all other Christians in the worship of our Lord, regardless of the church or organizational affiliation. Where the Spirit of the Lord is, there is liberty; where there is liberty, there is unity.

---

[22]*New Testament Evangelism* (Philadelphia: Judson Press, 1946), pp. 40,49.

[23]Horton, *op. cit.*, p. 75.

[24]For a good discussion of this view see W. R. Estep, *Baptists and Christian Unity,* especially chapter 10.

There are many encouraging signs today which point toward a growing spirit of unity among God's people. For example, the Roman Catholic Church's reform in its liturgy and its relaxing of certain practices among its people encourages dialogue with other Christian bodies. Also, many Protestant churches are giving serious study to the meaning of content and orderliness in worship, thus encouraging discipline in overcoming extreme individualism. Ministers and local congregations in various churches have been sharing pulpits with those of different denominational affiliation. Local churches in some denominations not affiliated with the National or World Councils of Churches work with local church councils at the community level.

In a number of instances Free Church groups and Roman Catholics have participated in joint worship services. For example, the Fort Worth Area Council of Churches, which includes various Protestant and Roman Catholic groups, sponsored a joint service of worship on January 23, 1966. The service was held in the sanctuary of the Holy Family Church, a Roman Catholic Church. Churches whose ministers participated in the service included an Episcopal church, a Baptist church, a Methodist church, a Presbyterian church, a Christian church, a Lutheran church, and the host Roman Catholic Church. The order of service included a call to prayer by minister and people, the hymn "The Church's One Foundation," an invocation, a Bible reading (1 Cor. 12:12-27), the hymn "Praise to the Lord," brief messages of meditation by the Roman Catholic priest and a Disciples of Christ minister, a litany of thanksgiving in three parts (thanksgiving, confession, petition) led by three different ministers, a choral amen, a benediction, and the hymn "Now Thank We All Our God." The sanctuary was crowded beyond capacity. The people entered into the service with zeal. The congregational singing of the hymns resounded in a spirit of joy and unity. A spirit of honesty pervaded the service as people from the various congregations acknowledged their differences. All of them seemed bent upon seeking unity in the spirit of Christ.

Convocations on world missions and evangelism are being held in various parts of the world. Into these meetings come people from various churches—Orthodox, Episcopal, Roman Catholic, Lutheran, Baptist, Methodist, Presbyterian, Disciples, Pentecostal, and other

Free Church groups. Reports on such a convocation held in Berlin, Germany, 1966, indicate a spirit of hope and enthusiasm. Whereas people with differing theological positions cannot agree thoroughly, they can join in a spirit of worship when Christ is acknowledged as head of his church.

F. D. Maurice gave this apostrophe to worship:

The worshiper has found that object to which the eyes of himself and all creatures were meant to be directed, in beholding which they attain the perfection of their being, while they lose all the feeling of selfish propriation which is incompatible with perfection. They gaze upon him who is the all-embracing Love, with whom no selfishness can dwell, the all-clear and distinguishing Truth, from which darkness and falsehood flee away; and they are changed into the same image, and their praises are only the responses to the joy with which he looks upon his redeemed creation and declares it very good.[25]

In every service of worship, whatever and wherever the congregation, hymns of praise and prayer point to the eschaton of God's kingdom. Every new vision of God is a foregleam of the triumphant appearance of the risen Lord. This hope was portrayed in the experience of John as he worshiped on the Lord's Day:

Then I saw a new heaven and a new earth; for the first heaven and the first earth had passed away, and the sea was no more. . . . And I heard a great voice from the throne saying, "Behold, the dwelling of God is with men. He will dwell with them, and they shall be his people, and God himself shall be with them; he will wipe away every tear from their eyes, and death shall be no more, neither shall there be mourning nor crying nor pain any more, for the former things have passed away. . . . I am the Alpha and the Omega, the first and the last, the beginning and the end." . . . He who testifies to these things says, "Surely I am coming soon." Amen. Come, Lord Jesus! (Rev. 21:1-4; 22:13-21).

---

[25]Quoted by Davies, *Worship and Theology in England: From Watts and Wesley to Maurice, 1690-1850*, p. 300 f.

Bibliography

General and Theological

ABBA, RAYMOND. *Principles of Christian Worship.* New York: Oxford University Press, 1957.

ABBOTT, WALTER M. (ed.). *The Documents of Vatican II.* New York: Guild Press (Angelus Books), 1966.

ALLEN, J. P. *Reality in Worship.* Nashville: Convention Press, 1965.

BAILLIE, DONALD M. *God Was in Christ.* New York: Charles Scribner's Sons, 1948.

BAILLIE, JOHN. *Our Knowledge of God.* New York: Charles Scribner's Sons, 1959.

————. *The Sense of the Presence of God.* New York: Charles Scribner's Sons, 1962.

BARTH, KARL. Translated by G. W. Bromiley. *Church Dogmatics,* Vol. IV, part 2. Edinburgh: T. & T. Clark, 1958.

BLACKWOOD, ANDREW W. "Public Worship," *Twentieth Century Encyclopedia of Religious Knowledge:* An Extension of the New Schaff-Herzog Encyclopedia of Religious Knowledge, ed. LEFFERTS A. LOETSCHER. Grand Rapids: Baker Book House, 1955.

————. *The Fine Art of Public Worship.* Nashville: Abingdon-Cokesbury, 1939.

BONHOEFFER, DIETRICH. *Life Together.* London: SCM Press, Ltd., n.d.

BRIGHTMAN, EDGAR S. *The Spiritual Life.* New York: Abingdon Press, 1942.

BRISTER, C. W. *Pastoral Care in the Church.* New York: Harper & Row, 1964.

BRUNNER, EMIL. *Revelation and Reason.* Philadelphia: The Westminster Press, 1958.

BYINGTON, EDWIN H. *The Quest for Experience in Worship.* Garden City, New York: Doubleday and Doran Co., 1929.

CASPARI, W. "Practical Theology," *The New Schaff-Herzog Encyclopedia of Religious Knowledge,* ed. SAMUEL M. JACKSON. New York: Funk & Wagnalls, 1912.

COFFIN, HENRY SLOANE. *The Public Worship of God: A Source Book.* Philadelphia: The Westminster Press, 1946.

COLEMAN, A. DUP. "Worship," *The New Schaff-Herzog Encyclopedia of Religious Knowledge.* Vol. XII.

COME, ARNOLD B. *Human Spirit and Holy Spirit.* Philadelphia: The Westminster Press, 1959.

CONNER, W. T. *Christian Doctrine.* Nashville: Broadman Press, 1949.

DANA, H. E. *A Manual of Ecclesiology.* Kansas City, Kansas: Central Seminary Press, 1944.

DARGAN, E. C. *Ecclesiology.* Louisville: Charles T. Dearing, 1897.

DAVIES, HORTON. *Christian Worship: Its History and Meaning.* New York: Abingdon Press, 1957.

————. *Worship and Theology in England: The Ecumenical Century, 1900–1965.* Princeton, N. J.: Princeton University Press, 1965.

————. *Worship and Theology in England: From Watts and Wesley to Maurice, 1690–1850.* Princeton, N.J.: Princeton University Press, 1961.

————. "Worship in the Old Testament." *The Interpreter's Dictionary of the Bible,* ed. GEORGE BUTTRICK. Nashville: Abingdon Press, 1962. Vol. IV.

DAVIS, H. GRADY. *Why We Worship.* Philadelphia: Muhlenberg Press, 1961.

DEVAN, S. ARTHUR. *Ascent to Zion.* New York: The Macmillan Co., 1942.

DOBBINS, GAINES S. *The Church at Worship.* Nashville: Broadman Press, 1962.

EDERSHEIM, ALFRED. *The Life and Times of Jesus the Messiah.* Grand Rapids: Wm. B. Eerdmans Publishing Co., n.d. Vol. II.

EDWALL, PEHR, HAYMAN, ERIC, and MAXWELL, W. D. (eds.). *Ways of Worship.* New York: Harper & Bros., 1951.

ESTEP, WILLIAM R. *Baptists and Christian Unity.* Nashville: Broadman Press, 1966.

FAIRBAIRN, A. M. *A Philosophy of the Christian Religion.* New York: The Macmillan Co., 1923.

FORSYTH, P. T. *The Person and Place of Jesus Christ.* Boston: Pilgrim Press, n.d.

GWALTNEY, L. L. *The World's Greatest Decade: The Times and the Baptists.* Birmingham: Birmingham Printing Co., 1947.

HAHN, WILHELM. *Worship and Congregation.* Translated by GEOFFREY BUSWELL. Richmond: John Knox Press, 1963.

HARDIN, H. GRADY, QUILLIAN, JOSEPH D., and WHITE, JAMES F. *The Celebration of The Gospel.* Nashville: Abingdon Press, 1964.

HAROUTOUNIAN. *God with Us: A Theology of Transpersonal Life.* Philadelphia: The Westminster Press, 1966.

HAYS, BROOKS and STEELY, JOHN E. *The Baptist Way of Life.* Englewood Cliffs, N. J.: Prentice-Hall Inc., 1963.

HEDLEY, GEORGE. *Christian Worship: Some Meanings and Means.* New York: The Macmillan Co., 1958.

————. *The Symbol of the Faith: A Study of the Apostles' Creed.* New York: The Macmillan Co., 1948.

HEILER, FRIEDRICH. *The Spirit of Worship.* London: Hodder & Stoughton, 1926.

HEIM, KARL. *Spirit and Truth: The Nature of Evangelical Christianity.*

Translated by EDGAR P. DICKIE. London: The Lutterworth Press, 1935.

HERBERT, A. G. *Liturgy and Society: The Function of the Church in the Modern World.* London: Faber and Faber Ltd., 1961.

HERRLIN, OLOF. *Divine Service: Liturgy in Perspective.* Translated by GENE J. LUND. Philadelphia: Fortress Press, 1960.

HERRMANN, WILHELM. *The Communion of the Christian with God.* Translated by J. S. STANYON. New York: G. P. Putnam's Sons, 1913.

HOCKING, WILLIAM EARNEST. *The Meaning of God in Human Experience.* New Haven: Yale University Press, 1912.

HORTON, DOUGLAS. *The Meaning of Worship.* New York: Harper & Bros., 1959.

HUME, DAVID. *The World's Living Religions.* New York: Charles Scribner's Sons, 1924.

JONES, RUFUS M. *New Studies in Mystical Religion.* New York: The Macmillan Co., 1927.

KALB, FRIEDRICH. *Theology of Worship in Seventeenth Century Lutheranism.* Translated by HENRY P. A. HAMANN. St. Louis, Missouri: Concordia Publishing House, 1965.

KAY, J. ALLEN. *The Nature of Christian Worship.* London: The Upworth Press, 1953.

KOENKER, ERNEST BENJAMIN. *The Liturgical Renaissance in the Roman Catholic Church.* St. Louis: Concordia Publishing House, 1966.

KRUMM, JOHN M. *Modern Heresies.* Greenwich, Connecticut: The Seabury Press, 1961.

LEE, F. G. *Glossary of Liturgical and Ecclesiastical Terms.* London: Bernard Quaritch, 1877.

LOCKHART, WILLIAM S. *The Ministry of Worship.* St. Louis: Christian Board of Publications, 1927.

MCNUTT, WILLIAM ROY. *Worship in the Churches.* Philadelphia: The Judson Press, 1941.

MACLEOD, DONALD. *Word and Sacrament: A Preface to Preaching and Worship.* Englewood Cliffs, N.J.: Prentice-Hall, Inc., 1960.

MAXWELL, W. D. *Concerning Worship.* London: Oxford University Press, 1949.

MICKLEM, NATHANIEL (ed.). *Christian Worship: Studies in Its History and Meaning.* London: Oxford University Press, 1936.

MILLER, SAMUEL H. *The Life of the Church.* New York: Harper & Bros., 1953.

MOODY, DALE. *Christ and the Church.* Grand Rapids: Wm. B. Eerdmans Publishing Co., 1963.

MULLINS, E. Y. *Freedom and Authority in Religion.* Philadelphia: Griffith and Rowland Press, 1913.

————. *The Christian Religion in its Doctrinal Expression.* Nashville: The Sunday School Board of the Southern Baptist Convention, 1941.

NIEBUHR, REINHOLD. "The Weaknesses of Common Worship in American Protestantism," *Christianity in Crisis,* May 28, 1951.

ORR, JAMES (ed.). *The International Standard Bible Encyclopaedia.* 5 vols. Chicago: The Howard-Severance Co., 1915.

OTTO, RUDOLPH. *The Idea of the Holy: An Inquiry into the Non-rational Factor in the Idea of the Divine and Its Relation to the Rational.* Translated by JOHN W. HARVEY. New York: Oxford University Press, 1950.

PATTISON, T. HARWOOD. *Public Worship.* Philadelphia: American Baptist Publication Society, 1900.

PAYNE, ERNEST A. *The Fellowship of Believers: Baptist Thought and Practice Yesterday and Today.* London: The Carey Kingsgate Press, Ltd., 1952.

PEARCE, J. WINSTON. *Come, Let Us Worship.* Nashville: Broadman Press, 1965.

PHIFER, KENNETH G. *A Protestant Case for Liturgical Renewal.* Philadelphia: The Westminster Press, 1965.

"Public Worship," *Review and Expositor,* LXIII, No. 2 (Spring, 1966).

"Public Worship," *Review and Expositor,* XII, No. 3 (Summer, 1965).

REED, LUTHER D. *Worship: A Study of Corporate Devotion.* Philadelphia: Muhlenberg Press, 1959.

RICHARDSON, ALAN (ed.). *A Theological Wordbook of the Bible.* New York: The Macmillan Co., 1955.

RICHARDSON, CYRIL C. *Library of Christian Classics, Early Christian Fathers.* Philadelphia: The Westminster Press, 1953. Vol. I.

ROBINSON, H. WHEELER. *Baptist Principles.* London: The Carey Kingsgate Press, Ltd., 1938.

_____. *Redemption and Revelation in the Actuality of History.* New York: Harper & Bros., 1942.

_____. *The Life and Faith of the Baptists.* London: The Carey Kingsgate Press, Ltd., 1946.

SANGSTER, W. E. *Secret of the Radiant Life.* New York: Abingdon Press, 1957.

SCHALM, BERNARD. *The Church at Worship.* Grand Rapids: Baker Book House, 1962.

SEGLER, FRANKLIN. *A Theology of Church and Ministry.* Nashville: Broadman Press, 1960.

SEIDENSPINNER, CHARLES. "Genius of Protestant Worship," *Religion in Life* (Spring, 1949).

SEIDENSPINNER, CLARENCE. *Form and Freedom in Christian Worship.* Chicago: Willet-Clark & Co., 1941.

SHEPHERD, MASSEY H., JR. *The Liturgical Renewal of the Church.* New York: Oxford University Press, 1960.

_____. *The Liturgy and The Christian Faith.* Greenwich: The Seabury Press, 1966.

_____. *The Worship of the Church.* Greenwich: The Seabury Press, 1961.

SKOGLUND, JOHN E. *Worship in the Free Churches.* Valley Forge: Judson Press, 1965.

SMART, JAMES D. *The Interpretation of Scripture.* Philadelphia: The Westminster Press, 1961.

SPERRY, WILLARD L. *Reality in Worship.* New York: The Macmillan Co., 1925.

STAGG, FRANK. *New Testament Theology.* Nashville: Broadman Press, 1962.

STANFIELD, V. L. *The Christian Worshiping.* Nashville: Convention Press, 1965.

STAUFFER, ETHELBERT. *New Testament Theology.* Translated by JOHN MARSH. London: SCM Press, Ltd., 1955.

TEILHARD DE CHARDIN, PIERRE. *The Phenomenon of Man.* New York: Harper, 1959.

TEMPLE, WILLIAM. *Nature, Man, and God.* London: Macmillan & Co., Ltd., 1956.

————. *The Hope of a New World.* New York: The Macmillan Co., 1942.

UNDERHILL, EVELYN. *Worship.* New York: Harper & Bros., 1937.

VAN DUSEN, HENRY P. *Spirit, Son and Father.* New York: Charles Scribner's Sons, 1958.

VOGT, VON OGDEN. *Modern Worship.* New Haven: Yale University Press, 1927.

VON ALLMEN, J. J. *Worship: Its Theology and Practice.* New York: Oxford University Press, 1965.

WHALE, J. S. *Christian Doctrine.* Cambridge: The Cambridge University Press, 1952.

————. *The Protestant Tradition.* New York: Oxford University Press, 1955.

WIEMAN AND HORTON. *The Growth of Religion.* New York: Willet-Clark & Co., 1938.

WINWARD, STEPHEN F. *The Reformation of our Worship.* Richmond: John Knox Press, 1965.

History

ASCHAM, JOHN B. *The Religion of Israel.* New York: Abingdon Press, 1918.

AUGUSTINUS, AURELIUS. *The City of God.* Book I, translated by MARCUS DODS. New York: Charles Scribner's Sons, 1877.

BAINTON, ROLAND. *Here I Stand.* New York: Abingdon Press, 1950.

BAKER, ROBERT A. *A Summary of Christian History.* Nashville: Broadman Press, 1959.

BARNES, W. W. *History of the Southern Baptist Convention.* Nashville: Broadman Press, 1954.

BRIGHT, JOHN. "Modern Study of Old Testament Literature," *The Bible and the Ancient Near East,* ed. G. ERNEST WRIGHT. Garden City, New York: Doubleday & Co., Inc., 1961.

BROWN, ROBERT MCAFEE. *The Spirit of Protestantism.* New York: Oxford University Press, 1961.

BUTTRICK, GEORGE (ed.). "The Faith of Israel," *The Interpreter's Bible*. Nashville: Abingdon-Cokesbury Press, 1952. Vol. I.

CULLMANN, OSCAR. *Early Christian Worship*. London: SCM Press, Ltd., 1953.

DAVIES, HORTON. *The Worship of the English Puritans*. London: Westminster, Dacre Press, 1948.

DELLING, GERHARD. *Worship in the New Testament*. Translated by PERCY SCOTT. Philadelphia: The Westminster Press, 1962.

DE VAUX, ROLAND. *Ancient Israel: Its Life and Institutions*. Translated by JOHN McHUGH. London: McGraw-Hill Book Co., 1961.

DIX, DOM GREGORY. *The Shape of the Liturgy*. London: A & C Black, 1945.

DUCHENSE, L. *Christian Worship: Origin and Evolution*. London: S.P.C.K., 1947. New York: The Macmillan Co., 1931.

ESTEP, WILLIAM R. *The Anabaptist Story*. Nashville: Broadman Press, 1963.

FRAZIER, JAMES F. *The Golden Bough*. 1 vol. ed. New York: The Macmillan Co., 1930.

————. *The Worship of Nature*. New York: The Macmillan Co., 1926.

FREUD, SIGMUND. *Totem and Taboo*. Translated by A. A. BRILL. New York: Moffat, Yard and Co., 1918.

HARDIMAN, OSCAR. *History of Christian Worship*. Nashville: Cokesbury Press, 1937.

HISLOP, H. D. *Our Heritage in Public Worship*. Charles Scribner's Sons, 1935.

JONES, ILION T. *A Historical Approach to Evangelical Worship*. Nashville: Abingdon Press, 1954.

JONES, RUFUS M. *Faith and Practice of the Quakers*. New York: Harper & Bros., 1927.

LINDSAY, THOMAS M. *A History of the Reformation*. New York: Charles Scribner's Sons, 1916.

————. *The Church and the Ministry in the Early Centuries*. London: Hodder & Stoughton, Ltd., 1902.

LITELL, FRANKLIN H. *The Anabaptist View of the Church*. Boston: Star King Press, 1958.

LUMPKIN, WILLIAM L. *Baptist Confessions of Faith*. Philadelphia: Judson Press, 1959.

MACDONALD, ALEXANDER B. *Christian Worship in the Primitive Church*. Edinburgh: Clark, 1934.

MARTYR, JUSTIN. *The First Apology*. Translated by THOMAS B. FALLS. New York: Christian Heritage, Inc., 1948.

MAXWELL, W. D. *An Outline of Christian Worship*. New York: Oxford University Press, 1936.

————. *History of Worship in the Church of Scotland*. New York: Oxford University Press, 1955.

MOULE, C. F. D. *Worship in the New Testament*. Richmond: John Knox Press, 1961.

MOWINCKEL, SIGMUND OLAF PLYTT. *The Psalms in Israel's Worship.* Translated by D. R. AP-THOMAS. New York: Abingdon Press, 1962.

NIEBUHR, H. RICHARD, and WILLIAMS, DANIEL D. *The Ministry in Historical Perspectives.* New York: Harper & Bros., 1956.

OESTERLEY, W. O. E. *The Jewish Background of the Christian Liturgy.* Oxford: Clarendon Press, 1925.

RICHARDSON, R. D. "Christian Worship in the New Reformation." *Modern Churchman.* Vol. XL.

ROBINSON, JOHN A. T. *Liturgy Coming to Life.* Philadelphia: The Westminster Press, 1960.

SHEPHERD, MASSEY H., JR. *The Reform of Liturgical Worship.* New York: Oxford University Press, 1961.

————— (ed.). *Worship in Scripture and Tradition:* Essays by Members of the Theological Commission on Worship (North American Section) of the Commission on Faith and Order of the World Council of Churches. New York: Oxford University Press, 1963.

SNYDER, ROSS. "Prayer and Worship Re-examined," *Pastoral Psychology,* XI (March, 1960).

SPIELMANN, RICHARD M. *History of Christian Worship.* New York: The Seabury Press, 1966.

STREETER, B. H. *The Primitive Church.* New York: The Macmillan Co., 1929.

STRONG, JAMES. *The Tabernacle of Israel.* Grand Rapids: Baker Book House, 1952.

SWEET, WILLIAM WARREN. *Religion in the Development of American Culture, 1765-1840.* New York: Charles Scribner's Sons, 1952.

SWETE, HENRY BARCLAY. *Church Services and Service Books Before the Reformation.* London: S.P.C.K., 1896.

TERRIEN, SAMUEL. *The Psalms and Their Meaning for Today.* New York: Bobbs-Merrill Co., Inc., 1952.

TERTULLIAN. *Against Marcion.* Ante-Nicene Fathers, VII, chap. IV, 351-354.

TYLER, EDWARD B. *Primitive Culture.* 2 vols. New York: Holt, Rinehart & Winston, 1874.

VERDUIN, LEONARD. *The Reformers and Their Stepchildren.* Grand Rapids: Wm. B. Eerdmans Publishing Co., 1964.

WILLIAMS, J. PAUL. *What Americans Believe and How They Worship.* Rev. ed. New York: Harper & Row, 1962.

Psychology

ALLPORT, GORDON W. *The Individual and His Religion.* New York: The Macmillan Co., 1962.

BUCKHAM, JOHN WRIGHT. *Christianity and Personality.* New York: Round Table Press, Inc., 1936.

CLARK, WALTER HOUSTON. *The Psychology of Religion.* New York: The Macmillan Co., 1958.

FRANKL, VIKTOR E. *The Doctor and the Soul: An Introduction to Logo-*

therapy. Translated from German by RICHARD and CLARA WINSTON. New York: Alfred A. Knopf, 1955.

GREEVES, FREDERIC. *A Theology of the Cure of Souls.* New York: Channel Press, Inc., 1962.

JAMES, WILLIAM. *The Varieties of Religious Experience.* New York: Modern Library, 1902.

JOHNSON, PAUL. *The Psychology of Religion.* Nashville: Abingdon-Cokesbury Press, 1945.

JUNG, C. G., *Psychology and Religion, West and East.* New York: Pantheon, 1958.

LEE, ROY STUART. *Psychology and Worship.* London: SCM Press, Ltd., 1955.

McKENZIE, JOHN G. *Guilt: Its Meaning and Significance.* Nashville: Abingdon Press, 1962.

————. *Psychology, Psychotherapy, and Evangelicalism.* London: George Allen & Unwin Limited, 1940.

MILLER, ALEXANDER. *The Man in the Mirror: Studies in the Christian Understanding of Selfhood.* Garden City, New York: Doubleday & Co., Inc., 1958.

OATES, WAYNE E. *Anxiety in Christian Experience.* Philadelphia: The Westminster Press, 1955.

————. *Christ and Selfhood.* New York: Association Press, 1961.

————. *Religious Factors in Mental Illness.* New York: Association Press, 1955.

PRATT, J. B. *The Religious Consciousness: A Psychological Study.* New York: The Macmillan Co., 1920.

ROBERTS, DAVID E. *Psychotherapy and a Christian View of Man.* New York: Charles Scribner's Sons, 1951.

SHERRILL, LEWIS JOSEPH. *The Gift of Power.* New York: The Macmillan Co., 1955.

TILLICH, PAUL. *The Courage to Be.* New Haven: Yale University Press, 1952.

TOURNIER, PAUL. *A Doctor's Casebook in the Light of the Bible.* New York: Harper & Bros., 1960.

————. *The Meaning of Persons.* New York: Harper & Bros., 1957.

————. *The Whole Person in a Broken World.* Translated by JOHN and HELEN ROBERSTEIN. New York: Harper & Row, 1964.

Music

ASHTON, JOSEPH N. *Music in Worship: The Use of Music in the Church Service.* 3rd ed. Boston: Pilgrim Press, 1944.

BACON, A. *The True Function of Church Music.* Stockton: The Printwell Press, 1953.

BAILEY, ALBERT EDWARD. *The Gospel in Hymns: Backgrounds and Interpretations.* New York: Charles Scribner's Sons, 1950.

BENSON, LOUIS F. *The Hymnody of the Christian Church.* New York: Doubleday, Doran & Co., 1927.

BREED, DAVID R. *The History and Use of Hymns and Hymn Tune.* Westwood, New Jersey: Fleming H. Revell Co., 1934.

Christian Worship: A Hymnal. St. Louis: Christian Board of Publication, and Philadelphia: Judson Press, 1941.

COON, ZULA EVELYN. *O Worship the King—Services in Song.* Nashville: Broadman Press, 1957.

DAVIDSON, ARCHIBALD T. *Protestant Church Music in America.* Boston: E. C. Schirmer, 1933.

DAVIES, WALFORD, and GRACE, HARVEY. *Music and Worship.* New York: H. W. Gray Co., 1935.

DAVISON, ARCHIBALD T. *Protestant Church Music in America.* Boston: E. C. Schirmer, 1933.

DICKINSON, EDWARD. *Music in the History of the Western Church.* New York: Charles Scribner's Sons.

DOUGLAS, W. and ELLINWOOD, L. *Church Music in History and Practice.* New York: Charles Scribner's Sons, 1962.

ELLINWOOD, L. *The History of American Church Music.* New York: Morehouse-Barlow Co., 1953.

ETHERINGTON, CHARLES L. *Protestant Worship Music.* New York: Holt, Rinehart & Winston, 1962.

HOOPER, WILLIAM LOYD. *Church Music in Transition.* Nashville: Broadman Press, 1963.

HUGHES, EDWIN HOLT, *et. al. Worship in Music.* New York: The Abingdon Press, 1929.

The Hymnal. Philadelphia: Presbyterian Board of Christian Education, 1933.

The Hymnal of the Protestant Episcopal Church in the United States of America, 1940. New York: The Church Pension Fund, 1940.

JULIAN, JOHN (ed.). *A Dictionary of Hymnology.* 2 vols. New York: Dover Publishing Co., 1957.

KEITH, EDMOND D. *Christian Hymnody.* Nashville: Convention Press, 1956.

LORENZ, EDMUND S. *Practical Church Music.* Westwood, New Jersey: Fleming H. Revell Co., 1909.

LOVELACE, AUSTIN C. *The Anatomy of Hymnody.* Nashville: Abingdon Press, 1965.

LOVELACE, AUSTIN C., and RICE, WILLIAM C. *Music and Worship in the Church.* Nashville: Abingdon Press, 1960.

McCUTCHAN, ROBERT GUY. *Our Hymnody: A Manual of the Methodist Hymnal.* New York: Abingdon-Cokesbury Press, 1937.

McKINNEY, HOWARD D., and ANDERSON, W. R. *Discovering Music.* New York: American Book Co., 1952.

McKINNEY, JAMES C. "Developing Musical Leadership for the Church," Chapel Message, Southwestern Baptist Theological Seminary, Ft. Worth, Texas, September 13, 1962.

————. *The Progressing Music Reader.* Nashville: Convention Press, 1959.

MARKS, HARVEY B. *The Rise and Growth of English Hymnody*. Westwood, New Jersey: Fleming H. Revell Co., 1937.

Methodist Hymnal, The. Nashville: Methodist Publishing House, 1939.

PHILLIP, C. HENRY. *The Singing Church: An Outline History of the Music Sung by Choir and People*. London: Faber & Faber, Ltd., 1945.

REYNOLDS, WILLIAM J. *Hymns of Our Faith*. Nashville: Broadman Press, 1964.

ROUTLEY, ERIK. *Church Music and Theology*. Philadelphia: Muhlenberg Press, 1959.

————. *Hymns and Human Life*. Wm. B. Eerdmans Publishing Co., 1952.

————. *The Church and Music*. London: Gerald Duckworth & Co., Ltd., 1950.

————. *Twentieth Century Church Music*. Oxford University Press, 1964.

SETTLE, MARTHA REEVES. *Music in the Small Churches*. Nashville: The Sunday School Board of the Southern Baptist Convention.

SIMS, WALTER HINES (ed.). *Baptist Hymnal*. Nashville: Convention Press, 1956.

————. "Church Music," *Encyclopedia of Southern Baptists*. Nashville: Broadman Press, 1958.

SMITH, H. A. *Lyric Religion*. Westwood, New Jersey: Fleming H. Revell Co., 1931.

WHITTLESEY, FEDERAL LEE. *A Comprehensive Program of Church Music*. Philadelphia: The Westminster Press, 1957.

WILLIAMS, LOREN R. *Graded Choir Hymnbook*. Nashville: Convention Press, 1958.

Prayer

BLACKWOOD, ANDREW W. *Leading in Public Prayer*. New York: Abingdon Press, 1958.

BUTTRICK, GEORGE A. *Prayer*. Nashville: Abingdon-Cokesbury Press, 1942.

CASTEEL, JOHN. *Rediscovering Prayer*. New York: Association Press, 1955.

FACULTY OF THE DIVINITY SCHOOL, UNIVERSITY OF CAMBRIDGE. *Prayer and Worship*. London: Hodder & Stoughton, 1945.

FOSDICK, HARRY EMERSON. *A Book of Public Prayers*. New York: Harper & Bros., 1959.

HARKNESS, GEORGIA. *Prayer and the Common Life*. New York: Abingdon-Cokesbury Press, 1958.

HEILER, FRIEDRICH. *Prayer*. New York: Oxford University Press, 1958.

MACLAREN, ALEXANDER. *Pulpit Prayers*. London: Hodder & Stoughton, n.d.

MILLER, JOSEPH HILLIS. *The Practice of Public Prayer*. New York: Columbia University Press, 1934.

NOYES, MORGAN PHELPS. *Prayers for Services: A Manual for Leaders of Worship.* New York: Charles Scribner's Sons, 1934.

PEARSON, ROY. *Hear Our Prayer: Prayers for Public Worship.* New York: McGraw-Hill Book Co., 1961.

RODENMAYER, ROBERT N. *The Pastor's Prayerbook.* New York: Oxford University Press, 1960.

SCOTT, E. F. *The Lord's Prayer: Its Character, Purpose, and Interpretation.* New York: Charles Scribner's Sons, 1951.

STEERE, DOUGLAS V. *Prayer and Worship.* New York: Association Press, 1938.

TITTLE, ERNST FREMONT. *A Book of Pastoral Prayers.* New York: Abingdon-Cokesbury Press, 1951.

WILLIAMSON, ROBERT L. *Effective Public Prayer.* Nashville: Broadman Press, 1960.

WYON, OLIVE. *The School of Prayer.* Philadelphia: The Westminster Press, 1944.

Preaching

ATKINS, GAIUS GLENN. *Preaching and the Mind of Today.* New York: Round Table Press, Inc., 1934.

BARTLET, GENE E. "When Preaching Becomes Real," *Pastoral Psychology,* Vol. 14, No. 137 (October, 1964).

————. "Worship: The Ordered Proclamation of the Gospel," *Review and Expositor.* LXII, No. 3. (Summer, 1965).

BEECHER, HENRY WARD. *Yale Lectures on Preaching.* Second series. New York: J. B. Bord & Co., 1874.

BROADUS, JOHN. *A Treatise on the Preparation and Delivery of Sermons.* Nashville: The Sunday School Board of the Southern Baptist Convention, 1926.

BROOKS, PHILLIPS. *Lectures on Preaching.* Grand Rapids: Zondervan Publishing House, n.d.

BROWN, H. C., CLINARD, H. G., and NORTHCUTT, J. J. *Steps to the Sermon.* Nashville: Broadman Press, 1963.

CLELAND, JAMES. *Preaching to be Understood.* Nashville: Abingdon Press, 1965.

CROCKER, LIONEL G. and EICH, LOUIS M. *Oral Reading.* 2d ed., Englewood Cliffs, New Jersey: Prentice-Hall, Inc., 1955.

CURRY, S. S. *Vocal and Literary Interpretation of the Bible.* Boston: The Expression Co., 1923.

DALE, R. W. *Nine Lectures on Preaching Delivered at Yale, New Haven, Connecticut.* London: Hodder & Stoughton, 1952.

DODD, C. H. *The Apostolic Preaching and Its Developments.* New York: Harper & Bros., 1936.

FORSYTH, P. T. *Positive Preaching and the Modern Mind.* London: Hodder & Stoughton, 1907.

HALL, JAMES T. "Measuring the Communication Feeling During Worship," *Pastoral Psychology* (October, 1963).

JACKSON, EDGAR N. *A Psychology for Preaching.* Great Neck, New York: Channel Press, Inc., 1961.

JONES, ILION T. *Principles and Practice of Preaching.* New York: Abingdon Press, 1956.

KNOX, JOHN. *The Interpretative Preaching.* Nashville: Abingdon Press, 1957.

MILLER, DONALD G. *Fire in Thy Mouth.* New York: Abingdon Press, 1954.

PEARSON, ROY. *The Preacher, His Purpose and Practice.* Philadelphia: The Westminster Press, 1963.

SANGSTER, W. E. *The Approach to Preaching.* Philadelphia: The Westminster Press, 1952.

STEWART, JAMES. *A Faith to Proclaim.* New York: Charles Scribner's Sons, 1953.

VON ALLMEN, JEAN-JACQUES. *Preaching and Congregation.* Translated by B. L. NICHOLAS. Richmond: John Knox Press, 1962.

WOOLBERT, CHARLES and NELSON, S. *The Art of Interpretative Speech.* New York: F. S. Crofts & Co., 1934.

Baptism and the Lord's Supper

BAILLIE, DONALD M. *The Theology of the Sacraments: And Other Papers.* New York: Charles Scribner's Sons, 1957.

BAKER, ROBERT A. "Baptist Sacramentalism," *Chapel Messages,* ed. H. C. BROWN. Grand Rapids: Baker Book House Co., 1966.

————. "Requisites to the Lord's Supper," *Encyclopedia of Southern Baptists.* II, 794-95.

BARCLAY, WILLIAM. *The Mind of Jesus.* New York: Harper & Bros., 1961.

BARNES, W. W. "Alien Immersion," *Encyclopedia of Southern Baptists.* I, 106-10.

BARTH, KARL. *The Teaching of the Church Regarding Baptism.* London: SCM Press, Ltd., 1950.

BEASLEY-MURRAY, GEORGE R. *Baptism in the New Testament.* London: Macmillan & Co., Ltd., 1962.

CLARK, NEVILLE. *An Approach to a Study of the Sacraments.* London: SCM Press, Ltd., 1958.

COPELAND, E. LUTHER. "Baptism and the Lord's Supper: A Positive Interpretation," *Review and Expositor,* XLVII, No. 3 (July 1950).

CULLMANN, OSCAR, and LEENHARDT, F. J. *Essays on the Lord's Supper,* Translated by J. G. DAVIES. Richmond: John Knox Press, 1958.

FORSYTH, P. T. *The Church and the Sacraments.* London: Longmans, Green & Co., 1917.

GILMORE, A. (ed.). *Christian Baptism: A Fresh Attempt to Understand the Rite in terms of Scripture, History, and Theology.* Philadelphia: Judson Press, 1959.

HIGGINS, A. J. B. *The Lord's Supper in the New Testament.* London: SCM Press, Ltd., 1960.

JEREMIAS, JOACHIM. *The Eucharistic Words of Jesus.* Translated by NORMAN PERRIN. New York: Charles Scribner's Sons, 1966.

McCLENDON, JAMES W. "Baptism as a Performative Sign," accepted for publication in *Theology Today.*

MILLER, SAMUEL. "Reducing the Reality of the Lord's Supper," *Foundations,* 1-4 (October, 1958).

Church Renewal

ALTIZER, THOMAS J. J. and HAMILTON, W. *Radical Theology and the Death of God.* Bobbs-Merrill Co., Inc., 1966.

BERGER, PETER L. *Noise of Solemn Assemblies.* Garden City, New York: Doubleday & Co., 1961.

BERTON, PIERRE. *The Comfortable Pew.* Philadelphia: J. B. Lippincott Co., 1965.

BONHOEFFER, DIETRICH. *The Cost of Discipleship.* New York: The Macmillan Co., 1959.

COX, HARVEY. *The Secular City.* New York: The Macmillan Co., 1965.

DEWOLF, L. HAROLD. *A Hard Rain and a Cross: Faith for a Church Under Fire.* Nashville: Abingdon Press, 1966.

EDGE, FINDLEY B. *A Quest for Vitality in Religion.* Nashville: Broadman Press, 1963.

ELMEN, PAUL H. *The Restoration of Meaning to Contemporary Life.* Garden City, New York: Doubleday & Co., 1958.

FERRÉ, NELS F. S. *Making Religion Real.* New York: Harper & Bros., 1955.

GIBBS, MARK, and MORTON, T. RALPH. *God's Frozen People.* Philadelphia: The Westminster Press, 1964.

GILKEY, LANGDON. *How the Church Can Minister Without Losing Itself.* New York: Harper & Row, 1964.

HEBERT, A. G. *Liturgy and Society.* London: Faber & Faber, Ltd., 1961.
————. *The Function of the Church in the Modern World.* London: Faber & Faber, Ltd., 1961.

KILBOURN, WILLIAM (ed.). *The Restless Church.* Philadelphia: J. B. Lippincott Co., 1966.

MILLER, DONALD G. *The Nature and Mission of the Church.* Richmond: John Knox Press, 1957.

MILLER, RANDOLPH C. *Christian Nurture and the Church.* New York: Charles Scribner's Sons, 1961.

MINEAR, PAUL S. *Horizons of Christian Community.* St. Louis: The Bethany Press, 1959.

MOSKIN, J. ROBERT. "Morality U. S. A.," *Look,* September, 1963.

RAINES, ROBERT A. *New Life in the Church.* New York: Harper & Bros., 1961.
————. *Reshaping the Christian Life.* New York: Harper & Row, 1964.

RAUGHLEY, RALPH C., JR. (ed.). *New Frontiers of Christianity.* New York: Association Press, 1962.

ROBINSON, JOHN A. T. *Honest to God*. Philadelphia: The Westminster Press, 1963.

SEGLER, FRANKLIN M., *The Christian Layman*. Nashville: Broadman Press, 1964.

SMART, JAMES D. *The Rebirth of Ministry*. Philadelphia: The Westminster Press, 1960.

THIELEKE, HELMUT. *The Trouble with the Church*. Translated by J. W. DOBERSTEIN. New York: Harper & Row, 1965.

THURMAN, HOWARD. *The Inward Journey*. New York: Harper & Bros., 1961.

TRUEBLOOD, ELTON. *The Company of the Committed*. New York: Harper & Bros., 1961.

————. *The Incendiary Fellowship*. New York: Harper & Row, 1966.

WEBBER, GEORGE W. *The Congregation in Mission*. New York: Abingdon Press, 1964.

Architecture and Symbolism

ABT, LAWRENCE. *Acting Out*. New York: Grune & Stratton, 1966.

BAILEY, ALBERT EDWARD. *Art and Character*. New York: Abingdon Press, 1938.

BEVAN, EDWYN. *Symbolism and Belief*. London: George Allen & Unwin, Ltd., 1938.

BOSTON, J. R. SCOTFORD. *The Church Beautiful: A Practical Discussion of Church Architecture*. Boston: Pilgrim Press, 1946.

CHRIST, ALBERT-JANER, and MARY MIX FOLEY (eds.). *Modern Church Architecture*. New York: McGraw-Hill Book Co., 1957.

CONOVER, ELBERT M. *Building the House of God*. New York: Methodist Book Concern, 1928.

————. *The Church Builder*. New York: Interdenominational Bureau of Architecture, 1948.

CRAM, RALPH ADAMS (ed.). *American Church Building of Today*. New York: Architectural Book Publishing Co., 1928.

CROCE, BENEDETTO. *Aesthetic: A Science of Expression and General Linguistic*. Translated by DOUGLAS AINSLIE. New York: The Noonday Press, 1962.

CURRY, LOUISE H. and CHESTER M. WETZEL. *Worship Services Using the Arts*. Philadelphia: The Westminster Press, 1966.

DILLISTONE, F. W. *Christianity and Symbolism*. London: Commons, 1955.

DRUMMOND, ANDREW L. *The Church Architecture of Protestantism*. Edinburgh: T. & T. Clark, 1934.

EVERSOLE, FINLEY (ed.). *Christian Faith and the Contemporary Arts*. New York: Abingdon Press, 1962.

FERGUSON, GEORGE. *Signs & Symbols in Christian Art*. New York: Oxford University Press, 1958.

HARNED, DAVID BAILEY. *Theology and the Arts*. Philadelphia: The Westminster Press, 1966.

IRWIN, K., and ORTMAYER, R. *Worship and the Arts*. Nashville: Board of Education of the Methodist Church, 1953.

JOHNSON, F. EARNEST (ed.). *Religious Symbolism.* New York: Harper & Bros., 1955.

MARITAIN, JACQUES. *Creative Intuition in Art and Poetry.* New York: Pantheon Press, 1953.

MAY, ROLLO (ed.). *Symbolism in Religion and Literature.* New York: George Braziller Co., 1960.

NATHAN, WALTER L. *Art and the Message of the Church.* Philadelphia: The Westminster Press, 1961.

NEALE, JOHN MASON, and REV. BENJAMIN WEBB. *The Symbolism of Churches and Church Ornaments.* 3rd ed. London: Gibbings, 1906.

PENNINGTON, JOHN (introductions by). *English Cathedrals and Abbeys.* London: Odhams Press, n.d.

PRENTICE, SARTELL. *The Heritage of the Cathedral: A study of the influence of history and thought upon cathedral architecture.* New York: William Morrow & Co., 1936.

PUGIN, A. WELBY. *The True Principles of Pointed or Christian Architecture.* Edinburgh: John Grant, 1895.

RITTER, RICHARD H. *The Arts of the Church.* Boston: The Pilgrim Press, 1947.

SCOTT, NATHAN A. *The Climate of Faith in Modern Literature.* New York: Seabury Press, 1964.

SHEAR, JOHN KNOX (ed.). *Religious Building for Today.* New York: F. W. Dodge Co., 1957.

SHORT, ERNEST H. *The House of God: A History of Religious Architecture and Symbolism.* New York: The Macmillan Co., 1926.

STAFFORD, THOMAS ALBERT. *Christian Symbolism in the Evangelical Churches.* Nashville: Abingdon Press, 1942.

VOGT, VON OGDEN. *Art and Religion.* Boston: Beacon Press, 1960.

Resources for Planning and Leading

BAILLIE, JOHN. *A Diary of Private Prayer.* London: Oxford University Press, 1947.

BAKER, EDNA DEAN. *The Worship of the Little Child.* Nashville: Cokesbury Press, 1927.

BALDWIN, JOSEPH L. *Worship Training for Juniors.* New York: The Methodist Book Concern, 1927.

BAYS, ALICE. *Worship Services for Purposeful Living.* New York: Abingdon Press, 1949.

Book of Common Prayer, The . . . according to the use of the Protestant Episcopal Church in the United States of America.

Book of Common Worship Approved by the General Assembly of the Presbyterian Church in the United States of America, The. Philadelphia: Publication Division of the Board of Christian Education of the Presbyterian Church in the United States of America, 1946.

Book of Worship, Church of the Brethren. Elgin, Illinois: The Brethren Press, 1964.

Book of Worship for Church and Home, With Orders for the Administration of the Sacraments and Other Rites and Ceremonies According to the Use of the Methodist Church, The. Nashville: The Methodist Publishing House, 1952.

Book of Worship for Free Churches, A. Prepared under the direction of the General Council of the Congregational Christian Churches in the United States. New York: Oxford University Press, 1948.

BOWMAN, CLARICE. *Restoring Worship.* Nashville: Abingdon-Cokesbury Press, 1951.

CASTEEL, JOHN L. *Renewal in Retreats.* New York: Association Press, 1959.

_____. *Spiritual Renewal Through Personal Groups.* New York: Association Press, 1957.

CHURCH USHERS ASSOCIATION. *Principles of Church Ushering.* New York: Church Association of New York, 1951.

Common Service Book of the Lutheran Church. Rev. ed. Philadelphia: Board of Publication of the United Lutheran Church in America, 1929.

EDDY, ROBERT L. *Pastoral Prayers Through the Year.* New York: Charles Scribner's Sons, 1959.

ELY, VIRGINIA. *Come, Let Us Adore Him.* Westwood, New Jersey: Fleming H. Revell Co., 1956.

GARRETT, WILLIS O. *Church Usher's Manual.* Philadelphia: Judson Press, 1924.

GIBSON, GEORGE M. *The Story of the Christian Year.* Nashville: Abingdon-Cokesbury Press, 1945.

HEAD, DAVID. *He Sent Leanness: A Book of Prayers for the Natural Man.* New York: The Macmillan Co., 1962.

HILL, CAROLINE MILES (ed.). *The World's Great Religious Poetry.* New York: The Macmillan Co., 1923.

HOBBS, JAMES RANDOLPH. *The Pastor's Manual.* Nashville: Broadman Press, 1934.

JACKSON, EDGAR N. *The Christian Funeral.* New York: Channel Press, 1966.

KEMPIS, THOMAS A. *Imitation of Christ.* Translated by ALOYSIUS CROFT and HARRY F. BOLTON. Milwaukee: Bruce Publishing Co., 1940.

LEACH, W. H. *The Cokesbury Marriage Manual.* Rev. ed. Nashville: Abingdon Press, 1959.

MCDORMAND, THOMAS BRUCE. *The Art of Building Worship Services.* Nashville: Broadman Press, 1942.

MAUS, CYNTHIA PEARL. *Christ and the Fine Arts.* New York: Harper & Row, 1938.

MORRISON, JAMES DALTON (ed.). *Masterpieces of Religious Verse.* New York: Harper & Bros., 1948.

OSBORN, EDWIN G. (ed.). *Christian Worship: A Service Book.* St. Louis: Christian Board of Publication, 1953.

PAGE, KIRBY. *Religious Resources for Personal Living and Social Action.* New York: Farrar & Rinehart, 1939.

PALMER, ALBERT W. *Aids to Worship.* New York: The Macmillan Co., 1944.

————. *The Art of Conducting Public Worship.* New York: The Macmillan Co., 1939.

PALMER, GORDON. *A Manual of Church Services.* Westwood, New Jersey: Fleming H. Revell Co., 1950.

PASCAL, BLAISE. *Pensees.* Translated by W. F. TROTTER. New York: E. P. Dutton & Co., Inc., 1947.

PAST, MARY E. *Intermediates' Worship Programs.* Westwood, New Jersey: Fleming H. Revell Co., 1942.

PAYNE, ERNEST A. and WINWARD, STEPHEN F. *Orders and Prayers for Church Worship.* London: The Carey Kingsgate Press, Ltd., 1960.

PHILLIPS, DOROTHY BERKLEY (ed.). *The Choice Is Always Ours.* New York: Richard R. Smith, 1951.

PORTER, DAVID R. (ed.). *Worship Resources for Youth.* New York: Association Press, 1948.

POWELL, MARIE COLE. *Boys and Girls at Worship.* New York: Harper & Bros., 1943.

SEBOLT, ROLAND H. A. (ed.). *God and Our Parish.* St. Louis: Concordia Publishing House, 1963.

SHEPHERD, MASSEY H., JR. *The Oxford American Prayer Book Commentary.* New York: Oxford University Press, 1950.

STEERE, DOUGLAS. *Doors Into Life.* New York: Harper & Bros., 1948.

STRODACH, PAUL ZELLER. *A Manual on Worship.* Rev. ed. Philadelphia: Muhlenberg Press, 1946.

STUBER, STANLEY I., and CLARK, THOMAS CURTIS. *Treasury of the Christian Faith.* New York: Association Press, 1949.

The Union Prayer Book for Jewish Worship. 2 vols. Cincinnati: Central Conference of American Rabbis, 1940.

WALLACE, J. SHERMAN. *Worship in the Church School.* Boston: Judson Press, 1930.

WALLIS, CHARLES L. (ed.). *The Treasure Chest.* New York: Harper & Row, 1965.

————. *Worship Resources for the Christian Year.* New York: Harper & Bros., 1954.

WYGAL, WINNIFRED. *How to Plan Informal Worship.* New York: Association Press, 1955.

Index of Subjects

Acts as worship, 5-6,7,8,155,172,175, 184
Adoration, 4,5,12,58,87-88
Advent, 187
Aesthetics, 55,182
  Sense of beauty, 78,165,168,173-74
Affirmation of faith, 159-60
Altar, 14,16,17,172
Amen, 30,162
Anabaptists, 41,47,48
Ancestor worship, 14
Anglican Church, 41,52
Announcements, 163
Apostles' Creed, 45,51
Architecture, 26,52,170-71,173
Art, 169,170,173
Attitudes in worship, 31,86-90
Auditorium, see Sanctuary

Baptism, 137-54
  Act of worship, 137-44
  Administration of, 146-47,153
  Alien immersion, 152,153
  History of, 28,31,140-41
  Of children, 145
  Problems in administration, 150-54
  Theology of, 143-45,151
  See Reformation; Radical Reformers
Baptistry, 147,172
Baptists, vii, 41,49-51,53,55,151-54, 219
  General, 49-50
  Particular, 50
  Southern, 54,152-53
Bible, worship in, 13-32
  As symbol, 171
  In worship, 65-70
  Preaching of, 30,126-33
  Reading of, 26,27,29,121-26
Book of Common Prayer, Episcopal, 119
Building, church, 25,29

See Architecture; Synagogue; Tabernacle; Temple

Call to worship, 155-56,190,193
Celebration, worship as, 8
Ceremony, 5,8,20,176,195,196
  See Ritual
Children, 44,50,133-36,145
Choir, see Music, choir
Christian life, 3,8,207,211,213
Christian Science, vii
Christian Year (calendar), 187
Christmas, 187
Christology, see Jesus Christ
Church, 1
  Building up, 210
  Early, 33
  Free Churches, 46-49
  Renewal, 54,206-20
  Theology of, 70-75
Commitment, 90 see Dedication
Communication, 121-36,167
  See Preaching; Reading of Scriptures
Communion, 6,7,190
  See Lord's Supper
Conducting worship
  See Leading worship
Confession, 31,89,115,160
  See Creed
Congregation, 73,202-205
  See Music, congregational singing; Worship, congregation and
Congregational Church, vii,51
Consubstantiation, 42
  See Lord's Supper
Council of Churches, 54,207,219
Creed, 47
  Apostles', 45-51
Cross, the, 27,62,171
Cult, 6,18-21

Dedication, 9,161,189,190

239

Index of Persons